Being Human

While there may be no one single characteristic that differentiates humans as a species, it is the combination of differences from other species that makes us unique. The new edition of *Being Human* examines the psychology of being human through exploring different psychological traditions alongside philosophy and evolutionary theory, covering themes such as culture, cognition, language, morality, and society.

Our nature – or 'essence' – is something that has preoccupied human beings throughout our history, beginning with philosophy and religion, and continuing through the biological, social, and psychological sciences. *Being Human* begins by describing some of the major philosophical accounts of human nature, from Ancient Greek philosophers, such as Plato and Aristotle, to major British and Continental philosophers, such as Locke and Nietzsche. The book considers religious accounts of human nature, with their focus on the nature of good and evil, and scientific accounts of genetics and the brain, which underpin the distinctively human cognitive ability of language. Attention then turns to the ideas of the behaviourists, such as Skinner, Freud, and other psychodynamic psychologists, and humanistic-phenomenological psychologists, such as Maslow. Finally, human culture is discussed as the ultimate defining characteristic of human beings: culture represents our 'natural habitat' and what defines us as a species.

This updated second edition includes increased coverage of social psychology and has a broader scope, in order to identify the defining characteristics of human beings. With reference to current psychological research and philosophical material, this is fascinating reading for students of psychology, philosophy, and the social sciences.

Richard Gross has been writing psychology texts for both undergraduate and A-level students for over 30 years. He has a particular interest in philosophical aspects of psychology, including what it means to be a human being.

Being Human

Psychological Perspectives on
Human Nature

Second Edition

Richard Gross

LONDON AND NEW YORK

Second edition published 2019
by Routledge
2 Park Square, Milton Park, Abingdon, Oxon, OX14 4RN

and by Routledge
52 Vanderbilt Avenue, New York, NY 10017

Routledge is an imprint of the Taylor & Francis Group, an informa business

First edition published by Routledge 2012

British Library Cataloguing-in-Publication Data
A catalogue record for this book is available from the British Library

Library of Congress Cataloging-in-Publication Data
A catalog record has been requested for this book

ISBN: 978-0-367-17550-4 (hbk)
ISBN: 978-0-367-15098-3 (pbk)
ISBN: 978-0-429-05500-3 (ebk)

Typeset in Bembo
by Deanta Global Publishing Services, Chennai, India

Printed and bound in Great Britain by
TJ International Ltd, Padstow, Cornwall

Contents

Figures

Tables

Preface to the second edition

The first edition of *Being Human* (2012) was an explicit attempt to compare human and non-human abilities and characteristics (including biological make-up, cognition, consciousness, and culture). There were also two chapters that focused exclusively on human abilities, dealing with fear of death, and memory and perception of time.

In this second edition, I've shifted the emphasis to exploring *human nature,* a much-used term in various sciences (including evolutionary biology, genetics, palaeoanthropology, primatology, anthropology, neuroscience, and psychology), as well as in philosophy, and religious – and everyday – discourse. Inevitably, there is still comparison between humans and non-humans, but the comparison is *secondary* to the attempt to identify the defining characteristics of human beings: *what we are like, what it means to be a human being.*

I've retained the basic logic of the first edition: discussion moves from basic biological features, through cognitive abilities that our brains make possible, to culture. While the biology of being human, and some of our cognitive abilities (such as memory) can be understood by studying – or imagining – an isolated individual, others (such as language), by definition, develop and are used within the context of interaction with others (other language users). In turn, all individuals are immersed in a culture which, typically, has evolved over hundreds/thousands of years and so is inherited by all its members. Claims that chimpanzees – and other non-humans – have culture only serves to highlight the uniqueness and all-pervasiveness of the human form: it's part of human nature to be cultural beings.

A major addition in this edition is a chapter on the *social psychology* of good and evil; both can take many different forms, such as volunteerism and heroism, and genocide, mass atrocities, and terrorism, respectively. Social psychology's *situationist* approach acts as counterbalance to the *dispositional* approach of biological and cognitive explanations of human behaviour; social psychology focuses on external, environmental influences, while still allowing for individual differences.

I've retained major features of the first edition, including:

- The 'Key Questions' at the beginning of each chapter, aimed at giving you a flavour of what's to follow and to get you thinking about the key issues that will be discussed.
- The 'Time for Reflection' breaks, intended to get you to think in a more focused way about particular theories, concepts, and issues. Often, the questions posed are answered in the text that follows; where they're not, you're either being asked to consider something very personal or the question is deliberately very general/wide-ranging (which might lend itself to a seminar paper or classroom discussion).

Acknowledgements

I'd like to thank Eleanor Reedy for showing faith in me and in this project. While not without difficulties along the way, writing this second edition has been a hugely stimulating and satisfying experience.

To Stephen Gross, my dearest brother, whose sharp mind has helped me to sharpen my own.

1 Introduction

How should we understand 'human nature'?

Key questions

- What's meant by the 'universalist assumption' (or *universalism*)?
- In what sense are humans part of nature?
- Is there necessarily a contradiction between those characteristics shared by all human beings and individual and cultural differences between people?
- How can we account for the apparent opposition between human beings' natural emotional responses and the ability to keep these under control?

Some preliminary thoughts

'Yes, he let himself down, but he's only human'; 'it's human nature to want to get married and have children'; 'wanting sex with another man is unnatural'; 'what makes human beings unique as a species is their use of language'.

These statements suggest a number of different views regarding the meaning of 'human nature' and how it is understood by both the layperson and the scientist.

1 'Yes, he let himself down, but he's only human after all'. The implication here is that human beings, despite all their outstanding abilities and achievements, are far from being 'perfect' or infallible beings, without weaknesses or faults. Put another way, it's 'natural' for individuals, on occasion, to fall short of the very highest standards of socially acceptable behaviour. Indeed, if someone never deviated from these standards, never showing human fallibility (such as losing self-control and displaying anger, or having too much to drink, or over-indulging in some other way), we may regard them as odd or strange (more automaton than human). These standards may derive from religious beliefs and codes and will differ between religious communities (within the same country) and between different countries and national cultures.

2 'It's human nature to want to get married and have children' implies that these wishes are 'normal'; this, in turn, implies that (i) society expects people to want these things; and (ii) the majority of people will, in fact, want

them. This is why those who choose not to get married and/or not have children may be seen as 'social deviants', having to justify themselves in a way that the majority don't need to (wanting marriage and parenthood is regarded as the 'default option' and so doesn't require justification). But as with the first example, the freedom to deviate from this norm – and any penalties for doing so – will differ hugely between different religious and cultural communities.

3 'Wanting sex with another man is unnatural (if you're a man)' implies a deviation that is much more of an aberration compared with the wish to remain single and not have children. For some, it represents a breach of fundamental *religious* principles and doctrine (e.g. 'the Bible condemns 'lying with another man as you would with a woman''); for others, it represents a breach of fundamental *biological* principles (e.g. 'sex is ultimately about reproduction'). Either way, it is judged to be *wrong* (either 'immoral' or 'perverse').

4 'What makes human beings unique as a species is their use of language' implies that it's 'natural' for human beings to speak and in other ways use language; any attempts to teach non-human animals to use language (in any form) – and any claims to have been successful – are 'unnatural' and likely to be unfounded. In turn, the implication is that language is a human *species-specific behaviour*: it's part of our biological make-up, reflecting our evolution as a species and distinguishing us from all other species. The ease with which humans acquire and use language demonstrates that it is, indeed, species-specific.

Human nature and universalism

What these examples illustrate are some of the different ways in which we commonly – and not so commonly (as in the last example) – understand the term 'human nature'.

- Whatever we think the distinguishing features of human nature may be, it conveys a set of characteristics, abilities, and tendencies that identify what human beings have in common and which set us apart from all other species. This possession of shared features is referred to as *universalism* (or the *universalist assumption)*: as human beings, we all display the same basic abilities, characteristics, behaviours, etc., making people *interchangeable*.
- These universal characteristics, abilities, and tendencies are sometimes referred to as the important 'deep' or 'hard-wired' structures of the mind; since we're all human and fundamentally alike with regard to these structures, national or cultural differences should have no effect on how they function.
- This raises fundamental questions regarding the validity of generalising research findings from the study of one particular cultural population to 'people in general'. If we start out by making the universalist assumption, then,

by definition, such generalisation is valid; but if we don't, then we're obliged to study different populations independently. If we find that certain features assumed to be 'hard-wired' do in fact vary between different cultural groups, do we then have to reject the concept of 'human nature' altogether?

- Perhaps, but not necessarily. The most common 'middle-ground' solution is to retain belief in a particular hard-wired feature (for instance, the capacity for language) but to acknowledge that it manifests itself differently according to varying environmental conditions (being born into different linguistic communities). If a child born in China to Chinese parents is raised from birth in England by English-only-speaking parents, the child will learn to speak – and understand – English as easily as if it had remained in China and acquired Chinese. What's hard-wired is, clearly, *not* knowledge of a specific language but the capacity to acquire *any* language the child is exposed to. (Language and other cognitive features of human nature are discussed in Chapter 5.) (This reasoning also applies to culture: see Chapter 9.)

- So, particular features of human nature don't have to come 'ready-made' for them to be considered deep or hard-wired. Other examples include what, arguably, are the most fundamentally important features, namely, our genetic make-up and the resulting human brain. In Chapter 3, we discuss what is distinctive about the *human genome* (the sum total of human genes) and the brain. The evidence for evolution is very powerful in both cases: we share so many of our genes, as well as major brain structures, with other species (not just our closest evolutionary relatives). From this, we could argue that underpinning human nature is a small set of genes that are only found in our species (or certain forms of which are unique to humans); these, in turn, determine the kind of brain that has evolved over millions of years and which is found only in human beings.

Are humans part of nature?

Just as it's commonly agreed that we have evolved from other animal species, so there's considerable – and constantly emerging – evidence that, like all evolving species, human beings ('*Homo*') had ancestors and cousins who shared some of our abilities but became extinct. The human family of species (*hominin*) comprises several extinct types (such as the *Australopithecines* – 'southern apes', Asian *Homo erectus,* and European *Homo neanderthalensis*). (Until quite recently, 'hominid' was used: but the great apes were then included following the discovery of close genetic relations with modern humans.)

According to Leakey (1994), it is the evolution of upright locomotion (*bipedalism*) that distinguishes ancient hominids from other apes of that time. But habitual bipedalism predates the appearance of modern humans *(Homo sapiens)* by at least four million years. The other fundamental change that occurred during the evolution of modern humans (who first appeared around 200,000 years ago) was an increase in brain growth (see Chapter 3).

Figure 1.1 Charles Darwin (1809–82), founder of evolutionary theory, aged about 45. (Permission granted by Mary Evans Picture Library.)

According to Reynolds (1980), life in the early hominid past can be thought of as the last phase of humans as a natural phenomenon, that is, an animal that's entirely subject to the processes of animal evolution generally (see Figure 1.1). Our now extinct hominid ancestors faced ecological and evolutionary challenges much like other, non-human, species did: we can describe their way of life in terms of adaptation to the environment, subject to all the normal 'rules' of natural selection with regard to the evolution of their physical form and behaviour. While being far from driven by instinct:

> Man was, at the Australopithecine stage, part of nature and any character-istics of the early hominids would be characteristics that one could com-pare on a one-to-one basis with those of closely related species, especially chimpanzees and gorillas.
>
> (Reynolds, 1980, p. 37)

Ironically, the concept of human nature only begins to be used and discussed once *Homo sapiens* had evolved, that is, once we had ceased being part of nature and started living as *cultural* creatures (see reference to Shotter, 1975, below). Once we'd ceased to be a part of nature, we began our *history* as human beings.

Human nature and the brain

Considering a single, isolated individual, there's a kind of in-built contradic-tion within his/her brain. The so-called *paleomammalian brain* comprises the limbic system which is responsible for emotional behaviour. While it's commonly believed that non-human animals are driven purely by instinct and have no control over their emotions (which is certainly not the case), it's generally accepted that what the *neomammalian brain* (namely, the neocortex) provides is the ability to control our emotions, think rationally, plan ahead, and everything that's implied by '(self-) consciousness'.

In other words, in terms of 'human nature', there's both the capacity to feel and overtly display, say, anger, and at the same time a capacity to control that anger (e.g. by channelling or sublimating it into some more constructive and socially acceptable behaviour: see Freud's psychoanalytic theory in Chapter 6). We're neither totally driven by our emotions nor always and totally in control of them (hence, 'Yes, he let himself down, but he's only human'). 'Human nature' denotes *both* of these tendencies. (This is consistent with the view that someone who is unable to exercise any or adequate control over his/her anger may be judged as psychopathic/sociopathic.)

There's a sense in which our brains point in *two directions*:

a We are clearly animals (flesh-and-blood, living creatures) as distinct from plants and have evolved from other animal species (unless you take an extreme creationist view).
b Our brains have evolved in ways that make conscious, rational thought possible (largely through the medium of language), which is essential for our ability to live with others in the way we do. (Again, while we're clearly not the only – or even the most highly developed – social species, the creation of social norms, rules, morality, etc. makes us unique (as far as we can tell!)).

In this latter sense, we're not simply immersed in nature but are *in a culture in nature* (Shotter, 1975). As biological organisms, we're special: we deal with nature through our immersion in culture (see Chapter 9). If there's such a thing as 'human nature', it lies in our ability to choose alternative courses of action within an indeterminate world. Indeed, it's the central task of such a *self-defining animal* to:

> Give form to the act of living itself; it is up to him to imagine new possibilities for being human, new ways of how to live, and to attempt to realize them in practice.
>
> (Shotter, 1975, p. 111)

What this implies is that 'human nature' is far from being a fixed, pre-determined set of attributes and behaviours shared by all human beings. Again:

> Human nature is not simply natural … On the one hand, human nature means that which expresses the *essence* of being human … On the other hand, it means that which is constituted by nature, in Darwinian terms, that which is the product of natural selection.
>
> (Malik, 2006, p. 170; emphasis added)

In non-humans, the two meanings are synonymous, but, unlike non-humans:

> The human essence – what we consider to be the common properties of our humanity – is as much a product of our historical and cultural development as it is of our biological heritage … Being both social and rational means that the common social goals, opportunities and constraints are often tackled in a similar fashion in different societies.
>
> (Malik, 2006, p. 170)

But equally, common goals, etc., are often tackled in characteristically *different* ways; these differences are what distinguish one culture from another. This means, in turn, that what is considered 'natural', 'normal', or 'part of human nature' in one culture may differ from, or even oppose, what's considered to be 'natural', etc., in another.

If genes and brain underlie what we call human nature, how do we account for both cultural differences and *individual* differences within the same culture? One way of beginning to answer this fundamental question is to consider the *plasticity* of the human brain. This is discussed in detail in Chapter 3.

Plan of the book

Chapter 2 focuses on the history of the concept of 'human nature', through examining major philosophical and religious accounts; it will also discuss the distinction between 'psychological and natural kinds'.

Chapter 3 provides a brief outline of basic genetic processes, before comparing and contrasting (i) human and chimpanzee genomes; and (ii) those of modern humans and Neanderthals. It will also consider the issue of genetics and race. The chapter then discusses the distinctive features of the human brain (such as its *plasticity*). Mirror neurons and theory of mind (ToM) provide a vital link between biological and socio-cognitive aspects of human nature (in Chapters 5 and 9).

Chapter 4 identifies different kinds of *consciousness* and the difference between this and self-consciousness. It also asks whether we need a body to be conscious, how we determine whether any non-human animals are conscious, and how and why consciousness evolved. The chapter also considers the relationship between consciousness and the brain.

Chapter 5 takes *recursion* as a fundamental – and uniquely human – feature of a range of *cognitive* abilities, including tool-making and use, abstract thought, mental time travel, and memory; *language* is central to all of these and the chapter will consider attempts to teach language to non-humans. Other apparently in-built features of human thought include *categorising* and *stereotyping* (crucial features of prejudice) and *heuristics* used in decision-making.

Chapter 6 brings together two *deterministic* accounts of human nature, namely *behaviourist* and *psychodynamic* approaches. Watson and Skinner, and Freud are the main protagonists, but the chapter will consider some of the challenges, extensions, and modifications of these major theorists/researchers (such as Bandura and Erikson, respectively). While diametrically opposed in most respects, Skinner and Freud agree in rejecting the existence of *free will*.

Chapter 7 examines what Maslow called the 'third force' within psychology, namely, the *humanistic-phenomenological* approach (Freud's and Skinner's approaches constituting the first two). The focus will be on Maslow's (and Rogers's) contribution and the relationship between humanistic psychology and existentialism (including Yalom's 'givens of existence' and terror management theory).

Chapter 8 focuses on one of the key debates within social psychology: is *antisocial* ('evil') behaviour a symptom of individuals' *dispositions* or is it the product of environmental, *situational* factors? Two much-cited studies discussed at length are Zimbardo's Stanford Prison Experiment and Milgram's obedience experiments. The chapter also discusses influences on terrorism, in particular, the Internet. In relation to *prosocial* behaviour (including helping, heroism, and volunteerism), two opposing accounts are *universal egoism* and the *empathy-altruism hypothesis*.

Chapter 9 begins by defining *culture* before exploring whether it is uniquely human. Central to this debate are the precise mechanisms by which cultural learning/transmission takes place (such as *true imitation vs. duplication*). *Cumulative cultural evolution* is uniquely human, central to which is *creative collaboration*. The chapter also discusses the relationship between *biological* and *cultural evolution*. The sex–gender distinction is discussed in the context of culture and history, as is the issue of *fair inequality*.

Chapter 10 is based on Harari's claim that, in seeking perfect happiness and immortality, *Homo sapiens* are actually trying to upgrade themselves into *gods*. With science at its centre, cultural evolution could be seen as beginning to override millions of years of biological evolution, as in *biological* and *cyborg engineering*.

So, after defining 'human nature' and looking at its philosophical and religious origins, we 'anchor' our scientific exploration within biology (genetics and brain: Chapter 3), then let psychology predominantly take over, combined with neuroscience (Chapters 4–7). The discussion then moves from focus on the *individual* to the *social* (Chapter 8) and the *cultural* (Chapter 9), where social anthropology comes into its own. Stir in some evolutionary theory and palaeoanthropology and we have completed a highly interdisciplinary mixture of 'human nature', but psychology – in its various forms – should be the major flavour that comes through.

Suggested further reading

Pasternak, C. (ed.) (2007) *What Makes Us Human?* Oxford: Oneworld.

Wells, R.H. and McFadden, J. (eds.) (2006) *Human Nature: Fact and Fiction*. London: Continuum.

2 Origins of the concept of 'human nature'

Views from religion, philosophy, biology, and psychology

Key questions

- How did Ancient Greek philosophers understand the soul and the relationship between reason and passion?
- How did belief in separation of the body and soul take shape?
- How does Descartes' *dualism* account for the uniqueness of human beings?
- In what ways are the philosophical theories of Hobbes, Locke, Rousseau, and Nietzsche reflected in modern psychological accounts of human nature?
- How have Judaism and Christianity defined sin/vice and virtue?
- What relevance, if any, do the 'Seven Deadly Sins' have to the modern world and can you add to the list by drawing on modern lifestyle and practices?
- What is the role of the brain in addictive behaviours such as gluttony?
- How do the *moral* and *disease* views of addiction differ and is there a middle-ground position (such as addiction as a disorder of *self-regulation*)?
- What's meant by the distinction between *psychological* and *natural* kinds?

The history of the concept of 'human nature'

Philosophical accounts of human nature

Plato (427–348 BCE)

Ancient Greece was probably the first culture that started to ask serious questions about the nature of the world it occupied. This marked the beginning of *philosophy* (love of wisdom) (around 600 BCE). One key question was whether the foundations of life are constant or ever-changing. Some argued that you can never do the 'same' thing twice (e.g. Heraclitus); others, however, most famously Plato (in *The Republic*), distinguished between the realm of eternal, never-changing *ideal forms* (of goodness, beauty, equality) and that of the ever-changing *material reality* in which the forms and ideas are imperfectly realised. We perceive only the *shadows* of the objects.

Plato also distinguished between *soul* and *body*, two radically different kinds of entity: the soul – which defines the person – is immortal, made from left-overs of the cosmos-soul travelling between the stars and the human body it temporarily inhabits. The human soul, which is 'imprisoned' in the body, comprises three interconnecting elements, as described in Box 2.1.

BOX 2.1 THE THREE INTERCONNECTING ELEMENTS OF THE HUMAN SOUL (BASED ON PLATO)

- ***Reason***, located in the brain, allows us access to the ideal realm, guiding us to a virtuous life in search of abstract, non-worldly perfection, the ideal fulfilment of human nature. The true path to (new) knowledge is the inward path of reasoning (as opposed to the outward path of perception). The attainment of wisdom is the highest human virtue.
- ***Sensation and emotion*** (e.g. anger/wrath, indignation, fear, pride, and courage) are mortal and situated in the heart. The neck separates reason from sensation/emotion in order to prevent it from polluting the divine soul.
- ***Lower passions/appetites*** (e.g. lust, greed, desire), located in the liver.

It's commonly believed (first with Stoic, then Christian ethical thinkers) that anger demeans: it reduces us to the level of bestiality (i.e. loss of control). Today, we see the expression of anger as desirable and keeping it in as positively harmful (e.g. anger management) (Walton, 2004). We should use reason to guide or restrain our passions/appetites, thereby achieving psychological harmony (Schimmel, 1997).

Aristotle (384–322 BCE)

Aristotle, a student of Plato, identified *psyche* (Latin: *anima*) as the animating force in the universe, which distinguished living from non-living things. Aristotle was interested in the place of the human in the natural world and in *On the Soul* (*De anima*), he described *psyche* as comprising:

- *Lowest, vegetative soul:* present in all living things (including plants), this enables organisms to nourish themselves and reproduce.
- *Animal (sensitive) soul* (humans and non-humans), which provides locomotion, sensation, memory, and imagination.
- *Rational soul* (*nous* = Greek for 'intellect'; '*intellectus*' = Latin translation): uniquely human, enabling us to reason consciously ('actively'); in turn, this makes us able to think abstractly and to develop universal principles.

It's also uniquely human to desire to know and understand and to lead virtuous lives. The concept of *nous* depended on an intimate connection between human reason and *logos*, the rational order of the world.

Time for reflection …

- Can 'psyche', 'anima', 'nous', 'intellectus', etc., be treated as having equivalent meanings?
- See Box 2.2.

BOX 2.2 LOSING ARISTOTLE IN TRANSLATION

- When translated from Greek to Latin, then from Latin into various modern languages, the categories used by Aristotle and his compatriots profoundly change their meaning (quite apart from the changes within one language over the centuries).
- For example, Aristotle's *psyche* isn't the *anima* of his Latin translators, and even less is the *soul* of the Middle Ages, let alone the *mind* of the moderns:
- 'There are therefore strong grounds for not including the ancient period in any history of psychological language' (Danziger, 1997, pp. 21–2).

Post-Aristotelian thinking

Starting with Galen (the 1st century BCE Roman physician, whose writings formed the basis of medicine for centuries), the body became increasingly important. For example, he related physiological functions to the body: mental activity was now increasingly seen as a function of the body and texts dealing with controlling the passions emphasised the dependency of the soul on the body. (Descartes took this further, separating the rational mind (not soul) and the physiological activity of the soul tied to the body: see below.)

The moral teaching of *Stoicism*, in particular, stressed rigorous self-control (rather than Aristotelian moderation): the things to be controlled were undesirable 'movement of the soul'. Four basic passions are pleasure, pain, fear, and desire. For the Stoics, unity and rationality of the soul remained paramount: passions include beliefs and judgements, so the opposition was between natural/unnatural expressions of the soul (not between cognition and passion): 'we are responsible for our emotions, just as we are for our more considered actions' (Annas, 1992).

In Medieval Christian theology, the opposition between (i) sensuous and intellectual striving; and (ii) endured passion and active will became enmeshed with that between flesh and spirit. According to St. Thomas Aquinas, the sensuous appetites/passions (including hope, despair, fear, courage, desire, pain, love, aversion) are all either good or evil: they aren't attributes of the (immortal) soul as such, but only affect the soul insofar as they're tied to the body.

> That idea incorporated a long tradition of blaming the body for feelings that were unwelcome yet hard to control, a tradition that was to survive in secular form right up to the twentieth century.
>
> (Danziger, 1997, p. 33)

René Descartes (1596–1650)

In *The Passions of the Soul* (1649), Descartes (see Figure 2.1) totally separated the body and soul; the former now seen mechanistically (no doubt reflecting his fascination with the then popular mechanical toys and other automata). The 'passions of the soul' originate in the body and include 'perceptions' of bodily appetites, like hunger and thirst; they're now distinguished from the 'actions of the soul' (which depend solely on the soul itself and owe nothing to the body). These actions are described as 'all our desires', including acts of will resulting in overt behaviour as well as pure thoughts. There could also be perceptions, feelings, and emotions that originate in the soul.

Figure 2.1 René Descartes (1596–1650), French dualist philosopher. (Permission granted by Mary Evans Library.)

Descartes disagreed with Aquinas's classification of the passions: all passions derive from six primitive ones: wonder, love, hatred, desire, joy, and sadness. Like those before him, he argued that the passions must be controlled in order to achieve the good life. The superior soul has to control the inferior body.

Descartes is probably best known for his *mind–body dualism*, which is described in Box 2.3.

BOX 2.3 DESCARTES' PHILOSOPHICAL DUALISM

- Descartes' belief in the material nature of the world (including the human body) is one side of a philosophical coin, the other being his belief that the human mind (or soul) is *non-material*.
- He divided the universe into two fundamentally different 'realms' or 'realities': (i) physical matter (*res extensa*), which is extended in time and space; and (ii) non-material, non-extended *res cogitans.*
- This distinction between matter and mind allowed scientists to describe the world objectively (without reference to the human observer); objectivity became the cornerstone of scientific activity. The material world consists of objects assembled like a huge machine and operated by mechanical laws that could be explained in terms of the arrangements and movements of its parts (*mechanism/machine-ism*).
- Descartes compared (non-human) animals to clocks composed of wheels and springs; likewise, the human body is a perfect cosmic machine, at least in principle controlled by mathematical laws. However, the mind, which only human beings possess, can only be known through *introspection*.
- So, while animals can be *reduced* to mere machines, humans are unique in being both matter (body) and mind; it's the mind that allows humans to act *voluntarily* (i.e. we have *free will*, which enables us to be both virtuous and sinful: see Gross, 2018).

By distinguishing between matter and mind and by attributing both to human beings, Descartes had to be able to explain how two qualitatively different entities can *interact* (i.e. how are we able to use our minds/free will to influence our bodies?). His solution was to propose that the *pineal gland* (as we now know to be part of the hormonal/*endocrine system* but located in the brain) is the meeting place of mind and matter; it's where God enters the brain.

Descartes wanted to keep a place for a religious notion of the soul as a distinct entity, essential to being human. This remains the position of the Orthodox and Catholic faiths. The soul is divine and independent of everything else in the universe and so can't be studied by natural science – only by philosophy and religion. Like Plato, he believed the soul had innate knowledge which could be recovered through reasoning.

Thomas Hobbes (1588–1679)

Hobbes rejected Descartes' dualism: the mind is wholly material and embodied in the brain. Like John Locke (see discussion later in this chapter), Hobbes believed that all knowledge comes through the senses. But whatever we perceive is illusory and biased: sensory qualities inhere in the perceiver – *not* in external objects (i.e. ears don't hear, only people do).

Passion and motivation

The central concept in Hobbes' theory of the passions (or affective states, including love, hate, desire, fear, joy, and sadness) is *conatus* (see Box 2.4)

BOX 2.4 HOBBES' CONCEPT OF CONATUS

- *Conatus* drives all human actions and comprises two mutually influencing passions: *desire* ('appetite') which represents efforts *towards* objects (present/absent) and *fear* ('aversion'), which represents efforts *away from* objects. (This basic distinction underlies Skinner's account of *operant conditioning* and to some extent, Freud's *psychoanalytic theory*: see Chapter 6.)
- Specific psychological functions (sensing, imagining, remembering, speaking, understanding) derive from, and mediate, these passions. But passions are distinct from *rational* desires that sustain individuals' well-being.
- Passions implicate the will and so have moral and religious connotations: they motivate us into action. They result from two basic motions: from senses to brain, from brain to heart; pleasure = *facilitative motion*; pain = *inhibitory motion*.
- '*Conatus*' was also used by other 17th century philosophers, including Leibniz and Spinoza.

According to Hobbes' first 'law' of human nature, appetites/passions are insatiable. The second 'law' states that reason enables individuals to avoid death and seek peaceful living. From this apparently *hedonistic* standpoint, humans avoid painful experiences and seek pleasurable ones. But Hobbes also understood that appetites have multiple causes, including familial, educational, cultural, and political ones. This means that people aren't radically autonomous, rational individuals who author their own actions: he denied self-determination and understood individuals as embedded in social relations. (But nor are they mere passive responders to stimuli.)

Individuals and society

In his famous *Leviathan* (1651), Hobbes discussed the complexities of human nature that a sovereign ruler/government must consider in order to rule effectively. One interpretation of the book is that humans aren't naturally sociable – yet we're social animals in that we satisfy our needs interdependently. Education works to contain radical individualism and resolve the tension between individuals and society, while actualising justice and charity enables social harmony (Walsh *et al.*, 2014).

Sociability is the product of a rational social order designed to neutralise *three motives* that cause social conflict: (i) *competition:* the desire for personal gain; (ii) *diffidence:* fear for safety; and (iii) *glory:* the desire for reputation.

What we label 'good' conduct is merely what gives us pleasure; 'evil' is what causes pain. (Again, this has echoes in Skinner's claim that what is 'good' is what is rewarded and what's 'bad' is what's punished: see Chapter 6. Altruism is simply an expression of self-preservation: see Chapter 8)

Hobbes was a determinist in a culture celebrating free will; his views tended to detract from the truth of the claims that church authorities made about nature and human nature. He was seen as an atheist and a heretic (which endangered his life). He's also been seen as advocating that you can modify human nature just as you can manipulate physical objects (Walsh *et al.*, 2014).

John Locke (1632–1704)

Locke was the most influential of the 17th/18th century British *empiricist* philosophers (the others being Hume and Berkeley) as far as the history of psychology is concerned (in particular, behaviourism). However, he never used the word 'psychology', nor imagined that he was contributing to a discipline separate from logic:

> His fame is that he wrote the canonical text displaying knowledge of mind beginning with sensory experience, and for those psychologists who identify themselves as natural scientists, *this* is the foundation of their field as objective research.
>
> (Smith, 2013, p. 24)

Locke (see Figure 2.2) is probably best known for *An Essay Concerning Human Understanding* (1690), which discussed the nature of human knowledge from an *empiricist* perspective, i.e. the result of concrete sensory *experience*. 'Empirical' means 'through the senses' and has become synonymous with 'scientific': experience is the only route to reliable knowledge and the best means of obtaining

Figure 2.2 John Locke (1632–1704), British empiricist philosopher. (Permission granted by Mary Evans Library.)

truth is through observation and experimentation. For Locke, the recent discoveries of Galileo, Newton, and other pioneering scientists represented the pinnacle of human knowledge.

Locke agreed with Aristotle's suggestion that the mind, at birth, is a *tabula rasa* ('blank slate'); it's capable only of recording impressions from the external world and subsequently recalling and reflecting upon them. This claim entailed a rejection of Descartes' belief in innate ideas (such as infinity, perfection, and other 'universals') (Fancher and Rutherford, 2012). For Locke, our character or personality is *made* – not born – through our experience and the social world we grow up in.

Locke and the self

As individuals became increasingly aware of the depth of gulf between themselves and the external world, so a new conception of the *self* became possible:

> The self now became the subjectively localized point of origin from which each individual experienced and acted on a world that had become no more than a source of these experiences and of the raw material for the individual's actions.
>
> (Danziger, 1997, p. 48)

> *Time for reflection ...*
>
> - For Locke, the self is a point within experience that is 'disengaged' and quite separate from any specific actions or experiences of the individual.
> - This psychological (individual) view mirror Locke's *political* viewpoint that society is the aggregate of strictly separate individuals, rather than a collective entity.
> - Do you agree with Locke's political viewpoint?
> - What kind of an argument is Locke putting forward?

In subsequent Anglo-Saxon writing, Locke's empiricist view became part of the taken-for-granted framework for understanding the nature of the self: it is an object that can be empirically known/studied much like any other object. According to empiricism, how we obtain knowledge about the external world becomes the model for how we obtain self-knowledge (Toulmin, 1977). This is revolutionary: the dispassionate observation used by 'natural philosophers' (later, 'scientists') to study the external world has to be directed *inward* at a world of mental objects waiting to be discovered. These mental objects were to be dissected into their most elementary components (the most 'real') (another example of *reductionism*).

For much of the 18th century, those scientists and philosophers whom we'd now call 'psychologists' usually wrote about knowledge of *human nature*: if we know human nature, we'll know how to educate people to build a better world: if we control experience, we'll control action. This was '*Enlightenment*', the word used by later historians to name the post-Locke age: once free of ignorance and religious prejudice, free from the vanity and greed of kings and tsars, people would use knowledge to control both physical nature and human nature, to reduce suffering and increase happiness (Smith, 2013).

Jean-Jacques Rousseau (1712–78)

Rousseau (see Figure 2.3) inspired early *Romanticism,* according to which feelings, love of nature, and social relations are primary in human psychology (a kind of counter-Enlightenment). Box 2.5 summarises the essential features of Rousseau's thinking.

BOX 2.5 ROUSSEAU'S FOUR CENTRAL IDEAS

- *The innate goodness of human nature:* humans are essentially good, but society's institutions corrupt human nature. We're naturally sociable, capable of living in harmony with others, and perfection is possible by reforming society through proper education. Preserving a simple life prescribed by nature can prevent most of humanity's ills. Although he didn't coin the term 'noble savage', he emphasised the superiority of 'savages'; however, his positive evaluation of 'racial' differences mor- phed into its opposite in 19th/20th century science (see Chapter 3).

- *Primacy of passions:* passions are more reliable for guiding human conduct than reason, but he didn't reject reason: careful thinking is *complementary* to the passions ('great thoughts come from the heart').
- *Child-centred education:* his famous *Emile* (1762) was partly a response to Locke's ideas (Richards, 2010). The best education aids actualisation of innate human potential (although he regarded girls as inferior, seeing females as 'naturally' inclined to serve men). He advocated that educators should combine permissiveness with firm control. He also advocated *discovery learning*, proceeding from concrete sensory experience to con- cept formation and eventually abstract ideas. The quality of stimulation should be adapted to the child's developmental level. (See the discussion of Piaget's theory of child development in Gross, 2015.) Most impor- tantly, educating emotions should take priority over educating reason.
- *Social relations:* as a first principle, all humans are equal; when they chose to live in society, competition and conflict associated with inequalities came to dominate behaviour. Private property was the original cause of social corruption and evil (Locke believed we have a natural right to private property.) Rousseau proposed a *social contract* that would allow us to live in harmony together: the 'general will' – in today's terms, 'the common good' – should take precedence over individuals' self-centred interests.

(Based on Walsh *et al.*, 2014)

Figure 2.3 Jean-Jacques Rousseau (1712–78), French philosopher and author. (Permission granted by Mary Evans Library.)

Friedrich Nietzsche (1844–1900)

For Nietzsche (see Figure 2.4), the *will to power* is the single most important explanatory principle of nature/human nature (comparable to Hobbes'
conatus). This is discussed in Box 2.6.

BOX 2.6 NIETZSCHE'S 'WILL TO POWER'

- *The will to power* is the fundamental reality and primary motive of life.
  He opposed Darwin's notion of basic struggle for survival; instead, it's
  the struggle for power/preservation of a great individual who rises
  above the tribe. Human beings can only exercise their will to power
  individually: one person cannot find another's path to greatness.
- While the Judaeo-Christian ethical system favours the weak over the
  strong/healthy, Nietzsche promoted notions of self-mastery of the
  strong and noble. The certainty of death imposes the responsibility of
  free choices on every individual; we should all become the artist of
  our own life (a key existentialist emphasis: see Chapter 7). We only
  have the present moment, so we must make the best of it by exercis-
  ing our will to power.
- The will to power is more important than the human capacity for
  reason. In fact, Nietzsche was highly sceptical of the Enlightenment's
  blind faith in reason: so-called universal and eternal truths are *culturally specific*, created by language, objectivity is an illusion, and personal
  prejudices precede thinking (including scientific reasoning).
- Alfred Adler was influenced by the will to power idea: he famously
  described the 'inferiority complex' as a part of the human condition and individuals' attempts to compensate for this by gaining
  power (see Chapter 6). The will to power notion is also reflected in
  Abraham Maslow's account of self-actualisation and the self-actualised individual (see Chapter 7).

Like Schopenhauer, Nietzsche stressed the *irrational* aspects of human nature,
but unlike him, he believed the 'instincts' (including aggression) should be
fully expressed, not repressed/sublimated (two of Freud's *ego defence mechanisms:* see Chapter 6). He argued for a return to the pre-Socratic tradition of
autonomous, strong-willed men who balance reason and passion.

The Übermensch

In opposition to Schopenhauer's belief that suffering is one's lot in life,
Nietzsche stressed joyful affirmation of the life-force. Nietzsche was influenced by Goethe, who in his literary, philosophical, and scientific activities

Figure 2.4 Friedrich Nietzsche (1844–1900), German philosopher. (Permission granted by Mary Evans Library.)

had embodied Nietzsche's 'Superhuman' (*der Übermensch*), a person who rises above the ordinary.

For Nietzsche, the greatest challenge facing human beings is to be an *Übermensch*, a person who transcends desire and exercises creative powers to the fullest; the fully alive individual is master of reality rather than its slave, accepts whatever occurs, knowing that sorrow and joy are inseparable. Heroic people create their own values, moved by the will to power to define truth for themselves (see Chapter 8).

What animated Nietzsche was his strong sense that society was in danger of imminent decline to a value-less state. His famous 'God is dead! God remains dead! And we have killed him!' (Nietzsche, 1882) isn't so much a declaration of atheism as a fierce criticism of conventional Christianity. In one sense, this liberates human beings, but at the same time, it brings us into the age of *nihilism*. Man's self-affirmation takes place therefore against the background of a godless and absurd world (MacQuarrie, 1972). In a godless world, man himself has to take God's place: in *Beyond Good and Evil* (1886), Nietzsche declares that Man is condemned to be free and so carries the weight of the whole world on his shoulders. Man is entirely abandoned to fixing his own norms/determining his values and what he'll become.

Nietzsche regarded women as essentially passive and less rational than men. But he opposed anti-Semitism and any judgement of others based on their ethnocultural origins rather than their behaviour. He wasn't a prophet of Nazi racial and social ideology. But, assisted by his sister, the Nazis distorted his concept of the *Übermensch* and made him the Third Reich's favourite philosopher (Walsh *et al.*, 2014).

> *Time for reflection …*
>
> - Reflecting on the theories of Hobbes, Locke, Rousseau, and Nietzsche, is there one which you believe captures human nature better than the others?
> - Give your reasons.

Religion and the Seven Deadly Sins

> *Time for reflection …*
>
> - What does 'sin' mean to you?
> - Are some more serious than others?
> - Does the concept only have meaning in the context of religion?

While sin is strongly associated with religion:

> The seven deadly [sins] are primarily concerned with what it means to be human and humane and the responsibilities that we have to fulfil if we want to be considered as such …
>
> … most sins or vices, and the seven deadly ones, in particular, concern the core of what we are, of what we can become, and most importantly, of what we should aspire to be…We need to reclaim the rich insights into human nature of earlier moral reflection if we want to lead more satisfying lives.
>
> (Schimmel, 1997, pp. 4–5)

This earlier moral reflection can be found in three great moral traditions: (i) Graeco-Roman moral philosophy; (ii) Judaism; and (iii) Christianity. The latter two adopted 'vice'/'virtue' from the Greek and Roman moralists, often renaming vices 'sins'. It's perhaps more accurate to call them 'vices': while 'sins' are specific acts of commission or omission, 'vices' are basic, perhaps universal human tendencies ('human nature') from which sins result. (Also, 'deadly' might be a misnomer: a distinction is usually made between (i) more serious *mortal (capital/cardinal)* sins; and (ii) less serious *venial* sins, the difference depending on the underlying *motive* (malicious/negligent or addiction-related, respectively.) The seven 'deadly' sins can be of either type.

Judaism

For the Hebrew Bible, sin is a violation of a divine command. Many laws and teachings are meant to be universal, applying to all mankind (not just the ancient

Israelites), dealing with moral and ethical responsibility. From the biblical perspective, sinning against our neighbour is also sinning against God; for example, the condemnation of Adam and Eve for eating the forbidden fruit (from the tree of knowledge) in the Garden of Eden teaches that we mustn't give in to temptation when we know it's wrong: if we do, it will bring discord into the world and our relationships (in this case, it brought about our mortality!) (see Figure 2.5).

From the Hellenistic period (roughly 320 BCE–31 BCE, i.e. the period of Ancient Greece, to end of the 5th century), the biblical moral tradition was expanded by Jewish spiritual leaders, whose teachings were collected in the Talmud and Midrash ('rabbinic literature'). They analysed human thoughts and feelings even more than the Bible in terms of good and evil behaviour. They taught how to express our impulses in an acceptable, constructive way; for example (i) the sexual impulse, which cannot/shouldn't be eradicated, should be channelled to procreation within the legitimate sexual satisfactions of marriage; (ii) envy should be transformed into emulation of the wise and virtuous (see below); and (iii) love of food should include sharing it with the hungry.

Christianity

Stoic ideas, synthesised by Hellenistic Jews with Hebrew Scripture, shaped Christian conceptions of sin/virtue. Among Stoic teachings were (i) the virtue

Figure 2.5 Adam and Eve are tempted by the serpent who wears a crown to show that, despite its diabolical nature, it is still king of the underworld. (Permission granted by Mary Evans Library.)

of living in accordance with the law of Nature, which is Reason; and (ii) the value of *asceticism* (i.e. self-denial) as a way of cultivating indifference to life's vicissitudes. Stoics (such as Epictetus and Seneca) combined moral philosophy with practical instructions regarding how to achieve these objectives. The better able we are in divorcing ourselves from worldly pursuits and in controlling/eliminating emotions, the freer and happier we'll be.

Jesus accepted the Hebrew biblical tradition that thoughts and feelings – not just deeds – can be sinful. But he went further, stressing almost exclusively faith, the ethical and inner states, and intention, making radical demands on our feelings.

Paul's views markedly influenced all subsequent understandings of human nature and sin. The struggle against sin is primarily the will versus temptation: the body is the source of sin and we're impotent in overcoming its temptations through our will alone: we must rely on faith in Christ as the means of freeing ourselves from sin.

Catholic theologians, such as Pope Gregory the Great (540–604), distinguished between *sins of the flesh* (gluttony, lust) and *sins of the spirit/psychological sins* (pride, anger, envy, greed, acedia (sloth)).

Medieval artists often portrayed the Seven Sins as demons, monsters, fiends, animals, wounds, or diseases (e.g. syphilis, cholera). The greatest poetic uses of the Seven Sins is in Dante's *The Divine Comedy* (1308–20), which describes his journeys through Purgatory, talking with souls about their sins and crimes: only after being cleansed from the stain of their sins can sinners ascend to Heaven.

Seven Deadly Sins in the modern world

The Seven Deadly Sins – pride, anger, envy, greed, gluttony, lust, and sloth – are as relevant today as ever. For the most part, these vices are manifestations of our refusal to master our physical and psychological impulses:

> All of us are engaged to one degree or another in a personal, ongoing battle with sin and vice, although we may not think of our conflicts with our natures in those terms…when we give in to our low passions we debase humanity.
>
> (Schimmel, 1997, pp. 3–4)

So, the vices operate at both individual and social levels. While 'sin' usually points towards individual actors, 'vice' perhaps points more outwards, implying the institutionalisation of those sins (such as sexism and racism in politics, commerce, popular culture and entertainment, the police or armed forces, corporate greed as in the banking crisis of 2008, and corruption in countries such as Zimbabwe):

> Every deadly sin fuels harmful social phenomena: lust – pornography; gluttony – substance abuse; envy – terrorism; anger – violence;

sloth – indifference to the pain and suffering of others; greed- abuse of public trust; and pride – discrimination.

(Schimmel, 1997, p.4)

Envy, pride, and wrath are recognised today as emotions with evolutionarily adaptive functions: envy and pride propel us to seek status and resources, while gluttony, lust, and greed are related to the unconstrained consumption of food, sex, and power. For example, Hill and Buss (2008) suggest that repeatedly comparing ourselves with our neighbours could have helped us assess how we were faring in the competition for resources. Furthermore, the frustration and inferiority feelings ignited by envy can warn us about a disadvantage, spurring us on to compensate for a deficiency: see Chapter 9.

There's also experimental evidence that envy can sharpen our attention to our social surroundings and heighten interest in potential competitors (Crusius and Mussweiler, 2013). Wrath ensues if our pursuit of any of these ends is thwarted or threatened. Sloth is like the mirror-opposite of the other sins – a lack of motivation/drive (Jarrett, 2011).

A unifying theme underlying all the sins is insufficient self-control, a failure to rein in the animal within.

(Jarrett, 2011, p.98)

Envy; the other side of greed?

> **Time for reflection ...**
>
> • How do you think envy and greed might be related?

Materialistic values are fostered by living in a competitive culture that inculcates the idea that wealth and status are needed for happiness. If greed motivates us to acquire wealth and status, then envy is the emotion that's triggered when another achieves what we want, and we think they don't quite deserve it. We want the envied other to lose their wealth and status, giving rise to *schadenfreude* if this happens (the pleasure we take in another's pain, first described by Aristotle). But it needn't always take this sinister form.

According to Crusius and Mussweiler (2013), envy is often defined as the pain of occupying an inferior position relative to another and a desire for what they possess. In its more benign form, it can involve more positive sentiments, such as admiration (e.g. 'I'd like what they've got – but I don't want to deprive them of it'). The envied person may be seen as deserving their good fortune and this may motivate us to try to reach their level.

Not only is envy socially undesirable, but it can also be extremely unpleasant and painful: we go to great lengths to either conceal our discontent or transform the attendant emotions, i.e. we exert *self-control* to quell an upsurge of envy.

(Crusius and Mussweiler, 2013, p. 37; emphasis added)

Envy versus jealousy

> **Time for reflection ...**
> * How would you distinguish between envy and jealousy?

Smith (2008) defines envy in the negative, sinister way outlined above. But in *jealousy,* we fear losing an important relationship with another person to a ((n) often *sexual*) rival.

So, we might say that in jealousy, we fear the loss of something (usually somebody) that is precious to us, while in envy, we feel that something has already been lost (such as pride, self-esteem, or status relative to others). Consistent with this, Epstein (2003) claims that '*one is jealous of what one has, envious of what other people have*' (p. 4).

While Iago warns Othello (in Shakespeare's *Othello*) that jealousy is 'the green eyed monster that doth mock/the meat it feeds on' (Act III, Scene iii), it's actually *envy* that's central to the plot, setting everything in motion and 'forging and forcing the denouement' (Epstein, 2003, p. 47). (According to Walton (2004), green was established as the colour of jealousy long before Shakespeare, perhaps because it's also the colour of immaturity, inexperience, newness. We're 'green with envy' at someone else's success or possessions because we haven't come to emotional maturity in such matters.)

Interestingly, two of the better known (and controversial) aspects of Freud's psychoanalytic theory (see Chapter 6) are (i) the Oedipus complex, which centres on the young boy's desire to keep his mother's affections all to himself (with the father becoming a sexual rival); and (ii) penis envy, the female's desire to have male genitalia (of which she feels she's already been deprived). So, the former is 'jealous of what he has', the latter 'envious of what other people (i.e. males) have'.

Again, while envy is the feeling we have for others who have something we haven't (but want), jealousy involves not wanting them to have it either (Walton, 2004); a classic example of the latter is the rejected lover (typically male) who is determined that no other man will have her either (which he guarantees by killing her!).

Gluttony

This is currently discussed in relation to *obesity*, considered as an eating disorder (the word 'gluttony' being rarely used).

According to Prose (2003), compared with the other sins, how gluttony has been viewed has evolved more in accordance with the changing obsessions of society and culture. From the early Middle Ages until the early Renaissance, mass consciousness was dominated by Christian tenets: the main danger of gluttony was seen as a form of idolatry, diverting the faithful from true, authentic religion. According to Prose (2003), the Renaissance and later the Industrial Revolution and 18th century rationalism refocused popular imagination from heaven to earth: the goals of labour now included rewards of this world as well as the next. So, gluttony lost some of its stigma and eventually became almost a badge of pride:

> Substance, weight, and the ability to afford the most lavish pleasures of the table became visible signs of vitality, prosperity.
>
> (Prose, 2003, p. 3)

In the past few decades, major cultural preoccupation with health has rendered being overweight an unacceptable, external sign of *poor* health and the likelihood of a shortened life expectancy. Obesity is commonly seen as related to high fat, high-calorie diets (fast food, etc.), those associated predominantly with the less well-off in society. Gluttony has changed from being a sin that leads to other sins to an illness that leads to other illnesses. However:

> The punishments suffered by the modern glutton are at once more complex and subtle than eternal damnation. Now that gluttony has become an affront to prevailing standards of beauty and health rather than an offence against God, the wages of sin have changed and now involve a version of hell on earth: the pity, contempt, and distaste of one's fellow mortals.
>
> (Prose, 2003, p. 5)

If envy is the only sin that's inherently unpleasant, gluttony is alone in being highly visible, written on the body; it's also the one that appears to be most under our control (with the possible exception of sloth). As observed by Prose (2003), the contempt and distaste that are often directed at obese individuals reflect a conscious or unconscious belief that they are responsible for their condition – because they choose to overeat! (This represents the *moral view of addiction*, which is discussed below.) However, this is clearly a reduction of a complex problem to a single, simple, cause: not only is obesity caused by a number of different factors (gluttony being but one), but gluttony itself (like so many behaviours) is less than completely under our control.

Gluttony as an addiction

While gluttony is defined in terms of over-consumption of food, and if it sometimes seems to meet the criteria for an addiction, it may be useful to consider other addictions in order to better understand why people overeat.

Simring (2013) cites a 2009 study which provides a snapshot of what food addiction might look like in the brain. The researchers showed pictures of chocolate milkshakes to 48 women (previously assessed for their degree of food–addiction) while they had a brain scan. The more strongly addicted women showed higher activity levels in four regions also implicated in drug cravings and expectation of reward: the *caudate nucleus, medial orbitofrontal cortex, anterior cingulate cortex,* and the *amygdala* (see Chapter 3). These women also had increased activity in the *dorsolateral prefrontal cortex,* known to be active when people try to resist pleasurable foods. When the women actually drank the milkshake, those prone to food addiction – like drug addicts – showed *reduced activity* in the *lateral orbitofrontal cortex,* a pattern linked to reduced ability to inhibit responses to cues for rewards (such as food or drugs). (Criticisms of the inferences drawn from brain scans are discussed in Gross, 2018.)

Models of addiction

- The punishments that Prose (2003) claims are faced today by obese individuals reflect the *moral view of addiction,* according to which the addictive behaviour is freely chosen, making the addicted person fully responsible; in turn, this means that they are blameworthy. This is most clearly associated with a pre-scientific mode of thinking, although it can also be found in some scientific thinking.
- At the opposite extreme is the *disease view,* stemming from the early 1800s and culminating in its latest manifestation the *brain disease model of addiction* (BDMA). This conceptualises addictive behaviour as completely involuntary: addicts are 'compelled' to act as they do. The implication here is that addicts shouldn't be blamed or punished for any crimes or unacceptable social behaviour and should instead receive compassion and treatment. This characterisation is now so common among scientists and professionals that any challenge to it seems heretical.
- According to Heather (2018; Heather and Segal, 2017), there's a mountain of evidence against the view that addictive behaviour is compulsive in any straightforward sense. Not only is the BDMA an example of 'greedy reductionism' (Dennett), but it depicts *brains* as being addicted when we can only properly talk about *people* who are (Heather, 2018). In addition, it may reduce addicts' chances of recovery by telling them they're powerless to change without special help: 'the language of irreversible brain disease and of compulsion is a strong disincentive to self-change and to the success of treatment aimed at helping people change' (Heather, 2018, p. 28).
- There's clearly need for a 'middle ground' between these two extreme positions. One possibility is *temporal inconsistency* (Levy, 2013): addicts cannot effectively exercise their will over an extended period of time: 'It is because addiction undermines extended agency, so that addicts are not able to integrate their lives and pursue a single conception of the good, that it impairs autonomy' (Levy, 2006, p. 427).
- Levy's account is consistent with the view of addiction as a *disorder of self-regulation* (or choice); in turn, this can be subsumed under a more

general proposal that addiction can be explained within the framework of a *dual-systems theory of human behaviour and experience*. Essentially, this framework claims that all behaviour and experience is the result of (i) implicit, automatic, non-conscious processes; and (ii) explicit, controlled, mainly conscious processes (see Chapter 5). Normally, these are balanced, but in addiction, the balance has become disturbed, with a bias towards (i) (Heather, 2018).

Some additional, modern-day sins

In 2008, Bishop Gianfranco Girotti announced that the Catholic Church has added seven new sins: polluting, genetic engineering, obscene wealth, drug abuse, abortion, paedophilia, and the perpetuation of social injustice (Gravotta, 2013).

In 2011, the first confessional iPhone app was developed, helping users to keep their sins straight and includes a 'custom examination of conscience' and the ability to 'choose from seven different acts of contrition' (Gravotta, 2013).

Jarrett (2011) identifies six new deadly sins for the 21st century (see Box 2.7).

BOX 2.7 NEW 21ST CENTURY DEADLY SINS

- *Truthiness:* the preference for concepts/facts that we *wish* to be true as opposed to those *known* to be true. It can have staggering – even apocalyptic – consequences for others, the community, even the world (such as denying global warming). But what about belief in God?

- *Iphonophilia:* constantly checking one's smartphone for texts, etc., while in actual conversation with others (see Figure 2.6).

- *Mobile abuse:* shouting into your mobile on the bus or other public places, and 'walking and talking' so that others have to deliberately avoid knocking into you.

- *Narcissistic myopia:* taking whatever one wants now and forgetting that future generations rely on the current generation to leave them a habitable world (global warming again!).

- *Entitlement:* the absolutist requirement that all one's egocentric demands for 'justice' not only be fully met but also be of keen interest to the rest of the world – no matter how trivial or inconsequential the injustices and irrespective of how great the redress of perceived inequality has been to date (cf. what Ellis called 'Musturbation').

- *Excessive debt:* individuals, politicians, and governments are guilty. (This can be thought of as an extension or modern manifestation of greed: but 'the more you have the more you want' is a deeply materialist-culture thing.)

(Based on Jarrett, 2011)

Figure 2.6 Three female students 'on' their electronic devices: do they enhance social interaction through conformity, or are they replacing it? (iStock.)

Summary and conclusions: psychological versus natural kinds

According to Smith (2013), after 1800, university disciplines came into existence in the natural sciences and humanities in something like their contemporary form (including social and psychological sciences). Needless to say, beliefs about human nature and conduct were being discussed long before this.

> It may even appear obvious that some kind of belief about mind has been present in all cultures around the world at all times. But we should be cautious. Any way we characterize people, using terms like human nature, human being, man and woman, race and ethnicity, mind and body, is weighted with meaning with a long history.
>
> (Smith, 2013, p. 9)

If, for example, you claim that everyone makes assumptions about human nature, you should be aware of cultures which relate human and animal in entirely non-Western ways, indeed, which think of animals as humans – not humans as animals. But hasn't Western science discovered the truth?

> If you are interested in how people live, or if you think that natural science is not the answer to every question … then the very terms in which different people think about the world has great significance.
>
> (Smith, 2013, p. 10)

Have psychological concepts always been the same?

Not only are psychological concepts culturally relative, but they're also *historically relative*. According to Danziger (1997), modern academic psychology is deeply *ahistorical*: it fails to see psychological categories and concepts from a historical perspective. The discipline of psychology had modelled itself on natural science, and because natural science is supposed to be concerned with *natural* – not historical – *objects* (such as rocks, electrons, DNA, and stars, which have always existed objectively, independently of the scientific researcher), psychologists have implicitly taken their objects of study (such as 'intelligence', 'emotion', motivation', 'personality') as natural kinds.

However, rather than being natural, tangible, historically invariant phenomena, 'intelligence', etc., are more accurately described as *psychological kinds:* people's actions, experiences, and dispositions *aren't* independent of how they're categorised (Danziger, 1997). The fact that 'intelligence' has been put in speech marks, implies that it doesn't exist in the way that rocks, etc., do. By not using speech marks, we create the impression that we all agree about what these terms denote and that they describe what people are actually ('really') like (their 'essence' or 'human nature' – both of which are timeless): they *seem* natural – but only to members of a particular linguistic community. While the concept of 'natural kinds' has nothing to do with culture, natural-*appearing* psychological kinds have *everything* to do with it (Danziger, 1997).

Even though pre-20th-century writers may not have structured their reflections around topics such as 'intelligence', etc., they're still presented as having had theories about them. If changes in such categories are acknowledged at all, it's their *present-day* form that's taken to define their 'true' nature: older work is interesting only in as much as it *anticipates* what we now know to be true.

Psychological kinds are *constructions* (or *hypothetical constructs*), abstract concepts used to make sense of observed behaviour; to understand them (and the real influence they can have on people's behaviour and experience), we need to analyse the historical conditions that gave rise to them. Even in the case of much older psychological categories (such as 'emotion', 'motive', 'consciousness', and 'self-esteem'), whose original meaning has been largely retained, this continuity of meaning may only apply within our Western cultural tradition (Gergen, 2001).

Suggested further reading

Blackburn, S. (2004) *Lust*. New York: Oxford University Press.

Dyson, M.E. (2006) *Pride*. New York: Oxford University Press.

Epstein, J. (2003) *Envy*. New York: Oxford University Press.

Prose, F. (2003) *Gluttony*. New York: Oxford University Press.

Schimmel, S. (1997) *The Seven Deadly Sins: Jewish, Christian and Classical Reflections on Human Psychology*. New York: Oxford University Press.

Thurman, R.A.F. (2005) *Anger*. New York: Oxford University Press.

Tickle, P.A. (2004) *Greed*. New York: Oxford University Press.

Wasserstein, W. (2005) *Sloth*. New York: Oxford University Press.

3 The biology of human nature

Genetics and the brain

Key questions

- What are the basic principles of genetics?
- How do the human and chimpanzee genomes compare with each other and with that of gorillas?
- Are there specifically human genes or (merely) human forms of the same basic genes shared by all mammals?
- What does genetic research tell us about the concept of 'race'?
- What physical, cognitive, and social consequences might becoming the 'naked ape' have had for *Homo sapiens*?
- How might the *loss* of certain genetic material account for uniquely human characteristics?
- What are the major structures and sub-divisions of the human brain?
- How are intelligence and brain size related?
- What's meant by the *plasticity* of the human brain?
- How are the long period of human immaturity and brain development related?
- How are mirror neurons and theory of mind related?
- What's distinctive about the human brain compared with those of other primates and mammals in general?

Religious versus evolutionary perspectives

As outlined in Chapter 2, for thousands of years philosophy and religion have been trying to answer fundamental questions about our nature, our essence, what it means to be human. From a religious perspective, the answer can sometimes appear quite straightforward: we are part of God's creation and are different from other animal species because that's how He determined we should be. However, since the mid-1850s in particular, evolutionary theory has fundamentally challenged this religious view and part of that challenge involves re-framing the questions we want to try to answer about human beings.

'Man' versus Homo sapiens

While philosophical and religious writings talk about us as 'Man' (i.e. 'human beings'), evolutionary biologists, palaeontologists (who study extinct and fossil species), palaeoanthropologists (who study hominin fossils in particular), and others interested in human evolution (including geneticists), refer to *Homo sapiens*. It's now widely agreed (at least by these and other scientific disciplines) that human beings ('*Homo*') are a distinct biological species, evolved over millions of years from now-extinct ancestors (including *Homo neanderthalensis*).

Along with this change of terminology comes a change in the very questions we ask about ourselves, and, hence, the possible answers. For example, (i) where and when did our species first appear?; (ii) where do we come from?; and (iii) who are we? How did people end up being everywhere? (Roberts, 2009).

Answers include the following: 'Modern humans are just the latest in a long line of two-legged apes, technically known as hominins' (Roberts, 2009, p.3). We're the only surviving *hominin* species alive today (as far as we know): 'By 30,000 years ago, it seems there were only two twigs left on the hominin family tree: modern humans and our close cousins, the Neanderthals. Today, only we remain' (Roberts, 2009, p. 3).

Palaeoanthropologists disagree amongst themselves about exactly how many species of ancient hominins there were; underlying this disagreement is an even more fundamental question: *what determines a separate species?* Basically, species are populations that are diagnosably different from each other, in terms of their *genes* (the basic units of heredity) or *morphology* (the way their bodies are constructed) – or both (Roberts, 2009). As a general rule, different species cannot interbreed. While *Homo sapiens* ('wise human' or modern human) and *Homo neanderthalensis* belong to the same *genus* (*Homo*), they're generally regarded as different species. Yet there's widely accepted evidence that these two populations did interbreed – and the most convincing such evidence is *genetic* (see below).

Before we look any further at this evidence, we need to consider some basic aspects of genetics.

An outline of genetics

Ridley (1999) asks us to imagine that the *human genome* (the total set of genes that distinguish modern humans from other species) is a book (see Figure 3.1).

- The book comprises 23 chapters (the number of human *chromosomes*, each of us inheriting one member of each of the 23 pairs, one from each parent).
- Each chapter contains several thousand stories (*genes*). (In fact, the number now appears to be about 23,500: Le Page, 2010.)

- Each story is composed of paragraphs (*exons*), which are interrupted by advertisements (*introns*).
- Each paragraph is made up of words (*codons*).
- Each word is written in letters (*bases*). (There are an estimated 3 billion bases: Pollard, 2009.)
- There are one billion words in the book (as long as 800 Bibles).

Genomes are written *entirely* in three-letter words, using only four letters: A (which stands for *adenine*), C (*cytosine*), G (*guanine*), and T (*thymine*). Also, instead of being written on flat pages, these words are written on long chains of sugar and phosphate called DNA (deoxyribonucleic acid) molecules; the bases are attached as side rungs. Each chromosome is one pair of very long DNA molecules. Ridley (1999) describes the genome as a 'very clever book': in the right conditions, it can both photocopy itself (*replication*), and read itself (*translation*).

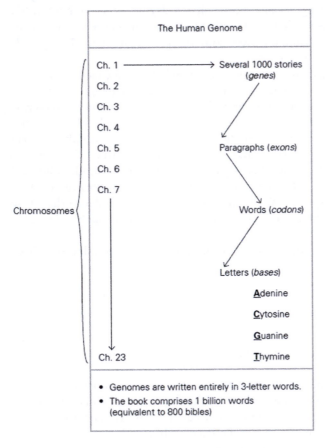

Figure 3.1 The human genome represented as a book.

BOX 3.1 REPLICATION AND TRANSLATION

- **Replication** works because of an ingenious property of the four bases: A pairs only with T, and G pairs only with C. So, a single strand of DNA can copy itself by assembling a complementary strand with Ts opposite all the As, As opposite all the Ts, Cs opposite all the Gs, and Gs opposite all the Cs. In fact, the usual state of DNA is the famous *double helix* of the original strand and its complementary pair intertwined (see Figure 3.2).

So, to make a copy of the complementary strand brings back the original text: the sequence ACGT becomes TGCA in the copy, which transcribes back to ACGT in the copy of the copy. In this way, DNA can replicate indefinitely, while still containing the same information.

- **Translation** begins with the text of a gene being *transcribed* (translated) into a copy by the same base-pairing process described above. But this time, the copy is made of RNA (ribonucleic acid) – a very slightly different chemical. RNA can also carry a linear code and uses the same letters as DNA – except that it uses U (*uracil*) instead of T. This RNA copy (called *messenger RNA*) is then edited by removing all introns and the splicing together of all exons (see text above).

Ribosomes (made partly from RNA) then move along the messenger RNA, translating each three-letter codon (word) in turn into one letter of a different alphabet; this consists of 20 different *amino acids,* each brought by a different version of a molecule called *transfer RNA.* Each amino acid is attached to the last to form a chain in the same order as the codons. When the whole message has been translated, the chain of amino acids folds itself up into a distinctive

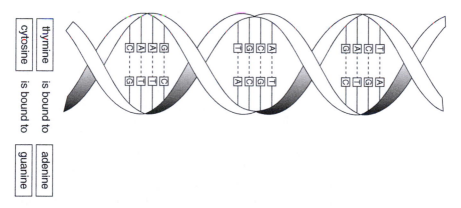

cytosine is bound to guanine
thymine is bound to adenine

Figure 3.2 Schematic representation of the structure of a DNA molecule.

shape that depends on its sequence. It's now referred to as a *protein*. Every protein is a translated gene.

Almost everything in the body is either made *of* proteins or made *by* them (Ridley, 1999). Proteins are also responsible for switching genes on and off. Different genes are switched on in different parts of the body. 'Somehow, those gene–words create a conversation telling one fertilised cell to multiply and change and multiply and change until an adult human being is produced' (Roberts, 2009, p. 186).

Mutations and mitochondria

The errors that can and do occur when genes are replicated are called *mutations*. As Ridley (1999) points out, many mutations are neither harmful nor beneficial; however, in the wrong place, even a single one can be fatal.

Not all human genes are found on the chromosomes; a few live inside little blobs called *mitochondria*, tiny capsules inside the cell, taking fuel – sugar – and burning it to produce energy. These gene 'power stations' are called 'mtDNA'. Also, there are long stretches of DNA that mean nothing to the cell: the bits between genes that are never 'read' to produce proteins.

Mutations accumulate more rapidly in mtDNA than in nuclear DNA (i.e. the genes inside the cell nucleus). Also, mtDNA doesn't get mixed up at each generation like nuclear genes; it remains untouched inside the mitochondria (which we all inherit from the mother). This means that maternal lineages can be traced back using mtDNA. There's a part of the Y (male) chromosome that also doesn't recombine (through sexual reproduction): this allows tracing back of paternal lineages. The branch points of family trees correspond with the appearance of specific mutations (Roberts, 2009).

'Junk DNA'

Not all DNA spells out genes: in fact, most of it is a jumble of repetitive or random sequences that's rarely or never transcribed (Ridely, 1999). According to Le Page (2010), 85–95 per cent of our DNA has no demonstrable function.

However, the blueprint for building a human (or any complex organism) lies not only in our genes but in other, neglected DNA, which might have shaped critical traits such as upright stance, opposable thumbs, large brains, capacity for language, even the tendency to form pair bonds. We now know that so-called 'junk DNA' controls genes like a conductor directs an orchestra, switching them on/off at different times and in different cells. This has emerged from comparisons of the human genome with that of chimps, mice and other mammals, Neanderthals, and other hominins (see below). The aim is to identify any bits that look suspiciously different in modern humans – that are uniquely ours (Barras, 2016). An example of junk DNA is given in Box 3.2.

BOX 3.2 HACNS1: 'JUNK DNA' AND HUMAN EVOLUTION

- HACNS1 has accumulated an unusually large number of mutations since humans split from chimps.
- According to Prabhakar *et al.* (2008), thumbs and feet are among the most distinctive human features. Evidence from the fossil record suggests that our ancestors evolved opposable thumbs about three million years ago – roughly when they began to use stone tools and only a few million years after the split from chimps.
- Standing upright (*bipedalism*) also appeared at around the same time or a little earlier. This was related to toes shrinking and foot arches becoming more rigid.
- All this could have been happening around the time that HACNS1 began altering gene activity in our hands and feet. This little piece of DNA, by subtly changing when and where genes were switched on, could have been modifying our hands and feet.

Junk DNA and methylation

Methylation refers to the process in which a chemical unit (a *methyl group*) is attached to a gene segment, influencing how much protein it produces. There's evidence suggesting that junk DNA is involved and represents another example of how *genetic controllers* – rather than genes themselves – played a crucial part in our evolution.

According to Hernando-Herraez *et al.* (2013), DNA methylation may have helped our transition to bipedalism and perhaps also our language skills. They compared methylation patterns in humans, gorillas, and orang-utans and found 171 genes with uniquely human patterns; these involved regulating blood pressure (BP), controlling development of the inner ear, and shaping facial muscles. Bipedalism lifted the brain: our ancestors had to change how they regulated BP to keep the brain fully oxygenated. It also required exceptional balance, typically improved by modifying the inner ear. Speech required an unprecedented level of control over facial muscles, especially around the mouth.

Gokhman *et al.* (2014) studied ancient DNA extracted from Neanderthals (and Denisovans). They found key differences in the genes that control limb movements: they were less active in archaic humans. By switching some genes on/off and making them pump out different amounts of proteins, methylation could have contributed to giving us longer legs.

Comparing the human and chimpanzee genome

According to Bodmer (2007), the obvious explanation for what makes us human must lie within the genetic differences that distinguish *Homo sapiens* from other species, especially chimpanzees.

On a purely *quantitative* level, it's well-known that humans and chimps have the overwhelming percentage of their genes in common: this figure ranges from 95 (e.g. Pasternak, 2007) to 98.4 per cent (Jones, 1994). According to Pasternak, the most likely interpretation of this dissimilarity is that it reflects not different genes, but merely *different mutations* within genes that are common to ape and man: specifically 'human genes' don't exist.

How similar are we?

Pasternak (2007) focuses on behavioural and cognitive *continuity* between humans and chimps (see Chapter 5). The *anatomical* differences between humans and chimps are also relatively minor, including the skeleton and the voice box.

According to Dunbar (2007), humans are genetically more closely related to the two chimpanzee species (the common chimpanzee and the bonobo) than any of the three of us is related to the gorilla. Indeed, it's since been shown that we're more closely related to each other than the two gorilla species (the physically barely distinguishable eastern and western gorillas) are related to each other! According to Dunbar, the universally accepted position is now that the big split in the great ape family isn't between humans and the other great apes, but between the Asian orangutan and the four (or should it be five?) species of African great apes (one of which is *Homo sapiens*). Humans are now, strictly speaking, firmly ensconced within the chimpanzee family (Dunbar, 2007). As Jones (1994) puts it:

> Any idea that humans are on a lofty genetic pinnacle is simply wrong. A taxonomist from Mars armed with a DNA hybridisation machine would classify humans, gorillas and chimpanzees as members of the same closely-related biological family.
>
> (p. 130)

What are the key differences?

While humans have 23 pairs of chromosomes, chimps, gorillas, and orangutans have 24 pairs! We're the exception to the rule among the great apes (Ridley, 1999). What has happened is that chromosome 2, the second largest of the human chromosomes, has formed from fusion of two medium-sized ape chromosomes.

Because most random genetic mutations neither benefit nor harm an organism, they accumulate at a steady rate that reflects the amount of time that has elapsed since two living species had a common ancestor (the 'ticking of the molecular clock'). An *accelerated* rate of change in some part of the genome is a hallmark of positive selection: those genes that have undergone the most modification since the chimp–human split are the ones that most likely shaped humankind (Pollard, 2009).

At the top of a list of rapidly evolving sequences is *human accelerated region 1* (HAR1), a stretch of 118 bases. HAR1 is found in the genomes of mice, rats, chickens, 12 other vertebrate species, as well as chimps and humans. However, until humans came along, HAR1 evolved extremely slowly; this abrupt revision in humans suggests that HAR1 performs some important function.

Pollard's research revealed that HAR1 is active in a type of *neuron* (brain cell) that plays a key role in the pattern and layout of the developing cerebral cortex. When something goes wrong in this process, it may result in a severe, often fatal, congenital disorder known as *lissencephaly* ('smooth brain'): the cortex lacks its characteristic folds (*convolution*) and there's a much-reduced surface area (see Figure 3.4). Malfunctions in these same neurons are also linked to the onset of schizophrenia in adults. So, HAR1 is active at the right time and place to be instrumental in the formation of a normal human cortex (Pollard, 2009).

As Pasternak (2007) observes, we might suppose that genes which play a role in the development of upright gait, mobile thumbs, vocal cords, and cortical neurons are the ones that show the greatest difference between chimpanzee and human. But we'd be mistaken. This is illustrated by the case of the *FOXP2* gene, which contains another of the fast-changing sequences (like HAR1) (see Box 3.3).

BOX 3.3 *FOXP2, LANGUAGE AND THE KE FAMILY*

- Half of the members of an extended English family (the KE family) are affected by *Specific Language Impairment* (SLI), a speech and language disorder evident from the affected child's first attempts to speak and persisting into adulthood (e.g. Vragha-Khadem *et al.*, 1995).
- By definition, SLI isn't a consequence of autism, deafness, mental retardation, or other non-linguistic problems – although they may co-occur (Pinker, 1994).
- While they have problems in speech articulation (especially as children) and in fine tongue/mouth movements (such as sticking out their tongue or blowing on command), their language disorder cannot be reduced to a motor problem: they also have trouble identifying phonemes (basic sounds that affect meaning), understanding sentences, judging grammar, and so on (Bishop and Norbury, 2002). On average, they have lower intelligence (IQ) test scores, but some affected members score in the normal range – and some score higher than unaffected relatives (Bishop and Norbury, 2002; Lai *et al.*, 2001).
- SLI is now known to be due to a point mutation on the *FOXP2* gene on chromosome 7 (Fisher *et al.*, 1998; Lai *et al.*, 2001). To acquire normal speech, two functional copies of *FOXP2* seem to be necessary.

Pinker (1994) went as far as identifying *FOXP2* as the 'grammar gene' – although he has more recently acknowledged that other genes probably also played a role in the evolution of grammar (Gentilucci and Corballis, 2007). However, subsequent research suggests that the core deficit in affected members of the KE family is one of *articulation* (i.e. speech), with grammatical impairment a secondary outcome (Watkins *et al.,* 2002a). Lai *et al.* (2001) reported that the disorder involves the inability to make certain subtle, high-speed facial movements needed for normal human speech – despite possessing the cognitive ability needed for processing language.

FOXP2 has been a target of selection in human evolution, probably during the last 200,000 years (when anatomically modern humans evolved) and probably within the last 100,000 (Enard *et al.*, 2002 in Corballis, 2002); it was selected for *directly* (rather than hitchhiking on an adjacent selected gene). The mutation of *FOXP2* was probably just the final step in a series of progressive changes (Gentilucci and Corballis, 2007), including freeing the hands for the development of technologies (allowing speech to become autonomous) (Corballis, 2002; see Chapter 5).

Clearly, merely possessing the *FOXP2* gene doesn't make speech possible. But perhaps having the peculiar human form of the gene is a prerequisite of speech (Ridley, 2003). Since the split with chimps ('a mere yesterday': Ridley, p. 215), there have already been another two very recent changes that alter the protein:

> Some time after 200,000 years ago, a mutant form of *FOXP2* appeared in the human race ... and that mutant form was so successful in helping its owner to reproduce that his or her descendants now dominate the species to the utter exclusion of all previous forms of the gene.
>
> (Ridley, 2003, p. 215)

Whole-genome comparisons in other species have shown that *where* DNA substitutions occur in the genome can make a big difference – rather than *how many* changes there are overall: you don't need to change very much of the genome to make a new species (Pollard, 2009).

Modern humans, Neanderthals, and FOXP2

Compared with other living primates, people lacking those human-specific changes to *FOXP2* have problems in both producing *and* understanding speech. Analysis in living people suggested the gene appeared and swept through the human population about 200,000 years ago (consistent with their appearance in Africa: see text below). It suggests that 'modern' language and symbolic behaviour are uniquely human attributes, with a biological basis (Roberts, 2009). (See Chapter 5.)

However, there's evidence for symbolic behaviour in the Neanderthal archaeological record (including intentional burial). Also, it's difficult to imagine how complex subsistence strategies would have appeared – from around 800,000 years ago – without complex social communication (see Chapter 9). And yet the 'human' version of *FOXP2* was initially estimated to have arisen well *after* the split between modern human and Neanderthal lineages.

Indeed, Krause *et al.* (2007) found the 'human' form of the gene in two Spanish Neanderthal fossils, showing that the 'much maligned Neanderthals' had a degree of human behaviour (Roberts, 2009).

BOX 3.4 MODERN HUMANS' NEANDERTHAL ORIGINS

- A long-awaited draft sequence of the Neanderthal genome (Green *et al.*, 2010), comprising more than four billion nucleotides from three individuals, was compared with the genomes of five present-day humans from different parts of the world.
- This has revealed that our own DNA contains clear evidence that early humans interbred with Neanderthals; nor were Neanderthals the only other *Homo* species that early *Homo sapiens* mated with. The genome of humans today is one to four per cent Neanderthal.
- These findings cast doubt on the familiar story that modern humans left Africa around 100,000 years ago and swept aside all other *Homo* species as they made their way around the globe. A more likely scenario is that as *Homo sapiens* migrated, they met and interbred with other *Homo* species that have all since died out (Callaway, 2010), (see text below).
- Pollard (2009) cites research (in 2007) which involved sequencing *FOXP2* extracted from a Neanderthal fossil and found that these extinct humans possessed the modern human version of the gene – perhaps enabling them to enunciate as we do.

Genes, language, and the brain

As important as *FOXP2* may be for understanding human language (especially speech), most of what distinguishes human language from vocal communication in other species reflects differences in cognitive ability; these, in turn, are correlated with brain size. Primates generally have a larger brain than would be expected from their body size (but see below). However, human brain volume has more than tripled since chimps and humans shared a common ancestor (Pollard, 2009).

One of the best-studied examples of a gene linked to brain size in humans and other species is *ASPM*. Genetic studies of people with *microcephaly*, in which the brain is reduced by up to 70 per cent, have revealed the role of *ASPM*, as well as three other genes – *MCPH1, CDK5RAP2,* and *CENPJ* – in controlling brain size. *ASPM* has been shown to have undergone several bursts of change over the course of primate evolution, suggesting positive selection. At least one of these bursts occurred in the human lineage since it diverged from that of chimps and so was potentially instrumental in the evolution of our large brain (Pollard, 2009).

Genes beyond the brain

In addition to undergoing morphological changes, our ancestors underwent behavioural and physiological shifts that helped them adapt to changed circumstances and migrate to new environments.

A much-cited example is *dietary adaptation* involving the gene for lactase (*LCT*), an enzyme that allows mammals to digest the carbohydrate lactose (or milk sugar). In most species, only nursing infants can process lactose. But around 9,000 years ago, changes in the human genome produced versions of *LCT* that allowed adults to also digest it. Today, adult descendants of ancient African and European herdsmen are much more likely to tolerate lactose in their diets compared with adults from other parts of the world; many Asian and Latin American adults are lactose-intolerant, having the ancestral primate version of the gene (Pollard, 2009).

A different kind of example of genetic change that can help explain the evolution of *Homo sapiens* as a distinct species relates to the loss of fur and the acquisition of dark skin. This is discussed in Box 3.5.

BOX 3.5 THE HUMAN *MC1R* GENE AND THE 'NAKED APE'

- Humans are the only primate species that has mostly naked (i.e. fur-less) skin. Loss of fur was an adaptation to changing environmental conditions that forced our ancestors to travel longer distances in search of food and water (Jablonski, 2010).

- Early human ancestors are thought to have had pinkish skin covered with black fur, much like chimpanzees, so the evolution of permanently dark skin was presumably a requisite evolutionary follow-up to the loss of our sun-shielding body hair.

- Going furless had profound consequences for subsequent phases of human evolution: the loss of most of our body hair and the gain of the ability to get rid of excess body heat through *eccrine* sweating (the epidermis comprises mainly eccrine glands, which permit improved cooling compared with furry animals) helped to make possible the dramatic enlargement of our brain – our most temperature-sensitive organ (Jablonski, 2010); 'shedding body hair was surely a critical step in becoming brainy' (Jablonski, 2016, p. 59), (see text below).

Time for reflection ...

- According to Jablonski (2016), our hairlessness also had *social* consequences.
- What do you think some of these might have been (bearing in mind that fur is a uniquely (and defining) *mammalian* characteristic?

We don't have body hair that cats, dogs, and chimps use to signal emotional states, nor do we have camouflage ('in-built advertising'). Perhaps human traits such as social blushing and complex facial expressions evolved to compensate for our lost ability to communicate through fur.

Likewise, body paint, cosmetics, tattoos, and other skin decoration are found in various combinations in all cultures: they convey group membership, status, and other vital social information (formerly encoded by fur). Non-verbal communication is also used to broadcast our emotional states and intentions, and language helps us speak our mind in detail. Viewed like this, 'naked skin did not just cool us down – it helped make us who we are' (Jablonski, 2016, p. 59).

Genetics and 'race'

Time for reflection ...

- What do you understand by 'race'?
- Do you believe that distinct races actually exist?

Marcia and Millie Madge Biggs are fraternal (non–identical or dizygotic/DZ) twins: one is white, one is black. How is this possible? It's actually more common than we might think.

DZ twins account for about 1 in 100 births. When a biracial couple has DZ twins, the traits that emerge in each depend on numerous variables, including the parents' ancestors' origins and complex pigment genetics. Skin colour isn't a binary trait: it's a *quantitative* trait and everyone can be placed on the *same spectrum*.

Morton, an American 19th century doctor and 'craniometrist', studied the volumes of craniums collected from all over the world. He claimed that people could be divided into five races, representing separate acts of creation; they had distinct characters, corresponding to their place in a divinely determined hierarchy. Whites/Caucasians are the most intelligent; then East Asians ('Mongolian'); then Southeast Asians, Native Americans, and finally Blacks ('Ethiopians').

In the decades before the American Civil War, Morton's ideas were quickly adopted by defenders of slavery and today, Morton is widely regarded as the father of scientific racism (Kolbert, 2018).

Geneticists now claim that the whole concept of race is misconceived. When the first complete human genome was assembled (2000), it was declared that the concept of race has no genetic/scientific basis. Race defined as 'genetically discrete groups' *doesn't* exist (Bamshad and Olson, 2003).

According to Kolbert (2018), genetic research over the past few decades has revealed two deep truths about people:

1   All humans are closely related – more so than all chimps (even though there are many more humans than chimps). We all have the same collection of genes, but (with the exception of identical or monozygotic/MZ twins) with slightly different versions of them.
2   Based on studies of this genetic diversity, scientists have reconstructed a sort of family tree of human populations: in a very real sense, all people alive today are Africans.

Consistent with these findings, genetic differences *between* the classically described races (European, Indian, African, East Asian, New World, and Oceanian) are, on average, only slightly higher (ten per cent) than those that exist between nations *within* a racial group (six per cent), and the genetic differences between individuals within a population are *far greater* than either of these (84 per cent) (Fernando, 1991).

Ethnic diversity and skin colour

The Khoe-San (of South Africa) represent one of the oldest branches of the human family tree, the Pygmies (of central Africa) also have a very long history as a separate group. This means that the deepest splits in the human family *aren't* between, say, whites or blacks or Asians or Native Americans: they're between African populations such as the Khoe-San and Pygmies who spent tens of thousands of years separated from one another even before humans left Africa (Kolbert, 2018). There's greater diversity in Africa than on all other continents combined: that's because modern humans originated there and have lived there the longest; they've had time to evolve enormous genetic diversity, including skin colour (and its 2,000-plus languages are used as a guide). There is *no* homogeneous African race; those who left Africa 60,000 years ago reflected only a fraction of Africa's diversity (Kolbert, 2018).

Less is more: is the loss of DNA the key to human uniqueness?

A ground-breaking study by McLean *et al.* (2011) has provided insight into how genetic changes helped us evolve our most prized asset – 'a large brain that enables us to reason, imagine, think forwards and backwards in time and unravel our own genetic and cosmological origins' (Coghlan, 2011, p. 6) (see below and Chapter 5).

The key changes are those that involve the *loss* of several hundred 'snippets' of DNA that McLean *et al.* believe are crucial in explaining human distinctiveness. (The snippets or chunks in question are bits of junk DNA: see above.)

McLean *et al.* compared the genomes of humans, chimps, macaques, chickens, and mice; they specifically looked for regulatory regions that are uniquely *absent* in humans but apparently vital to the other species. They identified 510 instances where the loss of DNA removed a sequence that's highly conserved in other animals, suggesting that the deletions were likely to have had functional consequences for humans. They then focused on two of these instances, both *enhancers* (they boost the production of a protein): the first is located next to *AR*, a gene that makes receptors for male hormones; the second switches on *GADD45G*, a gene that inhibits the growth of brain tissue.

The *AR* gene causes the growth of sensory whiskers on the faces of foetal mice and spines on the surface of the mouse penis. The loss of such spines may have allowed humans to prolong sex (which, in turn, may have made it more intimate) and helped establish the emotional bonds between partners (monogamous relationships) needed for the prolonged task of raising children.

In mice and chimps, the GADD45G *regulator* gene *suppresses* the development of brain regions which in humans are involved in higher cognitive functions (such as conscious thought and language). The loss of this gene may have been a pivotal moment in human evolution, allowing parts of the human brain to expand into the most complex known entity in the universe.

Evolution of the brain

A brief tour of the human brain

The brain, together with the spinal cord, comprise the *central nervous system* (CNS); the *peripheral nervous system* (PNS) subdivides into (i) the *somatic* (SNS), involved in voluntary bodily movements; and (ii) the *autonomic* (ANS), which controls the activity of the *viscera* (heart, stomach, intestines, glands, etc.). The ANS has two branches: the *sympathetic* and *parasympathetic*.

The NS as a whole comprises approximately 100 billion (100,000,000,000) *neurons*, 80 per cent of which are found in the brain (especially in the *cerebral cortex*, the topmost outer layer). However, there are several types of non-neuronal cells, including *glial cells* (or *glia*), and *spindle cells*.

During the first five weeks of foetal life, the neural tube changes its shape to produce five bulbous enlargements; these are generally accepted as the basic divisions of the brain, namely:

- The *myelencephalon* (comprising the medulla oblongata).
- The *metencephalon* (pons and cerebellum).
- The *mesencephalon* (tectum and tegmentum).
- The *diencephalon* (thalamus and hypothalamus).
- The *telencephalon* (cerebral hemispheres or cerebrum, basal ganglia, and limbic system).

('Encephalon' means 'within the head'.)

An overlapping, but broader, division, into hindbrain (*rhombencephalon*), midbrain (*mesencephalon*), and forebrain (*prosencephalon*) is shown in Figure 3.3.

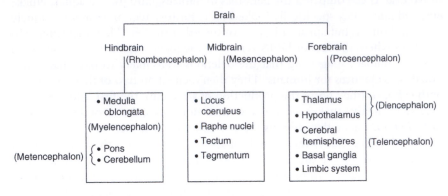

Figure 3.3 Division of the human brain into hindbrain, midbrain, and forebrain.

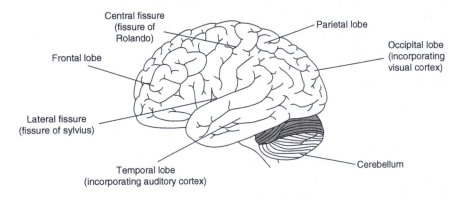

Figure 3.4 Lateral (side-on) view of the left cerebral hemisphere.

Mammalian brains

According to Rose (2005), the evolutionary development from the amphibians through the reptiles to mammals (including humans) resulted in the dominance of the furthest forward part of the brain (the *telencephalon*); in mammals this developed from the olfactory lobes (responsible for the sense of smell) so as to swell outwards, enlarging and folding over all other brain regions to form the *cerebral hemispheres* (or *cerebrum*) (see Figure 3.4). With the mammals, the cerebrum took over the task of co-ordination and control from the *thalamus*; some areas of the latter became mere staging posts or relay stations en route to the cortex.

However, the *hypothalamus* (with the thalamus, forming the *diencephalon*) and the *pituitary gland* (located near the hypothalamus, but actually the master *endocrine/hormonal gland* and not part of the brain at all) remain crucially important for controlling mood, emotion, and complex behavioural patterns. The hypothalamus contains groups of neurons concerned with the regulation of appetite, sexual drive, sleep, and pleasure; the pituitary (in conjunction with the hypothalamus) regulates the production of many key hormones and forms the major link between the nervous and endocrine systems.

Rose (2005) describes as 'popularising behavioural determinists' those who stress continuity with other species, pointing out as they do how critical these drives and behavioural states are for human beings, how they dominate the totality of human behaviour, and what a large proportion of human life is devoted to activities associated with or driven by them.

One very influential example of a serious scientific account, which is often depicted in cartoon form showing a straight line of fish emerging onto land to become reptiles, mammals, primates, then humans, is MacLean's (1973) *triune brain model* (TBM) (see following section). This specifies 'primitive' complexes in the human brain inherited from animal ancestors, reflecting traditional ideas about sequential evolution (Patton, 2008/2009). Originally proposed in the 1960s, MacLean's TBM has been widely popularised; it claims that human brains are the culmination of *linear* evolution progressing from simpler species.

Time for reflection ...

- What do you think is meant by '*linear* evolution'?

MacLean's triune brain model

According to MacLean's *triune brain model* (TBM), the human brain really comprises *three brains in one*, each with a different *phylogenetic* history, its own special intelligence, memory, sense of time and space, and motor functions (see Figure 3.5). In fact, he proposed *four* sequential steps:

1 A '*neural chassis*', corresponding to the brains of fish and amphibians.
2 A *reptilian complex*, comprising the *basal ganglia* (including the olfactory tubercle and nucleus acumbens, and part of the *corpus striatum,* dominant in the brains of reptiles and birds). This has remained remarkably unchanged since its appearance about 300 million years ago. Emotions had not yet evolved, and behavioural responses were largely controlled by instinct (Stevens and Price, 2000).
3 A *paleomammalian* component, consisting of the *limbic system,* (comprised of the hippocampus, hypothalamus, thalamus, and pituitary gland: see above). This supposedly emerged with the appearance of mammals and was responsible for emotional behaviour; it also functions as a *homeostatic mechanism,* maintaining control of hormone levels, eating, drinking, sleep, and sex. It also plays an indispensable role in memory (Stevens and Price, 2000). By this evolutionary stage, fear and anger have emerged, as well as love and attachment, together with their associated behavioural response patterns, bonding and mating. MacLean (1985) draws particular attention to three forms of behaviour that most clearly distinguish the evolutionary transition from reptiles to

mammals: (i) nursing and maternal care; (ii) audiovocal communication for maintaining mother–offspring contact; and (iii) play.

Conscious awareness is more evident at this evolutionary stage and behaviour is less rigidly determined by instincts (although they're still very apparent). The limbic system also includes the *paleocortex* – the most primitive part of the evolving cerebral cortex.

4 A *neomammalian* component, consisting of the *neocortex,* the site of higher cognitive functions, as opposed to emotional (limbic) and instinctive (basal ganglia) behaviour. According to Stevens & Price (2000), 'Behaviour arising in the neocortex is usually described as "conscious", "voluntary", and "rational", reflecting the fact that there is a sense of personal control over such behaviour' (p. 17). (See Chapter 4.)

An evaluation of MacLean's TBM

Rose (2005) agrees that in the brain's evolution, few structures have ever totally disappeared. Rather, as new ones have developed, the old ones have become less important and relatively smaller, but many of the connections and pathways remain. It's also true that the hypothalamus is of considerable importance in controlling mood and behaviour in mammals – including humans. However,

> To extrapolate from these facts towards the claim that because similar brain structures exist in people and frogs, people's behaviour is inevitably frog-like, is nonsense. It is like arguing that we think by smelling because the cerebral hemispheres evolved from the olfactory lobes.
>
> (Rose, 2005, pp. 43–4)

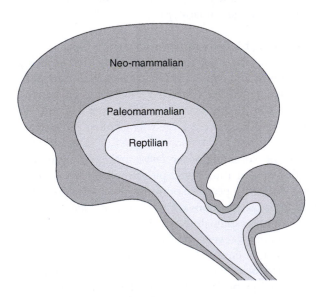

Figure 3.5 MacLean's three brains.

Brain regions may survive, but their functions are transformed or partially superseded by others. Fish, amphibian, reptiles, and birds survive today because they're fully 'fit' for the environmental conditions they find themselves in; they're all at least as fit and 'evolved' as humans are. As Rose says, 'our brains evolved as a strategy for survival, not to solve abstract cognitive puzzles, do crosswords or play chess' (p. 44).

Time for reflection ...

- Is there a case for claiming that human abilities/behaviours are *inherently* superior (or 'more evolved') or can they only be judged in terms of how they helped *Homo sapiens* adapt to its various environments (as with all other species-specific behaviours)?

Stevens & Price (2000) claim that the TBM provides a home for what might be called the 'triune mind'. Many thinkers, including Plato, St. Augustine (see Chapter 2), Freud, and Jung (see Chapter 6), have observed that the mind seems to possess separate functional components which compete with one another for overall control of behaviour.

> Variously attributed to such organs as the 'head', the 'heart', and the 'bowels', reason, emotion, and instinct may display differing intentions when it comes to choosing a mate during courtship ... MacLean's anatomical studies give useful support to this long-standing concept of three minds in one (the neurological 'holy trinity').
>
> (Stevens and Price, 2000, p. 18)

Not all mammalian brains are the same

The major development in the later-evolving mammals is the expansion of the area of neocortex between the sensory and motor regions; these contain *association areas*, which don't have direct connections outside the cortex. Instead, they 'talk' only to each other and to other cortical neurons: they relate to the outside world only after several stages of neuronal mediation. In humans, these association areas include the massive *prefrontal lobe* and regions of the *occipital, temporal,* and *parietal lobes* (Rose, 2005).

This relative ballooning of the cortex in humans endows it with far more neural tissue than is needed for the mundane tasks of keeping the rest of the body running (Oppenheimer, 2007); there's a huge volume of apparently redundant cortex without a civil service role (Deacon, 1997).

Intelligence and the brain: does size matter?

According to Patton (2008/9), in recent decades scientists have rejected the kind of linear, sequential view of brain evolution as provided by the TBM. This is partly because of the observation of abilities, in non-human species, previously taken to be limited to humans, or, at least, to primates. Among birds, for example, parrots and corvids (a group that includes crows, jays, ravens, and jackdaws) have been shown to be capable of some amazing cognitive feats (see Chapters 4 and 5).

Absolute versus relative size

Clearly, the brain of *Homo sapiens* isn't the biggest brain on the planet in *absolute* terms: whales and elephants outdo us by up to six times, and the dolphin brain is also larger than ours (Motluk, 2010; Rose, 2005). However, it's equally clear that larger bodies require bigger brains (Oppenheimer, 2007; Rose, 2005).

So, perhaps brain weight *relative* to body weight might be a better measure. In general, brain weight and body weight increase in step and the *brain weight/ body weight ratio* is fairly predictable in most mammals. Humans (2.00 per cent body weight) come out ahead of whales, elephants, and great apes (chimps: 0.61; bonobos: 0.69; gorillas: 0.64; orang-utans: 0.55); bottlenose dolphins: 0.94; Asian elephants: 0.15; and killer whales: 0.094. But for mice, it's 3.2 per cent and for small birds 8 per cent; their light bodies help inflate the ratio, but they seem to contradict every means of trying to prove human superiority (Corballis, 2011).

Also, the brain weight/body weight ratio in higher mammals has been distorted in several fundamental ways; for example, primates have proportionately larger adult brains than other mammals, because they have bodies that, from early life, grow more slowly for the same absolute rate of brain growth (Oppenheimer, 2007).

Another problem is that small animals have larger ratios than larger animals. A more sophisticated measure is *encephalisation quotient* (EQ) (Jerison, 1973): (brain weight)/(.12 x body weight); it is calibrated so that the ratio of the mass of the brain of the species under investigation relative to a standard brain belonging to the same taxonomic group = 1.

For example, if we consider all mammals and compare them against the cat as reference animal, this produces EQs of 7.4416 (humans); 5.3055 (dolphins); 2.4865 (chimps); 1.8717 (elephants); 0.4029 (rats); and 0.5 (mice). So, the human brain is seven times bigger than that of a typical mammal weighing as much as we do (Koch, 2017).

How did humans come to have bigger brains?

Functions such as language and episodic memory (EM) placed new demands on neural storage and may have driven the dramatic increase in brain size during the Pleistocene period (beginning just under two million years ago). *Recursion* too must have added to the pressure – it requires hierarchical structure, enhanced short-term memory (STM), and sequential programming (Corballis, 2011) (see Chapter 5).

According to Dunbar (1993), intelligence is driven by *social interaction*: the larger the social group, the greater the need for an enlarged neocortex, simply to cope with all the social pressures. The *neocortical ratio* (NR) is the ratio of neocortex to the rest of the brain; it increases with size. Humans have the largest NR (4.1); chimps (3.2), gorillas (2.65), orang-utans (2.99), and gibbons (2.08). According to the equation relating group size to the NR, humans should belong to groups of 148 ($\pm$ 50); this is reasonably consistent with the estimated size of early Neolithic villages.

Fossil evidence shows that brain size remained fairly static in hominins for some four million years after the split from apes. It was with the emergence of the genus *Homo* that brain size increased at a rapid rate, reaching a peak with Neanderthals (average brain size of 1450 cc). The present-day average of *Homo sapiens* is 1350 cc, still about three times the size expected of an ape with the same body size. (Neanderthals' believed larger body size accounts for their larger average brains.) The final increase seems to have coincided with advances in technological invention compared with the previous 1.5 million years (Corballis, 2011).

Looking elsewhere for what makes human brains special

According to Rilling and Insel (1999), the human *neocortex* is significantly larger than expected from a primate of our brain size; also, the human brain is significantly more *convoluted* than expected for our brain size: the neocortex (independently of overall brain size) was uniquely modified throughout hominid evolution. These modifications may constitute part of the neurobiological substrate that supports some of *Homo sapiens'* most distinctive cognitive abilities (Rilling and Insel, 1999) (see Chapter 5).

It's also been proposed that it's the way the human brain develops that makes it unique. This is discussed in Box 3.6.

BOX 3.6 THE UNIQUE DEVELOPMENT OF THE HUMAN BRAIN

- According to Oppenheimer (2007), compared with other apes, humans have a slower clock for brain maturation.
- In all mammals, brain growth switches off before body growth in a way that matches the functional needs of the adult body size. But in the case of humans, our internal clock keeps our brains growing for longer than would be expected for our final body size as primates. (This mirrors the finding cited above that the great apes differ from other primates in that their bodies are bigger than would be expected from their brain size.)
- The result of this prolongation of foetal and infant development (*ontogenesis*) is a brain size more appropriate for a 1,000 kg ape such as the extinct *Gigantopithecus* (Deacon, 1997).

Developmental cognitive neuroscience and brain plasticity

Developmental cognitive neuroscience (DCN) is a relatively new subfield in which researchers are specifically interested in relating developmental changes in perception, cognition, and behaviour in the developing child to the underlying growth of the brain.

DCN has produced increasing evidence for the *plasticity* of the brain, that is, its ability to change in response to changing conditions); in turn, this is critically related to the slower clock for brain maturation described above. For humans especially, the postnatal structural and functional development of the brain is influenced by the environment in which it is raised since our postnatal brain development is considerably slowed down, even relative to our most closely related primate cousins (Johnson, 2009).

The environment that helps shape our brains involves not only the *physical world* of objects, surfaces, gravity, etc., but also the *social world* of other human beings. For Gerhardt (2004), it is the baby's responsiveness to human interaction that is the distinguishing characteristic of human beings compared with other new-born mammals. Humans share with other mammals a core brain which ensures survival (echoing MacLean's TBM: see above). A new-born baby has a basic version of these systems in place; what makes the human infant special is its *sociability*:

> Human beings are the most social of animals and are already distinctive in this way at birth, imitating a parent's facial movements and orienting themselves to faces very early on.
>
> (Gerhardt, 2004, p. 33)

BOX 3.7 DEVELOPMENT OF THE SOCIAL BRAIN

- According to Turner (2000), as the emotional (i.e. mammalian) brain evolved in humans, we became more emotionally complex and sophisticated: more alternatives and choices arose in our social interactions.
- This required a capacity for thinking about and reflecting on our emotions, which led to the development of the cortex, in particular, the *prefrontal cortex* (PFC).
- The PFC has a unique role, linking the sensory areas of the cortex with the emotional and survival-oriented subcortex; it's found only in humans (Gopnik, 2010).
- A key region within the PFC, and the first to mature, is the *orbitofrontal cortex* (OFC) (lying behind the eyes, next to the amygdala and anterior cingulate gyrus).

Time for reflection ...

- According to Gerhardt (2004), the OFC, together with other parts of the PFC and anterior cingulate gyrus, is probably the most responsible for '*emotional intelligence*' (Gelman, 1996).
- What do you understand by 'emotional intelligence'?

Without an intact and properly functioning OFC, it becomes impossible to empathise with other people (to mentally put yourself in their shoes). Gerhardt (2004) describes it as 'so much about being human' (p. 37). Not only is it larger in the right hemisphere, but Schore (2003) believes that the OFC is the controller for the whole right hemisphere, which is dominant throughout infancy. It develops almost entirely postnatally, not maturing until toddlerhood. However, while the functions supported by the PFC clearly become more advanced during childhood, this region is active from at least the first few months after birth (Johnson, 2005).

Crucially, there's nothing automatic about the maturation of the OFC: it's very experience-dependent (Gerhardt, 2004). This makes good evolutionary sense: precisely because we're so dependent as babies, and our brains at this stage are so 'plastic', we can learn to fit in with whatever culture and circumstances we find ourselves in (Gerhardt, 2004).

Similarly, Johnson (2009) observes that the influence of the environment on the brain includes not only aspects of the social and physical world that are specific to individuals (such as being exposed to spoken English), but also aspects that are common to almost all human beings (such as being exposed to language of some kind or other). This suggests that some of the common aspects of human brain structure and function could arise not only because we have genes in common, but also because we share a common environment (Johnson, 2009).

The self-organising brain

What Gerhardt claims for the OFC, in particular, a majority of researchers involved in DCN claim for the brain as a whole. There's considerable evidence that human functional brain development is a *constructive process*, in which the state of the brain at one (earlier) stage helps it to select the appropriate experience needed for advancing to the next (later) stage (Johnson, 2009). In other words, human post-natal brain development is a *self-organising process* (Mareschal *et al.*, 2007).

The relatively primitive nature of babies' brains has been explained in terms of our evolutionary history (see Chapter 1). Our upright posture and bipedal lifestyle sets limits on pelvic size, so women can only squeeze out a baby with a relatively small head; this means that its brain is only partially developed. However, humans also take relatively longer to complete their development because they have more functions (especially cognitive ones) to add – we have further to go. This helps explain the relative under-developed nature of new-borns' brains: it's to allow them to learn to add these additional functions. Echoing Mareschal *et al.*'s concept of brain development as a self-organising process, Eliot (1999) states that:

> Babies' brains are learning machines. They build themselves, or adapt, to the environment at hand. Although the brain is often appropriately compared to a computer, this is one way in which they differ: The brain actually programs itself.
>
> (p. 8)

> While genes program the *sequence* of neural development, at every turn the *quality* of that development is shaped by environmental factors.
>
> (p. 9)

Time for reflection …

- What other differences between brains and computers can you think of? (See Gross, 2014, 2015.)

Box 3.8 discusses the complementary nature of plasticity and specificity.

BOX 3.8 SPECIFICITY AND PLASTICITY

- Rose (2005) describes the two intertwined, complementary processes of *specificity* and *plasticity* as a 'developmental double helix'.
- Without *specificity*, the brain wouldn't be able to become accurately wired; for example, nerves wouldn't be able to make the right connections between the retina and the visual cortex to enable binocular vision, or between the motor cortex and muscles (via the spinal cord).
- Without *plasticity*, the developing NS would be unable to repair itself following damage or to mould its responses to changing aspects of the outside world in order to create an internal model or representation of that world (a plan of how to act on the world).

Perhaps the clearest example of babies seeking out those aspects of the environment necessary for their own later brain development is the attention and effort they devote to interacting with other humans, especially their primary caregivers (Johnson, 2009). This brings us neatly back to the social brain.

According to Gopnik (2010):

> Far from being mere unfinished adults, babies and young children are exquisitely designed by evolution to change and create, to learn and explore.

Those capacities, so intrinsic to what it means to be human, appear in the purest forms in the earliest years of our lives. Our most valuable human accomplishments are possible because we were once helpless dependent children and not in spite of it. Childhood, and caregiving is fundamental to our humanity.

(p. 61)

Task-sharing, mirror neurons, and theory of mind

According to Ramachandran (2011), it's not possible to isolate a specific brain region that makes humans unique. At the anatomical level, every part of the brain has a direct analogue in the brains of the great apes. However, recent research has identified brain regions that have been so radically elaborated that at the *functional* (or cognitive) level, they actually seem to be novel and unique (including Wernicke's language-related area in the left temporal lobe, the PFC, and the inferior parietal lobules (IPLs), offshoots of which (the supramarginal and angular gyri) are anatomically non-existent in apes).

The extraordinarily rapid development of these areas in humans suggests something crucial must have been going on there; clinical observations confirm this.

Mirror neurons

BOX 3.9 THE DISCOVERY OF MIRROR NEURONS (MNs)

- In a monkey's frontal lobes, certain cells fire when it performs a very specific action (e.g. one fires when it pulls a lever, a second when grabbing a peanut, a third for putting it in its mouth): they're part of a *circuit* performing a very specific task.
- While studying these motor-command neurons in the late 1990s, Rizzolatti *et al.* observed that some of these neurons fired when the monkey saw another monkey perform the same action.

  These neurons ... were for all intents and purposes reading the other monkey's mind, figuring out what it was up to. This is an indispensable trait for intensely social creatures like primates.

  (Ramachandran, 2011, p. 121)

- One of the main sites of MNs in the monkey brain is the ventral premotor area; this may be the precursor of Broca's area (in the left frontal lobe, important for representation of word meaning). The left hemisphere inferior parietal lobe in monkeys is rich in MNs.

While in monkeys MNs enable the prediction of simple goal-directed actions of other monkeys, in humans (alone), they've become sophisticated enough to interpret even *complex intentions* of other people; this, in turn, enables us to *anticipate* their next action. In other words, humans are capable of 'reading' (aspects of) other people's *minds*, not just *imitating* others' movements.

However, MNs are clearly not sufficient for the evolution of culture: even monkeys have them, but they don't possess culture (but see Chapters 5 and 9): 'Their mirror neuron system is either not advanced enough or is not adequately connected to other brain structures to allow the rapid propagation of culture' (Ramachandran, 2011, pp. 134–5). But innovations would only be valuable if they spread rapidly; in this respect:

> Mirror neurons served the same role in early hominin evolution as the Internet, Wikipedia, and blogging do today. Once the cascade was set in motion, there was no turning back from the path to humanity.
>
> (Ramachandran, 2011, p. 135)

The mirror neuron system (MNS) is well documented in humans and involves characteristics that are more language-like than monkeys'. (Indeed, both Broca's and Wernicke's areas are part of the MNS.) For example, only humans' MNs respond to both *transitive* acts (e.g. reaching for an actual object) and *intransitive* acts (miming with no object present); the latter would have paved the way for understanding *symbolic* acts. Brain scanning studies show that the MN region of the premotor cortex is activated not only when people watch movements of the foot, hand, or mouth, but also when they read text pertaining to such movements (Aziz-Hadeh *et al.,* 2006).

Mirror neurons and theory of mind

Accurate imitation of others' actions may depend on the uniquely human ability to 'adopt another's point of view' – both visually (literally) and metaphorically. (Imitation is discussed in detail in Chapter 9.) This ability to see the world from another's perspective is also essential for *theory of mind* (ToM). The term was originally coined by Premack and Woodruff (1978) based on their work with chimps; they defined it as the ability to attribute mental states (knowledge, wishes, feelings, beliefs) to oneself and others.

Humans' highly sophisticated ToM is one of the most unique and powerful faculties of the human brain. Our ToM ability doesn't rely on our general intelligence but on a specialised set of brain mechanisms that evolved to endow us with our equally important degree of *social* intelligence. Much of what we know about ToM comes from the study of children and adults on the *autistic spectrum:* 'it's precisely [the] presumed functions of mirror neurons – such as empathy, intention-reading, mimicry, pretend play, and language learning – that are dysfunctional in autism' (Ramachandran, 2011, p. 140). (See Gross, 2012b.)

As De Waal (2016) points out, ToM derives from primate research (see above). He prefers to talk about *perspective taking* than ToM (and even more so than '*mindreading*'). There's plenty of evidence (from apes and corvids, such as scrub jays and crows) that non-humans do perspective taking, from being aware of what others want to knowing what others know. In view of this evidence of PT:

> There is little doubt that the blanket assertion that theory of mind is uniquely human must be downgraded to a more nuanced, gradualist view… Humans probably possess a fuller understanding of one another, but the contrast with other animals is not stark enough that extraterrestrials would automatically pick theory of mind as the chief marker that sets us apart.
>
> (De Waal, p. 148)

Summary and conclusions: so what, if anything, is special about the human brain?

As Rose (2005) points out, our biochemistry is virtually identical to that of species without a brain, and even under the most powerful microscope our neurons look the same as those of any other vertebrate species; they communicate with one another using exactly the same electrical and chemical signals.

As we've seen, our brains aren't the biggest, either in absolute terms or in terms of brain weight/body weight ratio. But they do have some unique features, such as the relative enlargement of the frontal lobe and, specifically, the PFC.

Although humans may not be unique in displaying handedness or the related hemispheric specialisation, the *nature* of that specialisation may still distinguish us from all other species (including chimps), as in our possession of left hemisphere areas (Broca's and Wernicke's) devoted to language. We've also noted that the long period of infancy and childhood has evolved in order to allow the 'learning machine' that is the human brain to develop and mature. That learning machine is also special in the way it constructs itself, adapting to the unique environmental conditions it confronts; for humans, namely, *culture*, which both creates and is created by human brains (see Chapter 9).

Rose (2005) believes that part of what makes us unique is our *versatility*:

> we are the only species that can…run a kilometre, swim a river and then climb a tree. And for sure we are the only species that can then go on to tell others of our kind of our achievements, or write a poem about them. We have above all a deeper range of emotions, enabling us to feel empathy, solidarity, pity, love, so far as we can tell, well beyond the range of any other species…We have language, consciousness, foresight.
>
> (p. 55)

We've also noted that *brain development* is critically different in humans: we're the only primate (and perhaps hominin) that passes through *stages* of development. According to Locke and Bogin (2006), childhood (two–seven years) is especially critical to the emergence of grammatical language, episodic memory (EM), mental time travel (MTT), and theory of mind (ToM) (Corballis, 2011). These are major features of human *cognition* and are discussed in Chapter 5.

Suggested further reading

Jones, S. (1993) *The Language of the Genes: Biology, History and the Evolutionary Future.* London: Flamingo.

Ramachandran, V.S. (2011) *The Tell-Tale Brain: Unlocking the Mystery of Human Nature.* London: Windmill Books.

Ridley, M. (1999) *Genome: The Autobiography of a Species in 23 Chapters.* London: Fourth Estate.

Ridley, M. (2003) *Nature Via Nurture: Genes, Experience and What Makes Us Human.* London: Fourth Estate.

Rose, S. (2005) *The 21st Century Brain: Explaining, Mending and Manipulating the Mind.* London: Vintage.

4   Consciousness and
self-consciousness

Key questions

- What do we mean by the term 'consciousness'?
- What's the difference between consciousness and self-consciousness?
- How do we know that other people are conscious?
- Do we need to have a body in order to be conscious?
- How do we determine whether any non-human animals are conscious?
- How and why did consciousness evolve?
- What's (self-) consciousness for?

The nature of consciousness

According to Chalmers (2007), 'consciousness' is an ambiguous term, referring to many different phenomena, some of which are easier to explain than others. The 'easy' problems of consciousness are those that seem directly accessible to the standard methods of science (in terms of computational or neural mechanisms) even if we don't currently have a complete explanation for them. They include:

1   The ability to discriminate, categorise, and react to environmental stimuli.
2   The integration of information by a cognitive system.
3   The reportability of mental states.
4   The ability of a system to access its own internal states.
5   The focus of attention.
6   The deliberate control of behaviour.
7   The difference between wakefulness and sleep.

For Chalmers, the 'hard' problem of consciousness is the problem of *experience*:

> When we think and perceive, there is a whir of information-processing, but there is also a subjective aspect. As Nagel (1974) has put it, there is something it's like to be a conscious organism. The subjective aspect is experience. When we see, for example, we experience visual sensations: the felt quality of redness, the experience of dark and light, the quality of depth in a visual field. Other experiences go along with perception in different

modalities: the sound of a clarinet, the smell of mothballs. Then there are bodily sensations, from pains to orgasms; mental images that are conjured up internally; the felt quality of emotion, and the experience of a stream of conscious thought. What unites all these states is that there is something it's like to be them.

(Chalmers, 2007, p. 226)

> *Time for reflection ...*
>
> - If you haven't already done so, try to focus on something red, close your eyes and experience the darkness, open them and experience the light, focus on depth in the room you're reading this in, and so on.
> - What are those experiences like?

While this might seem relatively straightforward, even 'natural', for Chalmers the 'hard problem of consciousness' is trying to explain the *relationship* between (i) an individual's subjective experience; and (ii) his/her brain activity or information-processing. Philosophers have been discussing this for centuries in the form of the *mind-brain* (or *mind-body*) *problem* (see Gross, 2014).

Consciousness and qualia

These personal, subjective experiences, feelings, and sensations that accompany awareness that Chalmers describes are known as *qualia*. According to Edelman (1992), qualia are phenomenal states, 'how things seem to us as human beings' (p. 114), how consciousness manifests itself.

For Edelman, what Chalmers calls the hard problem amounts to an apparent discrepancy between subjective and objective:

> The dilemma is that phenomenal experience is a *first-person matter*, and this seems at first glance, to prevent the formulation of a completely objective or causal account.
>
> (Edelman, 1992, pp. 114–15; emphasis added)

Since science is a *third-person account*, how can we produce a scientific account of consciousness that (must) include qualia?

> *Time for reflection ...*
>
> - As 'real' as subjective experience is, discussion of qualia seems to raise a number of fundamental issues:

a   The age-old philosophical problem of other minds. It's all very well having access to our own consciousness (if not to our 'mind'), but how do we know that *anybody else* is conscious? (This is discussed below – see Box 4.2.).

b   Are non-humans conscious in the same way as humans are? This is partly answered by Edelman's distinction between *primary* and *higher-order consciousness* (see below), partly by studies of self-recognition in children and other species (see below), and partly by studies of what's called animal cognition (see Chapter 5 and Gross, 2012).

c   Could a machine have consciousness? (see Gross, 2014).

Edelman's proposed solution to the 'first-person/third-person dilemma' is to accept that other people and oneself do experience qualia, to collect first-person accounts, and to correlate them in order to establish what they all have in common – bearing in mind that these reports are inevitably incomplete, imprecise, and relative to personal context.

BOX 4.1 WHAT'S IT LIKE TO BE A BAT?

- A potential danger involved in trying to solve the 'first-person/third-person dilemma' (although not in Edelman's case) is *reductionism*: a powerful third-person account, such as neuroscience, is likely to take precedence over the subjective, first-person qualia account, with the consequence that qualia are 'explained away' (reduced to brain processes).

- A well-known attempt to protect first-person experience (qualia) from reduction to third-person talk (as in neuroscience) is Nagel's (1974) 'What is it like to be a bat?' (see the quote from Chalmers in the text above).

- The essence of Nagel's argument is that no amount of descriptive knowledge could possibly add up to the experience of how it feels to be a bat, or what it's like to perceive by sonar.

- Conscious experience is 'what it's like' to be an organism to the organism. Attempts to reduce that subjective experience must be considered unsuccessful as long as the reducing theory (for example, pain is the firing of neurons in some brain centre) is logically possible without consciousness (the 'zombie problem'). A theory of consciousness should be able to distinguish us from zombies (Bem and Looren de Jong, 1997).

Nagel (1974) argues that subjective experience is *real*; this coincides with one of Searle's (2007) seven criteria for defining conscious states. These are described in Box 4.2.

BOX 4.2 MAJOR CRITERIA FOR DEFINING CONSCIOUS STATES (SEARLE, 2007)

1 Conscious states are *qualitative*: there's a qualitative feel to being in any particular conscious state. This is Searle's way of describing qualia and mirrors Nagel's 'batness' argument, albeit at the level of different conscious states (e.g. tasting beer and listening to a Beethoven Symphony) as opposed to whole organisms (e.g. bats).

2 Such states are also *ontologically subjective*: they only exist as experienced by a human being or non-human animal. While physical objects, as well as natural features such as mountains, have an objective (or third-party) ontology/existence, conscious states (such as pains and itches) exist only when experienced by a person or animal (they have a subjective or first-person ontology).

3 At any moment in your conscious life, all your conscious states are experienced as part of a *single, unified conscious field*. The unity of consciousness is the starting point for Edelman and Tononi's (2000) *information integration theory* of consciousness (see text below and Figure 4.1).

4 Most, but not all, conscious states are *intentional*, in the philosophical sense that they are *about*, or refer to, something (objects or states of affairs); this is in contrast with undirected, generalised feelings of well-being or anxiety. Edelman (1992) makes the same observation.

5 Conscious states are *real* parts of the real world and cannot be reduced to something else (they are *irreducible*) (see Box 4.1). According to Searle:

> where the very existence of consciousness is in question we cannot make the appearance–reality distinction, because the appearance of the existence of consciousness is the *reality* of its existence.
>
> (p. 327; emphasis added)

Wise (1999) extends this argument to consciousness in non-human animals (see text below).

6. We cannot reduce consciousness to more fundamental neurobiological processes (again, see Box 4.1). We cannot show that the subjective, first-person ontology of consciousness is 'nothing but' brain processes (with their third-person, objective ontology). However, this is different from the claim that conscious states are *caused by* brain processes, which Searle believes isn't in dispute (although exactly how this happens is still unknown).

7. Conscious states have *causal efficacy*. (This is discussed at the end of the chapter in relation to how – and why – consciousness evolved.)

Even if we accept that mental states are the product of brain states, it's not possible for a neuroscientist to peer inside your brain and see what you're thinking (despite recent claims to the contrary!) (Caldwell, 2006).

According to Tallis (2013), the grip of neuroscience on the academic and popular imagination is extraordinary. One recent, extreme example is the claim made by Taylor (cited in Tallis, 2013) that Muslim fundamentalism may be categorised as mental illness and cured by science as a result of advances in neuroscience.

The 'jewel in the neuroscientific crown' is fMRI (see Chapter 3) and the findings of almost any study using it seem to be taken, implicitly, as valid. Underlying this, in turn, may be the belief that you are your brain and that consciousness is identical with brain activity, so that 'peering into the intracranial darkness is the best way of advancing our knowledge of humankind' (Tallis, 2013, p. 13). However:

> Our moment-to-moment consciousness – unlike nerve impulses – is steeped in a personal and historical past and a personal and collective future...We belong to a community of minds, developed over hundreds of thousands of years, to which our brains give us access but which is confined to the stand–alone brain.
>
> (Tallis, 2013, p. 13)

Studies that locate irreducibly *social* phenomena, such as love, the aesthetic sense, wisdom, or Muslim fundamentalism in the function (or dysfunction) of specific areas of the brain are *conceptually misconceived* (Tallis, 2013). It involves a confusion between different levels of explanation (or *universes of discourse*) (Rose, 1976).

Consciousness and self-consciousness

Time for reflection ...

- What do you understand by the term 'self-consciousness' and how does it differ from 'consciousness'?

Edelman (1992) makes what he believes is a fundamental distinction between *primary* and *higher-order* consciousness.

a   *Primary consciousness* refers to the state of being mentally aware of things in the world, of having mental images in the present. An animal with only primary consciousness is strongly tied to the succession of events in *real time*, unaccompanied by any sense of being a person with a past and a future. So, to be conscious in this sense doesn't necessarily imply any kind of 'I' who is aware and having mental images. (Another term for primary consciousness is *sentience*, the ability to have bodily sensations, including hunger, thirst, pain, and more emotional states, such as fear and anger.) Edelman believes that chimpanzees are almost certainly conscious (see Chapter 5), and, probably, so are most mammals and some birds; probably those animals without a cortex (or its equivalent) are not (see Chapter 3).

b *Higher-order consciousness* involves the recognition by a thinking subject of his/her own acts or affections, embodying a model of the personal, and of the past and future as well as the present. It involves *direct awareness* – 'the noninferential or immediate awareness of mental episodes without the involvement of sense organs or receptors. It is what we as humans have in addition to primary consciousness. We are conscious of being conscious' (p. 112).

Edelman believes that human beings are in a 'privileged position':

[W]e are, with the possible exception of the chimpanzee, the only self-conscious animals. We are the only animals capable of language, able to model the world free of the present, able to report on, study, and correlate our phenomenal states with the findings of physics and biology.

(p. 115)

The primary/higher-order consciousness distinction is a central feature of *information integration theory* (IIT) (Edelman and Tononi, 2000; Koch, 2009; Koch and Tononi, 2011). As we noted in Box 4.1, the unity of consciousness is the starting point for IIT, according to which consciousness corresponds to the capacity of a system to integrate information (Tononi, 2007). This is summarised in Figure 4.1. The figure shows a *re-entrant loop*, which appeared during the evolution of *hominids* and the emergence of language. The acquisition of a new kind of memory via semantic capabilities, and ultimately language, produced a conceptual explosion. As a result, concepts of the self, the past, and future could be connected to primary consciousness (see the discussion of mental time travel/MTT in Chapter 5). Consciousness of consciousness now became possible (Blackmore, 2010).

The distinction between primary and higher-order consciousness corresponds to that between *consciousness* and *self-consciousness,* respectively; it also corresponds to that between *phenomenal consciousness* and *self-consciousness* (Allen and Bekoff, 2007). *Self-consciousness* usually refers to an organism's capacity for *second-order representations* of its own mental states ('thought about thought'); this is closely related to questions about theory of mind (ToM) in non-humans, i.e. the ability to attribute mental states to others (see Chapters 3 and 5).

Some modern philosophers who reject *philosophical dualism* (see Chapter 2) support Descartes' views regarding the necessary involvement of linguistic processing in human consciousness:

Such insistence on the importance of language for consciousness under-writes the tendency of philosophers such as Dennett (1969, 1997) to deny that animals are conscious in anything like the same sense that humans are.

(Allen and Bekoff, 2007, pp. 62–3)

The special role of language is discussed in Chapter 5.

How do we know that anyone else – or any non-human animal – is conscious?

Time for reflection ...

- Do we just *assume* that everyone else is conscious, like us?
- Or is there some kind of *evidence* that we base our assumption on?
- What *social* processes depend on us making this assumption?

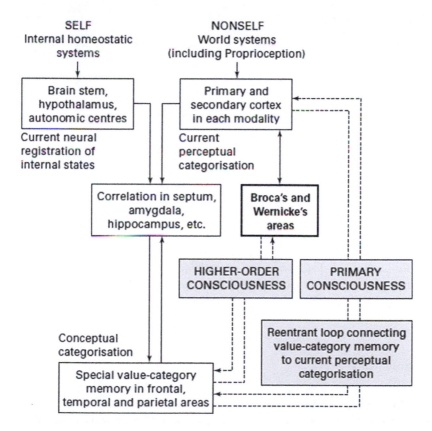

Figure 4.1 A re-entrant loop.

According to Wise (1999), the strongest available argument that you (as well as chimpanzees and baboons) are conscious is 'by analogy':

1   I know I am conscious.
2   We are all biologically very similar.
3   We all act very similarly.
4   We all share an evolutionary history.
5   Therefore, you (and other great apes, and other species too) are conscious.

The basic argument is that 'if it walks like a duck and quacks like a duck'. If something behaves in all respects as if it is conscious, and there's no good reason to believe otherwise, then it (almost certainly) *is* conscious.

But doesn't this beg the question? Since we don't have direct access to other people's minds (one of Watson's – the founder of behaviourism – arguments against the possibility of the scientific study of consciousness: see Chapter 6), our belief that others are conscious remains no more than an assumption.

Time for reflection …

- A second argument against the view that specifically non-humans are conscious is that anyone who adopts it is guilty of *anthropomorphism*.
- What do you understand by the term?
- Can you think of any counter-arguments?

As we noted in Box 4.2, Searle (2007) claims that if it consciously appears to me that I am conscious, then I am conscious: we can never be mistaken (or deluded) about consciousness. Wise (1999) extends this argument to non-human animals and, at the same time, argues *against* the anthropomorphism objection:

Most mammals and every primate act in ways that cause most reasonable people to think that they have minds of some kind…It is circular thinking to dismiss this belief as mere *anthropomorphism*…as some do. They begin by assuming that only humans are conscious, then label any contrary claim as anthropomorphic. Why? Because only humans are conscious.

(pp. 123–4; emphasis added)

Time for reflection …

- Can you think of any possible objections to Wise's position?
- For example, is his extension of Searle's argument valid, i.e. even if you accept the 'appearance = reality' argument in relation to other people, does it inevitably apply to non-humans?

An evaluation of the 'argument from homology'

According to Allen and Bekoff (2007), similarity arguments for animal consciousness clearly have roots in common-sense observations (of our pets,
for example). But they may also be bolstered by scientific study of behaviour
and neurology, as well as considerations of evolutionary continuity (*homol-
ogy*) between species. For example, the reactions of many animals, especially
other mammals, to bodily events that humans would report as painful are easily
and automatically recognised by most people as pain responses. High-pitched
vocalisations, fear responses, nursing of injuries, and learned avoidance are
examples of responses to noxious stimuli that form part of the common mammalian heritage.

Again, as we noted in Chapter 3, all mammals share the same basic brain
anatomy, and much is shared with vertebrates more generally. A large amount
of scientific research that's directly relevant to the treatment of conscious
human pain, including that on the efficacy of analgesics and anaesthetics, is
conducted on rats and other mammals; the validity of this research depends on
the similarity of the mechanisms involved.

Time for reflection ...

- While the similarity arguments may be scientifically valid, is the use
  of animals for such (largely medical) research *ethically* acceptable?
- Some researchers stress the *dissimilarities* between, say, rats and
  humans, leading them to question even the scientific validity of
  using these non-human mammals for such research.

(For both issues, see Gross 2014, 2015)

In Allen and Bekoff's view:

[T]he mere fact that humans have a trait does not entail that our closest
relatives must have that trait too. There is no inconsistency with evolutionary continuity to maintain that only humans have the capacity to learn
to play chess. Likewise for consciousness.

(2007, p. 66)

A case, perhaps, of the whole being greater than the sum of its parts: while
humans and other mammals, especially other great apes, might share a great
deal (behaviourally, physiologically, and morphologically), in humans these
'parts' simply produce a different 'whole' compared with other species.

Literature and consciousness

A different approach to demonstrating the existence of consciousness is taken
by the novelist David Lodge (2002). He quotes Sutherland, who states (in the

International Dictionary of Psychology, 1989) that 'Consciousness is a fascinating but elusive phenomenon; it is impossible to specify what it is, what it does, or why it evolved. Nothing worth reading has been written about it'. In making this claim, Sutherland was, inadvertently, dismissing the entire body of the world's literature, the richest and most comprehensive record of human consciousness we have.

Lodge contrasts science's pursuit of universal explanatory laws with literature's description:

> [I]n the guise of fiction the dense specificity of personal experience, which is always unique, because each of us has a slightly or very different personal history, modifying every new experience we have; and the creation of literary texts recapitulates this uniqueness.
>
> (Lodge, 2002, p. 5)

Both science and literature demonstrate the *symbolic* nature of human beings; in their very different ways, they allow us to stand back from 'reality' to ask if things could have been different from how we experience them.

However, while Lodge emphasises the contrast between literature's treatment of the *uniqueness* of personal experience with science's attempt to identify *universal* laws, other novelists (such as Ian McEwan) point out that great literature is great partly because it too deals with universal aspects of human experience. This is discussed further in Box 4.3.

BOX 4.3 LITERATURE, SCIENCE, AND HUMAN NATURE (BASED ON MCEWAN, 2006)

When we read great novels such as *Anna Karenina* or *Madame Bovary*,

> Imaginary people appear before us, their historical and domestic circumstances are very particular, their characters equally so.

And yet:

> By an unspoken agreement, a kind of contract between writer and reader, it is assumed that however strange these people are, we will understand them readily enough to be able to appreciate their strangeness.
>
> (McEwan, 2006, p. 40)

It is our *theory of mind* (ToM) that enables us to get inside the minds of people living in historical and socio-cultural conditions that we've never ourselves experienced (see text below and Chapter 5). Through our ToM,

---

we're able to appreciate what fictional characters all have in common – both with each other and with ourselves and other real people – namely, their individuality, which at the same time is one of the universals of human experience (see Chapter 7). As McEwan puts it:

> At its best, literature is universal, illuminating human nature at precisely the point at which it is most parochial and specific.
>
> (p. 41)

Also in the context of literature, Carroll (2006) argues that:

> If people were truly 'unique' in any very radical way, it would not be possible for ordinary empathy, ordinary insight into others' minds to take place…the sense of individual uniqueness is itself one of those human universals that we all recognise in one another.
>
> (p. 75)

In other words, part of our ToM is the recognition that every human being experiences the world from a unique position. But at the same time, this recognition is part of the shared, universal understanding of what it is to be a person.

McEwan concludes by saying:

> That which binds us, our common nature, is what literature has always, knowingly and helplessly, given voice to. And it is this universality which science, now entering another of its exhilarating moments, is set to explore.
>
> (p. 58)

The 'exhilarating moment' that McEwan refers to is the period following the sequencing of the human genome (see Chapter 3). He asks whose genome was this anyway? What lucky individual was chosen to represent us all? Who is this universal person? In fact,

> [T]he genes of 15 people were merged into just the sort of composite, plausible, imaginary person a novelist might dream up, and here we contemplate the metaphorical convergence of these two noble and distinct forms of investigation into our condition: literature and science.
>
> (McEwan, 2006, p. 58)

Consciousness and the importance of having a body

According to Humphrey (1992), the subject of consciousness, 'I', is an *embodied* self. In the absence of bodily sensations, 'I' would cease: *Sentio, ergo sum* ('I feel, therefore I am') – this is a variant of Descartes' famous *Cogito, ergo sum* ('I think, therefore I am': see Chapter 2).

If there's something distinctive about human consciousness, where should we look for it? According to Eiser (1994):

> Even if we could build a machine with [a] full capacity of a human brain [immensely interactive parallelism] we would still be reluctant to attribute to it the *kind* of consciousness, the sense of self, to which we ourselves lay claim.
>
> (p. 238)

> To ask what is special about human consciousness, therefore, is not just a question about process. It is also to ask what is special about our experience of the world, the experience we have by virtue of physical presence *in* the world.
>
> (p. 239)

Any distinction we try to draw between mind and body (mind–body dualism) is, according to Eiser, objectionable precisely because it divorces mental from physical experience. The most continuous feature of our experience is our own body: *personal* identity (and that of others) depends on *physical* identity, we feel our body and we feel the world *through* it, and it provides the anchor and perspective from which we experience other things.

A similar position to those of Humphrey and Eiser is taken by Merleau-Ponty (1962, 1968). He distinguishes between 'one's own body' (the *phenomenal body*) and the *objective body* (the body-as-object). Experience of our own body is not, essentially, experience of an object. In fact, most of the time we're not aware of our body as such – it is, as it were, *transparent* to us. But without our body, we could not *be*.

For Merleau-Ponty, mind and body, mental and physical, are two aspects of the same thing, namely a person. The mind is embodied in that it can be identified with one aspect of something that has two aspects, neither of which can be reduced to (explained in terms of) the other (Teichman, 1988). The body provides us with a continuous patterned stream of input, and (simply from the fact that we cannot be in two places at the same time) imposes constraints on the information received by the brain about the outside world (Eiser, 1994). This, in turn, relates to the intentionality ('aboutness') of consciousness (see Box 4.2).

Time for reflection ...

- Eiser is arguing for the importance of having a body by focusing on our sense of self. How does this relate to Edelman's distinction above between primary and higher-order consciousness?
- If Eiser is claiming that machines would need a body (as well as a human-like brain) in order to display consciousness, where does that leave non-human animals, especially those whose brains and bodies are most similar to our own (i.e. chimpanzees and other primates)?

Self-recognition: a way of assessing consciousness

Time for reflection ...

Look in a mirror.

- What do you see?
- How do you know it's you?
- Do you ever look in the mirror and *not* recognise yourself?
- If so, how do you account for such experiences?

Many non-human animals (including fish, birds, cats, and chickens) react to their mirror image as if it were another animal: they don't seem to recognise it as their own reflection at all. But self-recognition has been observed in the higher primates – chimpanzees and other great apes. (See Povinelli, 1993.)

In order to determine that an image in a mirror (or a person depicted in a photograph or on film) is oneself, particular knowledge seems to be necessary:

- At least a rudimentary knowledge of oneself as *continuous through time* (necessary for recognising ourselves in photographs or movies) and *space* (necessary for recognising ourselves in mirrors).
- Knowledge of particular features (what we look like).

Although other kinds of self-recognition exist (such as one's voice or feelings), only visual self-recognition has been studied extensively, both in humans and non-humans. Some of the earliest, and still the most cited research, was conducted by Gallup (1970, 1977); this is described in Box 4.4.

BOX 4.4 MIRROR SELF-RECOGNITION IN CHIMPANZEES (GALLUP, 1970, 1977)

- Gallup, working with pre-adolescent, wild-born chimps, placed a full-length mirror on the wall of each animal's cage.
- At first, they reacted as if another chimp had appeared – they threatened, vocalised, or made conciliatory gestures.
- But this behaviour quickly faded out, and after three days had almost disappeared. They then used their image to explore themselves (e.g. picking up food and placing it on their face, which they couldn't see without looking in the mirror).
- After 10 days' exposure, each chimp was anaesthetised and a bright red spot was painted on the uppermost part of one eyebrow ridge, and a second spot on the top of the opposite ear.
- After recovery from the anaesthetic, the chimp was returned to its cage, from which the mirror had been removed; it was observed to see how often it touched the 'spotted' parts of its body.
- The mirror was then replaced, and each chimp began to explore the spotted areas about 25 times more often than it had done before.
- The procedure was repeated with chimps that had never seen themselves in the mirror: they reacted to the mirror image as if it were another chimp (they didn't touch the spots); lower primates (monkeys, gibbons, and baboons) showed no evidence of self-recognition.

A number of researchers (e.g. Lewis and Brooks-Gunn, 1979) have used modified forms of Gallup's technique with 6–24-month-old children. The mother applies a dot of rouge to the child's nose (while pretending to wipe its face) and the child is observed to see how often it touches its nose; it's then placed in front of a mirror, and again the number of times it touches its nose is recorded.

While touching the dot in the mirror reflection was never seen before 15 months, between 15 and 18 months, 5–25 per cent of children did so, compared with 75 per cent of the 18–24-month-olds.

Interpreting Gallup's findings: self-concept and mind-reading

Time for reflection …

- How would you interpret Gallup's findings?
- Does a chimp's ability to recognise itself necessarily mean the same as a child's ability to do so?
- What can we infer about the evolution of (primitive) self-consciousness from the findings using different primate species?

According to Mitchell (1997), while seeing itself in a mirror isn't exactly an everyday experience for a chimp in the wild, opportunities do sometimes present themselves for self-reflection (such as when it looks into water). Success in self-recognition might be a sign not only that chimps can build up a conception of themselves when presented with the relevant visual evidence (i.e. their mirror-reflection), but that their ability to interpret their own image may rest on their holding a *pre-existing* self-concept.

Compared with monkeys, chimps appear to hold a concept that *self* is *me*. But what does 'me' mean? At the very least, it may imply an ability to differentiate between oneself and other individuals.

> This remarkable capacity might signal the dawning of consciousness about self as a sentient and thinking organism with a unique subjective experience, one that differs from other individuals. Hence, being able to recognise oneself in a mirror might be an important manifestation of a primitive and rudimentary conception of mind.
>
> (Mitchell, 1997, p. 35)

It's generally agreed that passing the mirror test is strong evidence that a chimp has a self-concept, and that only chimps, orang-utans, and humans consistently pass it. However, Gallup (1998) infers much more than this: species that pass the mirror test are also able to sympathise, empathise, and attribute intent and emotions to others – abilities that some consider to be uniquely human.

Gallup also believes that a by-product of self-awareness is the ability to infer the existence of mental states in others (ToM or mental state attribution): if you're self-aware, then you're in a position to use your experience to model the existence of comparable processes in others (Gallup *et al.*, 2002). (This is similar to Humphrey's (1986, 1993) account of the evolution of human consciousness: see below.) This view is called the *mind-reading hypothesis* (MRH). Evidence relating to Gallup's' claim regarding the MRH is discussed in Box 4.5.

BOX 4.5 EVIDENCE RELEVANT TO THE RELATIONSHIP BETWEEN SELF-CONSCIOUSNESS AND THE MRH?

- Gallup believes that the best support comes from the mirror studies discussed above. But doesn't this claim involve *circular reasoning?:* (i) passing the mirror test implies self-awareness and, in turn, the ability to read others' minds; and (ii) the best evidence for self-awareness and, in turn, the ability to read others' minds, is passing the mirror test. Is there any additional, *independent* evidence?

- Gallup's research also points to the *right prefrontal cortex* as the brain area that mediates self-awareness and mental states (such as deception and gratitude) – and this is the brain region that grows most rapidly between 18–34 months (see Chapter 3).
- Gallup cites studies by Povinelli and his colleagues involving chimps. These studies are often taken to show that chimps have a ToM, but, ironically, Povinelli (1998) himself disagrees with Gallup's interpretation. While agreeing that passing the mirror test indicates that chimps possess a self-concept, he disagrees that that this means they also possess the deep psychological understanding of behaviour that seems so characteristic of humans.

If chimps *don't* genuinely reason about mental states, what can we say about their understanding of self based on the mirror test? Povinelli has tried to address this by shifting his attention from chimps to two-, three-, and four-year-old children. These studies are described in Box 4.6.

BOX 4.6 STICKERS, LIES, AND VIDEOTAPES (POVINELLI, 1998)

- In a series of experiments, children were videotaped while playing an unusual game. The experimenter secretly placed a large, brightly coloured sticker on top of the child's head.
- Three minutes later, they were shown either (i) a live video image of themselves; or (ii) a recording made several minutes earlier, which clearly depicted the experimenter placing the sticker on the child's head.
- Two- and three-year-olds responded very differently, depending on which video they saw. With the *live image* (equivalent to seeing themselves in a mirror), most reached up and removed the sticker from their head. But with the *recording* (the 'delayed self-recognition test'), only about one-third did so.
- However, this wasn't because they failed to notice the stickers; they also 'recognised' themselves in the recording. But this reaction didn't seem to be much more than a recognition of facial and bodily features. When asked 'Where is that sticker?', they often referred to the 'other' child (e.g. 'It's on his/her head'), as if they were trying to say 'Yes, that looks like me, but that's not me – she's not doing what I'm doing right now'.
- By about four, a significant majority of the children began to pass the delayed self-recognition test. Most four- and five-year-olds confidently reached up to remove the stickers after watching the delayed video image of themselves. They no longer referred to 'him/her' or their proper names.

Autobiographical memory or kinaesthetic self-concept?

According to Povinelli (1998), these results are consistent with the view that genuine *autobiographical memory* (AM) appears to emerge in children between three-and-a-half and four-and-a-half (not the two-year mark favoured by Gallup). AM implies understanding that memories constitute a genuine 'past' – a history of the self leading up to the here and now. (AM is considered by many researchers to be a uniquely human form of memory: see Chapter 5.) It also suggests that self-recognition in chimps – and human toddlers – is based on recognition of the self's *behaviour* and not the self's psychological states.

When chimps and orang-utans see themselves in a mirror, Povinelli (1998) believes they form an *equivalence relation* between the actions they see in the mirror and their own behaviour: every time they move, the mirror image moves with them. These apes can pass the mirror test by correlating coloured marks on the mirror image with marks on their own bodies. Instead of 'That's me!', they conclude 'That's the *same* as me!'

In short, chimps possess explicit mental representations of the positions and movements of their own bodies, which Povinelli calls the *kinaesthetic self-concept*.

Is it just apes that pass the mirror test?

Three major exceptions to the 'only apes display self-consciousness' rule are dolphins and whales (Reiss and Marino, 2001), and elephants (Plotnik *et al.*, 2006, 2014); these are all both extremely intelligent and communicative species.

Prior *et al.* (2008) gave the mirror test to five European magpies (who belong to the crow family or *corvids*); after displaying the usual looking-for-another-animal-behind-the-mirror response, three attempted to remove spots placed on their throats by looking in the mirror. (See Chapter 5.) What makes these findings so remarkable is that corvids' brains are quite different from those of great apes or elephants. As we saw in Chapter 3, bird brains are tiny compared with human brains and lack the convoluted cortex. However, as Blackmore (2010) notes, in all the species that have passed the mirror test, the *brain weight/ body weight ratio* is very high.

Drawing conclusions from the mirror test research

Since crows are so far removed phylogenetically from chimps and humans, their success on the mirror test begs the question: does passing the mirror test necessarily tell us the same thing regarding the animal's self-consciousness? For example, having a self-concept and a ToM are part of our concept of a person – but not of a crow or an elephant! But doesn't this beg its own fundamental question, reflecting the *human exceptionalism* argument (i.e. only humans possess a self-concept and ToM)?

Perhaps a way forward is to break ToM down into some of its component parts, such as *deception*, and understanding *intention*. (See the discussion of mirror neurons in Chapters 3 and 5, and Gross, 2012a.)

De Waal (2016) describes himself as a *gradualist*: there are many stages of mirror understanding, ranging from utter confusion to a full appreciation of the reflected images. These stages are demonstrated not just in a range of non-human species, but also in human infants; the latter show curiosity about their mirror image long before they pass the mirror (mark) test. According to De Waal:

> Self-awareness develops like an onion, building layer upon layer, rather than appearing out of the blue at a given age. For this reason, we should stop looking at the mark test as the litmus test of self-awareness. It is only one of many ways to find out about the conscious self.
>
> (2016, p. 243)

What is (self-)consciousness *for*?

According to Humphrey (1986), when we ask what consciousness does, what difference it makes to our lives, there are three possibilities that might more or less make sense:

1   *It might be making all the difference in the world*: it might be a necessary pre-condition of all intelligent and purposive behaviour, both in humans and non-humans.
2   *It might be making no difference whatsoever*: it may be a purely accidental feature that happens (at least) sometimes to be present in some animals and has no influence on their behaviour.
3   *It might, for those animals that have it, be making the difference between success and failure in some particular aspect of their lives.*

> **Time for reflection …**
> - Which of these do you consider is the most likely to be true?
> - Which corresponds to the common sense view?

Humphrey believes that common sense must back the first of these. Our everyday experience is that consciousness makes all the difference in the world (just as our experience tells us that we have free will: see Gross, 2014): when we lose consciousness, we lose touch with the world.

The cognitive unconscious

According to Frith and Rees (2007), perhaps the major development in consciousness research during the past 50 years has been the demonstration of unconscious, automatic, psychological processes in perception, memory, and action (the *cognitive unconscious*: Kihlstrom, 1987. See Chapter 5). One major example is *blindsight* (Weiskrantz, 1986), which is described in Box 4.7.

BOX 4.7 BLINDSIGHT: CAN WE SEE WITHOUT REALLY 'SEEING'?

- According to Humphrey (1986, 1993), there's increasing evidence that the higher animals, including humans, can demonstrate perception through their behaviour without being aware of what they're doing.
- During the 1960s, Humphrey worked with a monkey called Helen, who'd had her visual cortex removed (as part of a study of brain damage in humans); but her lower visual centres were intact. Over a six-month period following the operation, she began to use her eyes again, and over the next seven years, many of her visual abilities returned.
- At that time, there were no comparable human cases, but what relevant evidence existed suggested that people wouldn't recover their vision. Then, in 1974, Weiskrantz *et al.* reported the case of D.B., a young man who'd recently undergone surgery to remove a tumour at the back of his brain. The entire right-side primary visual cortex had been removed, resulting in blindness in the left side of the visual field. So, for example, when he looked straight ahead, he couldn't see (with either eye) anything to the left of his nose. Or could he?
- While there was no doubt that he was genuinely unaware of seeing anything in the blind half of his visual field, was it possible that his brain was nonetheless still receiving and processing visual input?
- Weiskrantz asked him to forget for a moment that he was blind and to 'guess' at what he might be seeing if he could see. To D.B.'s own amazement, it turned out that he could locate an object accurately in his blind field and he could even guess certain aspects of its shape. Yet he continued to deny any conscious awareness.
- Weiskrantz (1986) called this phenomenon *blindsight*: a condition, caused by brain damage, in which a person is able to respond to visual stimuli despite not consciously perceiving them.
- Other cases have since been described, and unconscious vision appears to be a clinical reality (Humphrey, 1986). As Weiskrantz (2007) says, 'Blindsight has made us aware that there is more to vision than seeing, and more to seeing than vision' (p. 179).

However, despite the fact that perception (and other fundamental cognitive and behavioural processes) may not *require* consciousness, these processes are very often *accompanied* by consciousness. If most other species lack the kind of consciousness that humans possess, isn't it reasonable to suppose that it evolved in humans for some purpose?

Humphrey (1986) asks us to imagine an animal that lacks the faculty of conscious or self-reflexive 'insight'. It has a brain that receives inputs from conventional sense organs and sends outputs to motor systems, and in between runs a highly sophisticated information processor and decision maker. But it has no picture of what this information processing is doing or how it works: the animal is 'unconscious'.

Now imagine that a new form of sense organ evolves, an 'inner eye', whose field of view isn't the outside world *but the brain itself*. Like other sense organs, it provides a picture of the informational field (the brain) that's partial and selective; but, equally, like other sense organs it's been designed by natural selection to give a useful ('user-friendly') picture – one that will tell the subject as much as he/she needs to know: the animal is conscious. These two different types of animal are shown in Figures 4.2a and 4.2b.

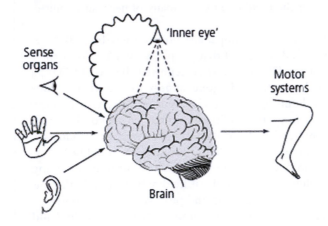

Figure 4.2a How an animal without insight works.

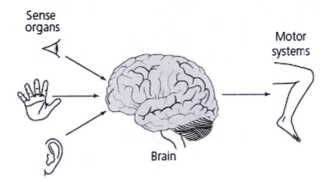

Figure 4.2b How the addition of an 'inner eye' affects the animal. (Re-drawn from Humphrey, 1986.)

Suppose our ability to look in upon ourselves and examine our own minds at work is as much a part of human biology as our ability to walk upright or to perceive the outside world. If Darwin's evolutionary theory is correct, consciousness must have come into being because it conferred some kind of biological advantage on those creatures that possessed it:

> In evolutionary terms it must have been a major breakthrough. Imagine the biological benefits to the first of our ancestors that developed the ability to make realistic guesses about the inner life of his rivals: to be able to picture what another was thinking about, and planning to do next, to be able to read the minds of others by reading his own. The way was open to a new deal in human social relationships: sympathy, compassion, trust, treachery and double-crossing – the very things which make us human.
>
> (Humphrey, 1986, p. 43)

This, of course, is a way of looking at people as *natural psychologists* (*Homo psychologicus:* Humphrey, 1986; see Gross, 2018). It's no accident that humans are both the most highly social creatures to have evolved and are unique in their ability to use self-knowledge to interpret others. This view of people as natural psychologists is consistent with Whiten's (1999, 2007) 'deep social mind' account.

The deep social mind

According to Whiten (1999, 2007), humans are more deeply social than any other species on earth (including chimps). By 'deep', Whiten means a special degree of cognitive or mental penetration between individuals: this goes beyond the sociality of species such as ants, which often involves self-sacrifice and innate infertility.

The *deep social mind* comprises four major elements:

- *Mind-reading* (theory of mind/ToM): as important as the evolution of human *practical* intelligence may have been (bipedalism, tool-making, hunting, fire-lighting), the real mark of a human-like ape would have been the ability to manipulate and relate himself – in human ways – to the other apes around him (i.e. *social* intelligence). (See Chapters 3 and 5.)
- *Culture:* mind-reading plays a crucial role in the processes of *cultural transmission* and *cultural evolution*. (See Chapter 9.)
- *Language and communication:* while language is often cited as a uniquely human ability, it could equally be seen as a *tool* through which mind-reading and cultural transmission operate particularly powerfully. (See Chapter 5.)
- *Cooperation:* this is a crucial feature of culture and is discussed at length in Chapter 9.

Overlapping with the deep social mind is the distinctively human *socio-cognitive niche* (e.g. Whiten and Erdal, 2012), comprising cooperation, egalitarianism, mindreading (ToM), language, and cultural transmission. In *Homo sapiens,* these components go far beyond the most comparable phenomena in other primates, but primate research has increasingly identified related capacities in those species.

Summary and conclusions: the problem of causation

Part of the common sense understanding of consciousness (Humphrey's 'it makes all the difference in the world' possibility) is that conscious processing and the subjective experience of volition (i.e. having free will) do just what they seem to. In other words, we normally take our conscious decision to, say, get out of our chair and go into the kitchen, as the *cause* of those actions: it's 'I' who decides (the *causal efficacy hypothesis*/CEH).

But what if it could be shown that my brain begins to become activated *before* I have made the (conscious) decision? Wouldn't this seriously detract from belief in free will and the causal properties of consciousness? Some very influential – and highly controversial – experiments by Libet (1985; Libet *et al.,* 1983) claim to have shown that:

a   The conscious decision to act (in this case, flexing the finger or wrist) comes about 200 milliseconds (ms) (one-fifth of a second) *before* the action (*consistent* with the concept of free will); but
b   The 'readiness potential' (i.e. gradually increasing electrical activity in the motor cortex) begins about 300–500 ms *before that* (i.e. 500–700 ms before the action – *contrary* to what belief in free will would predict).

(For a more detailed discussion of Libet's research, including a review by Banks and Pockett, 2007, see Gross, 2014.)

According to Velmans (2003), Libet's findings show that our conscious experiences typically occur too late to causally affect the processes to which they most obviously relate. Rather than the conscious wish/decision causing the action, Velmans takes a feeling of volition to be an accurate representation of a *preconscious* voluntary decision. This is consistent with the general finding that consciousness often contains the *results* of cognitive processing, rather than the processing details (Mangan, 2007). In a much-cited article, Nisbett and Wilson (1977) argue that there's no direct access to cognitive processes at all but only to the ideas and inferences that are the *outputs* resulting from such processes. They claim that our common-sense, intuitive belief that we can accurately account for our own behaviour is *illusory*: what really guides our behaviour is unavailable to consciousness.

However, we can certainly be ignorant of the details of a complex process and yet still have the power to initiate, influence, or control it, especially in conjunction with a little feedback (such as driving a car, using a computer, and making a baby) (Mangan, 2007). Higher levels of neural organisation control – but don't themselves contain – the information used to execute lower level functions. If there's sufficient information *in* consciousness in some form (that is, relevant phenomenological contents) to support making volitional decisions, then consciousness *can* be a locus of volition (that is, consciousness does indeed do what common sense assumes).

While it's difficult to deny that we sometimes need to choose a course of action (such as ducking to avoid an approaching missile) faster than could be achieved consciously (i.e. they're made preconsciously, as Libet has shown):

> [T]he mechanisms of consciousness do still have a say: they are able to *veto* plans that would lead to disadvantage in the long run, and to permit only the beneficial ones to proceed. 'Free will' is thus expressed in the form of selective permission of automatically generated actions, rather than as the (Cartesian) initiation of action by an independent mind (Libet, 1985)...Libet's (1994) philosophical conclusion is that consciousness exists as a *dualistic mental field*.
>
> (Rose, 2006, p. 353; emphasis added)

Returning to the evolutionary argument, if consciousness evolved because of its survival value, could it have equipped human beings with such survival value unless it had causal properties? (Gregory, 1981) That is, unless it could actually bring about changes in behaviour? There's no doubt that our subjective experience tells us that our mind affects our behaviour, that consciousness has causal properties.

Lodge (2002) quotes the physicist James Trefil, according to whom:

> [N]o matter how my brain works, no matter how much interplay there is between my brain and my body, one single fact remains...I am aware of a self that looks out at the world from somewhere inside my skull...that is not simply an observation, but the central datum with which every theory of consciousness has to grapple. In the end the theory has to go from the firing of neurons to this essential perception.
>
> (p. 6)

According to Blakemore (1988), Humphrey's evolutionary theory raises two important questions:

1   Why does consciousness use such strange symbolism? For example, the biological value of finding a partner obviously has to do with the nitty-gritty of procreation. But we feel we're in love, a sensation that tells us nothing about the crude necessity of reproduction.
2   Why does the inner eye see so little? It gives us only a tiny glimpse, and a distorted one at that, of the internal world (as we noted above in relation to the cognitive unconscious, much of what our brains do is entirely hidden from the 'spotlight' of consciousness).

For Blakemore, our only answers to these questions are in terms of the structure and organisation of the brain: 'to understand the organ that allows us to understand would be little short of a miracle. The human brain makes us what we are. It makes the mind' (Blakemore, 1988, p. 16). We discussed in Chapter 3 some of the distinctive features of the human brain's structure and organisation; perhaps the most distinctive feature of all is the (kind of) consciousness it produces. What that consciousness allows us to do, in conjunction with other special abilities such as language (see Chapter 5), is to try to understand the 'organ that allows us to understand'.

Suggested further reading

Blackmore, S. (2010) *Consciousness: An Introduction* (2nd edition). London: Hodder Education.

Edelman, G. (1992) *Bright Air, Brilliant Fire: On the Matter of the Mind*. Harmondsworth: Penguin.

Humphrey, N. (1986) *The Inner Eye*. London: Vintage.

Velmans, M. and Schneider, S. (Eds.) (2007) *The Blackwell Companion to Consciousness*. Oxford: Blackwell Publishing.

5 Cognitive aspects of human nature

The recursive mind

Key questions

- What does Hauser mean by '*humaniqueness*'?
- Are there different kinds of *generative computation*?
- How is *recursion* (or *embeddedness*) demonstrated in language and thought?
- How do *levels/orders of representation* illustrate recursion?
- How does tool use demonstrate generative computation?
- What are the essential differences between human and non-human use and manufacture of tools?
- How are tool use and *causal understanding* related?
- What conclusions can we draw from attempts to teach language to non-human animals?
- Is language uniquely human?
- How is *meta-representation* related to *theory of mind* (ToM) (or *mind-reading*)?
- How are ToM and language related?
- What's meant by *mental time travel* (MTT) and is *episodic memory* (EM) unique to humans?
- How are memory, fiction, and religion related?
- Are we naturally prejudiced and are stereotypes inherently bad?
- What's meant by *modern, symbolic,* or *aversive racism*?
- Are *heuristics* a built-in feature of human decision-making?
- What is the cognitive basis of religious belief?
- How is the use of *metaphor* central to what it means to be a *symbolic creature*?

In contrast with Darwin's (1871) view that the difference between human and non-human minds is 'one of degree and not of kind' (i.e. *continuity*), Hauser (e.g. 2009) believes there's mounting evidence that a 'profound gap' exists between them. While some of the 'building blocks' of human cognition have been found in other species (consistent with the evolutionary perspective), these building blocks constitute only 'the cement footprint of the skyscraper' of the human mind. Human cognition has evolved so far beyond other species' abilities that it has become *qualitatively* different.

Hauser (2009) argues that:

> If we scientists are ever to unravel how the human mind came to be, we must first pinpoint exactly what sets it apart from the minds of other creatures.
>
> (p. 45)

The rearranging, deleting, and copying of universal genetic elements shared with other species (see Chapter 3) created a brain with special properties. This 'deep chasm' (*human exceptionalism*) argument is captured in Hauser's term '*humaniqueness*', which denotes the key ingredients of the human mind. The four major ingredients of humaniqueness are:

- *Generative computation.*
- *Promiscuous combination of ideas.*
- *Mental symbols.*
- *Abstract thought.*

Generative computation

Generative computation refers to the ability to create a virtually limitless variety of 'expressions' (such as arrangements of words, sequences of notes, combinations of actions, or strings of mathematical symbols). Generative computation encompasses two types of operation: *recursive* and *combinatorial*.

The fundamental importance of recursion

Recursion is the repeated use of a rule to create new expressions. For example, a short phrase can be *embedded* within another phrase, repeatedly, in order to create longer, richer descriptions of our thoughts.

According to Jackendoff (1993), recursion is an example of a *pattern* in the mind, which, along with words and their meanings, overcomes the limitations of human memory (we couldn't possibly store all the sentences we're likely to hear or want to use.) Recursion prepares us for any possible sentence we might encounter (most of which we've never heard before in that exact form and are therefore countless.) One such pattern corresponds to the different levels or orders of representation which characterise theory of mind (ToM); for example:

(a)   Bill thinks that Beth is a genius.
(b)   Sue suspects that Bill thinks that Beth is a genius.
(c)   Charlie said that Sue suspects that Bill thinks that Beth is a genius.
(d)   Jean knows that Charlie said that Sue suspects that Bill thinks that Beth is a genius.

This sequence can be extended *indefinitely* – we can always add one more element (or level/order of representation). But according to Dunbar (2004, 2007), most adult humans are limited to five. This example demonstrates the important relationship between language and memory. Indeed, for Corballis (2011), while recursion may be the main ingredient that distinguishes human language from all other forms of animal communication (see below), recursion is the primary feature distinguishing the human *mind* from that of other animals:

> It underlies our ability not only to reflect upon our own minds, but also to simulate the minds of others … to travel mentally in time.
>
> (Corballis, 2011, p. 1)

For Corballis (and others), recursion *originates* in thought (rather than language): 'The only reason language needs to be recursive is because its function is to express recursive thoughts' (Pinker and Jackendoff, 2005, p. 230).

What Jackendoff calls patterns in the mind form part of what others (notably Chomsky, e.g. 1957, 1979) have called *mental grammar*. The notion of a mental grammar stored in the brain of a language user is *the* central theoretical construct of modern linguistics and is central to the view that (the capacity for) human language is *innate* – and uniquely human (see Gross, 2012a). Up until very recently, recursion had been included in the list of *linguistic universals*, which are essentially what mental grammar comprises; this claim has been challenged (see Gross, 2015).

Time for reflection …

- Music is another example of generative computation. Jackendoff (1993) claims that, like language, music is a uniquely human activity; at the very least, they are both human universals (Williamson, 2009).
- In what ways can music be thought of as a (kind of) language?

Combinatorial generative computation

This second type of generative computation – refers to the mixing of discrete elements to produce new ideas, which can be expressed as novel words (e.g. 'Walkman') or musical forms, among other possibilities (Hauser, 2009).

Generative computation and the use and making of tools

Hauser (2009) claims that generative computation by humans, but not other animals, is reflected in the use of tools. He gives the example of an orang-utan using a large, single leaf as an umbrella (see Figure 5.1); this is typical of non-humans' making of implements from a single material and for a single purpose.

By contrast, humans routinely combine materials to form tools and often use a given tool in a number of ways (they're *multi-purpose*): Hauser's example is the No. 2 pencil (see Box 5.1).

BOX 5.1 THE NO.2 PENCIL: DRAWING ON HUMAN VERSATILITY (HAUSER, 2009)

- Hauser describes the No. 2 pencil as one of our most basic tools, illustrating the exceptional freedom of the human mind as compared with the limited scope of animal cognition.
- You hold the pencil's painted wood, use the lead for writing and drawing, and erase with the pink rubber held in place by a metal ring: four different materials, each with a particular function, all wrapped up into a single tool.
- Although that tool was designed as a writing implement, it can also be used to pin long hair up into a bun, as a bookmark, or to stab an annoying insect.
- By contrast, animal tools – such as the stick chimps use to fish termites out from their mounds – consist of a single material, designed for a single purpose, and is never used for any other. None has the *combinatorial properties* of the pencil.

According to Oakley (1957), in *Man The Toolmaker*, only humans make tools. Oakley discounted Köhler's (1925) famous observations of Sultan and other chimps stacking boxes in order to reach an inaccessible banana (what Köhler called 'insight learning') as tool manufacture, since it was done in response to a given situation rather than in anticipation of an imagined future. But De Waal (2016) believes that chimp survival is often (even if indirectly) dependent on the use of tools (in order to find scarce or inaccessible food sources).

Beck (1980) defined *tool use* as 'the external deployment of an unattached environmental object to alter more efficiently the form, position, or condition of another object, another organism, or the user itself' (p. 10). *Tool manufacture* can be defined as the active modification of an unattached object to make it more effective in relation to one's goal. (Note the importance of *intentionality*.) According to De Waal (2016):

> By making suitable tools out of raw materials, chimpanzees are exhibiting the very behaviour that once defined *Homo faber*, man the creator.
>
> (p. 78)

De Waal claims that 'wild chimps not only use and make tools, but they learn from one another, which allows them to refine their tools over generations'

(p. 78, see also Chapter 9 of this book). For example, Jane Goodall (1988) describes two older chimps, David Greybeard and Goliath (in Gombe National Park, Tanzania), who on several occasions picked small leafy twigs and prepared them for termite-fishing by stripping off the leaves. She refers to it as the first recorded example of a wild animal not merely using an object as a tool, but actually modifying an object and thus showing the crude beginnings of tool *making* (Goodall, 1988). De Waal also points out that in addition to corvids (such as crows), even crocodiles, alligators, and octopi have been observed making and using tools (see Figure 5.1).

According to Goodall (1988):

> The point at which tool-using and toolmaking, as such, acquire evolutionary significance is surely when an animal can adapt its ability to manipulate objects to a wide variety of purposes, and when it can use an object spontaneously to solve a brand-new problem that without the use of a tool would prove insoluble.

> (Goodall, 1988, p. 232)

Figure 5.1 Chimpanzee (*Pan troglodytes*) using a stick to retrieve food from underground (as in the wild in Central African forests, but now set up as behavioural enrichment). (Permission granted by Mary Evans Library.)

This sounds very much like Hauser's generative computation, which, he claims, is only demonstrated through human tool use and tool making. Goodall also provides evidence that chimps use objects for many different purposes, illustrating generative computation.

Tool use and causal understanding

According to Wolpert (2007), causal understanding is unique to humans. While there are, of course, similarities between human and mammalian – especially primate – cognition, primates have little understanding of the causal relationships between inanimate objects.

> They [primates] do not view the world in terms of underlying 'forces' that are fundamental to human thinking. They do not understand the world in intentional or causal terms (Povinelli, 2000; Tomasello, 1999). Non-human primates do not understand the causal relation between their acts and the outcomes they experience.
>
> (Wolpert, 2007, p. 168)

Contrary to evidence presented by Goodall and the much-cited New Caledonian crows that manufacture and use several types of tools (including straight and hooked sticks) (Chappell and Kacelnik, 2002), Wolpert concludes his review by saying:

> While primates and some birds use simple tools there is an almost total absence of causal beliefs in animals other than humans … they [animals like crows and monkeys] have a very limited capacity for refining and combining objects to make better tools. The tools chimpanzees use have a narrow range of functions and there is little evidence that they can think up new functions for the same tool. Compare this with the way humans use a knife for a whole variety of purposes.
>
> (Wolpert, 2007, pp. 170–1)

Tools, evolution, and technology

Perhaps the most critical difference of all (although arguably *not* part of Hauser's concept of generative computation – and going beyond it), is that chimps (unlike humans) have never been observed using one tool to make another (*secondary tools*) (Goodall, 1988; Wolpert, 2007). Even simple stone tools require a hammer stone, like those used by chimps to break hard-shelled fruits or nuts; these were later used by our hominin ancestors to shape rocks for cutting tools.

According to Wolpert (2007), one cannot make a complex tool (i.e. one that has a well-characterised form for the use it will be put to) without a concept of cause and effect; even more importantly, a complex tool describes any tool made out of two pieces put together (such as a spear and a stone head).

According to Schick and Toth (1993), it's the technological path that humans took that has separated us most profoundly from our primate ancestry and from our extant primate relatives.

Promiscuous combination of ideas, mental symbols, and abstract thought

It's useful to consider the other three components of Hauser's 'humaniqueness' in the context of his discussion of the differences between human language and animal communication (see Box 5.3).

BOX 5.3 PROMISCUOUS COMBINATION OF IDEAS, MENTAL SYMBOLS, AND ABSTRACT THOUGHT

Promiscuous combination of ideas

Time for reflection …

Hauser (2009) poses the following task:

- For the numbers 0, 0.2, and −5, add the most appropriate word: 'apple' or 'apples'.
- Which word would you select for 1.0?

If you're like most native English speakers, you opted for 'apples'. Hauser says it's good if you're surprised by this. If you think about it rationally, 'apple' (i.e. singular) is the correct choice, so we couldn't have learnt this as a grammatical rule in school. It's part of the universal grammar we're born with; the rule is simple but abstract: anything that's not '1' is pluralised.

This example demonstrates how different systems − syntax and the concept of sets − interact to produce new ways of thinking about or conceptualising the world. But the creativity process in humans doesn't stop there: we apply our language and number systems to cases of morality (saving five people is better than saving one), economics (if I'm giving £10 and offer you £1, that seems unfair, and you'll reject the £1), and taboo trade-offs (in Western Europe and the U.S., selling our children, even for lots of money [or especially for lots of money?] isn't acceptable) (Hauser, 2009).

Mental symbols and abstract thought

We can spontaneously convert any sensory experience – real or imagined – into a symbol that we can either keep private or share with others through language, art, music, or computer code.

Abstract thought

Unlike animal thoughts, which are largely anchored in sensory and perceptual experiences, many human thoughts aren't; 'We alone ponder the likes of unicorns, nouns and verbs, infinity and God' (Hauser, 2009, p. 48).

Almost by definition, domains of knowledge/systems of understanding are *abstract*, that is, the terms we use to refer to them (e.g. economics, morality, language, grammar) don't denote anything that's tangible or perceptible in any other way: they're collective, 'higher-level' representations of real individual objects, events, activities, and so on. But even here, things are far from straightforward: in that list given in the previous sentence, the terms all refer to abstract categories. For example, while we can visualise a specific object (say, a vase), we cannot visualise the category of 'object' (not, at least, without trying to picture a *particular* object). The category 'object' embraces an enormous range of things (e.g. cars, food, furniture, cleaning products, electrical goods), and each of these examples itself illustrates another abstract concept (but at a lower level in the mental hierarchy made up of all these concepts). Go into any supermarket, and you'll see how 'food' (and, increasingly, other 'products') is separated into categories (e.g. the large signs above each aisle, then smaller labels on the shelves within each aisle).

Imagine how chaotic – and time-consuming – it would be if supermarkets weren't organised in this way – and imagine how chaotic a place our *minds* would be if they weren't also organised in this way. However, it's only minds that are/need to be organised *hierarchically* and it's *language* that makes this possible. The world doesn't come naturally categorised or 'cut up' in this way: it's something the human mind creates or constructs out of the 'raw material' of sensory experience. As we've seen, language frees us from the here-and-now, our immediate environment, allowing us to explore what *could* be (or might have been) through the use of *imagination* (Dunbar, 2007). Literature and science both, in their very different ways, try to address this question, and both are deeply symbolic activities.

Differences between human and non-human communication

Like other animals, humans have a non-verbal communication system that expresses our emotions and motivations to others. But humans alone have a system of linguistic communication based on the manipulation of mental symbols, with each example of a symbol falling into a specific and abstract category (such as noun, verb, and adjective).

Even if the famous honeybee's waggle dance (which 'informs' the hive of the precise location of a pollen source) *symbolically represents* that location, these uses of symbols differ from ours in five fundamental ways (Hauser, 2009):

1   They're triggered only by real objects or events, never imagined ones.
2   They're restricted to the present (see below).
3   They're not part of a more abstract classification scheme, such as organising words into nouns, verbs and adjectives.
4   they're rarely combined with other symbols – and when they are, the combinations are limited to a string of two, with no rules.
5   they're fixed to particular contexts.

Another remarkable difference between human language and animal communication is that language operates equally well in the visual and auditory modes: a deaf person using sign language can convey anything that a hearing person can communicate via speech: they're equally expressive and structurally complex. But if a songbird loses its voice and a honeybee its waggle, their ability to communicate would be eradicated.

Humans as symbolic creatures

Tattersall (2007) sees human beings (unlike other primates) as *symbolic* creatures, with language the ultimate symbolic activity. The world we occupy is not the one presented to us directly by nature, but rather the one we've created in our heads through the use of language. According to Cassirer (1944):

> in the human world we find a new characteristic which appears to be the distinctive mark of human life … Man has … discovered a new method of adapting himself to his environment. Between the receptor system and the effector system, which are to be found in all animal species, we find in a man a third link which we may describe as the *symbolic system*…As compared with the other animals man lives not merely in a broader reality; he lives, so to speak, in a new *dimension* of reality.
>
> (p. 24)

And again:

> No longer in a merely physical universe, man lives in a *symbolic universe*. Language, myth, art, and religion are parts of this universe. They are the varied threads which weave the symbolic net, the tangled web of human experience.
>
> (p. 25; emphasis added)

Both Cassirer and Langer (1951) cite the cases of Helen Keller and Laura Bridgman, both of whom were blind and deaf-mute, and so deeply reliant on the sense of touch. According to Langer (1951), despite these disabilities, both women were capable of 'living in a wider and richer world than a dog or an ape with all his senses alert' (p. 34). Their cases are described in Box 5.4.

BOX 5.4 HELEN KELLER (1902, 1908) AND LAURA BRIDGFORD (LAMSON, 1881)

- Helen Keller had previously learned to combine a certain thing or event with a certain sign of the manual alphabet, through a fixed association between these things and particular tactile impressions.
- But to grasp what human speech is and means, requires the understanding that *everything has a name* – 'that the symbolic function isn't restricted to particular cases but is a principle of *universal* applicability which encompasses the whole field of human thought' (Cassirer, 1944, pp. 34–5).
- As usually happens some years earlier, Helen, aged seven, had come to use words as symbols – rather than mechanical signs or signals.
- Laura Bridgman was greatly inferior to Helen Keller, both in intellectual ability and development. Yet Laura also suddenly reached the point where she began to understand the symbolism of human speech (having learned to use the finger alphabet) (Cassirer, 1944).

According to Cassirer (1944), the case of Helen Keller, who reached a very high degree of intellectual development, shows 'clearly and irrefutably' that in constructing our human world we're not dependent upon the 'raw material' that reaches the brain via the sense organs. While speech may confer great technical advantages compared with a tactile language (the finger alphabet), Helen Keller and Laura Bridgman were certainly not 'exiles from reality': if the child has succeeded in grasping the meaning of human language, it doesn't matter through which medium this has come about (Cassirer, 1944).

Teaching language to non-humans

Cassirer's arguments are highly relevant to the claims made regarding non-human animals' capacity to *acquire* language (in particular – and most famously – chimps and bonobos). Some of the most commonly cited *production-based* studies are summarised in Table 5.1.

Table 5.1 The major studies which have attempted to teach language to non-human primates

Study	Subject	Method of language training
Gardner and Gardner (1969)	Washoe (female chimp)	American Sign Language (ASL or Ameslan). Based on a series of gestures, each corresponding to a word. Many gestures visually represent aspects of the word's meaning.
Premack (1971)	Sarah (female chimp)	Small plastic symbols of various shapes and colours, each symbol standing for a word; they could be arranged on a special magnetised board; e.g. a mauve [triangle] = 'apple'; a pale blue [star] = 'inert'; a red [square] = 'banana'.
Rumbaugh *et al.* (1977)/ Savage-Rumbaugh *et al.* (1980)	Lana (female chimp)	Special typewriter controlled by a computer. Machine had 50 keys, each displaying a geometric pattern representing a word in a specially devised language ('Yerkish'). When Lana typed, the pattern appeared on the screen in front of her.
Patterson (1978, 1980)	Koko (female gorilla)	ASL
Terrace (1979)	Nim Chimpsky (male chimp)	ASL

Time for reflection ...

- In all the studies described in Table 5.1, positive reinforcement ('reward') was used when signs, etc., were used correctly (see Chapter 6).
- Can you think of any limitations to studies using such a reward-based system for teaching language to non-humans?

Chimps' and gorillas' lack of speech clearly doesn't automatically disqualify them from acquiring language in some other form (such as American sign language), but at the same time their ability to use sign language doesn't necessarily imply that they grasp the *meaning* of those signs. One contentious issue in this area of research relates to the understanding that 'everything has a name' (see Box 5.4).

Cassirer points out that symbols are not only *universal*, but, as a complementary characteristic, also extremely *variable*: the same meaning can be expressed in different languages; even within the limits of a single language, a particular thought or idea can be expressed in quite different ways. By contrast, a sign or a signal is related to the thing it refers to in a fixed and unique way. Cassirer gives the example of the unconditioned/conditioned stimuli in Pavlov's (1927) famous classical conditioning experiments with dogs (see Chapter 6).

Unlike signs and signals, a genuine human symbol is versatile, not rigid or inflexible but mobile and dynamic. However, Cassirer observes that the full *awareness* of this mobility seems to be a rather late achievement in human intellectual and cultural development. For example, in mythical thought the name of a god is an integral part of the nature of the god: if I don't call the god by his right name, then the spell or prayer becomes ineffective. The same holds good for symbolic actions: a religious rite, a sacrifice, must always be performed in the same invariable way and in the same order if it is to have its effect (Cassirer, 1944).

Langer (1951) regards the *need for symbolisation* as a basic – and uniquely – human need.

Is language unique to humans?

One major criticism of the production-based studies summarised in Table 5.1 is that the animals fail to show any evidence of understanding *grammar* (specifically *syntax* or basic 'grammatical rules'), which is generally accepted as a fundamental feature of a true language. A second major limitation is that they involve *rote learning*: the animal is being *trained* to build up a vocabulary, one symbol at a time.

Partly to meet these criticisms, since the 1980s Sue Savage-Rumbaugh has adopted an alternative approach, in which a large vocabulary of symbols is used from the start, using them in naturalistic settings as language is used around human children – through the use of *observational exposure* (see Gross, 2015). This represents a move away from an emphasis on grammatical structure (at least in the beginning) and towards *comprehension*.

According to Aitchison (1983), the apparent ease with which children acquire language, compared with apes, supports the claim that they're innately programmed to do so. Similarly, although these chimps have grasped some of the rudiments of human language, what they've learned, and the speed at which they learn it, are *qualitatively* different from those of human beings (Carroll, 1986).

Aitchison and Carroll seem to be talking for a majority of psychologists; belief in human exceptionalism (or uniqueness) is especially powerful – and widely held – in relation to language. However, Savage-Rumbaugh believes the difference between ape and human language is merely *quantitative*.

Jackendoff (1993) believes that asking whether apes have language or not is a 'silly dispute', preferring to ask: do the apes succeed in *communicating*? He thinks the answer is undoubtedly yes. He also believes that they appear to successfully communicate *symbolically*. However, beyond that, it doesn't look as though apes are capable of constructing a mental grammar that regiments the symbols coherently. In short, Universal Grammar appears to be exclusively human (Jackendoff, 1993). This ability to communicate symbolically represents a necessary precursor for language that evolution has equipped them with, but they have no use for it in their natural environment.

Finally, when Jane Goodall was asked in a recent interview what sets the human mind apart from the chimp mind, she answered 'The explosive development of intellect':

> You can have very bright chimps that can learn sign language and do all kinds of things with computers, but it doesn't make sense to compare that intellect with even that of a normal human, let alone an Einstein...the evolution of our intellect quickened once we began using the kind of language we use today, a language that enables us to discuss the past and to plan the distant future.
>
> (Goodall, 2010, p. 63)

Time for reflection ...

- Is it ethically acceptable to use chimps and other apes for this kind of research?
- For example, is it right that they're treated *as if* they're human when they're not?

Mental time travel, memory, and language

At the end of the quote above from Goodall, she's referring to what we've previously called *mental time travel* (MTT). Corballis and Suddendorf (2007) believe that the ability to transcend time is what makes human beings unique. While other animals react to what's happening in their immediate environment, humans are able to remember the past and think about the future. Corballis and Suddendorf believe that language and MTT probably co-evolved; in turn, these are both related to memory.

Episodic memory

Episodic memory (EM) is a conscious projecting oneself back *in time* (*autonoetic*/self-knowing) in order to re-experience some earlier event or episode (Tulving, 2002). This is contrasted with *semantic memory* (SM) or 'knowing' (which is *noetic*); simply knowing something ('facts') doesn't imply any shift of consciousness. (Both EM and SM are forms of *explicit* or *declarative* memory, dependent on the hippocampus: see Chapter 3.) (See Figure 5.2.)

Autonoetic awareness is *recursive*: we can insert previous personal experience into present awareness (comparable to embedding phrases within phrases or

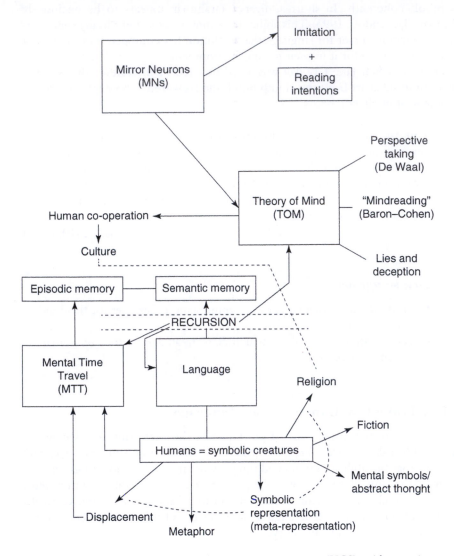

Figure 5.2 Schematic summary of the human cognitive system (HCS), with recursion as a common feature linking the major components. The HCS is central to the view of humans as symbolic creatures.

sentences within sentences: see above). We can also remember remembering something. This kind of embedding may have set the stage for the recursive structure of language itself (Corballis, 2011).

Storage of EMs depends on SMs that are already in place: we can hardly remember a specific visit to a restaurant without already knowing what a restaurant is and what happens there, but the former is related to the self in subjectively sensed time (Corballis, 2011).

Projecting ourselves into the future is sometimes referred to as *episodic future thinking* (EFT) (Atance and O'Neill, 2005); Suddendorf (2010) also suggests 'episodic foresight'. EFT develops in children at around the same time as EM itself (three to four years). Amnesic patients are as unable to answer simple questions about past events as they are to say what might happen in the future. Amnesia for specific events, then, is at least partly a loss of time awareness (Corballis, 2011). This is dramatically illustrated by the case of Clive Wearing (see Box 5.5).

BOX 5.5 CLIVE WEARING

- Clive Wearing was the chorus master of the London Sinfonietta and a world expert on Renaissance music, as well as a BBC radio producer.
- In March, 1985, he contracted a rare brain infection caused by the cold sore virus (*Herpes simplex*), which attacked and destroyed his hippocampus, along with parts of his cortex.
- He lives in a snapshot of time, constantly believing he's just awoken from years of unconsciousness. For example, when Deborah, his wife, enters his hospital room for the third time in a single morning, he embraces her as if they'd been apart for years, saying, 'I'm conscious for the first time' and 'It's the first time I've seen anyone at all'.
- He can still speak, walk, read music, play the organ, and conduct; he can also acquire new skills (based on *implicit, unconscious,* or *non-declarative memory*), although he doesn't know/remember that he has those skills. His memory for his earlier life is extremely patchy.
- According to his wife, 'Without consciousness, he's in many senses dead'; in his own words, his life is 'Hell on earth – it's like being dead – all the bloody time'.

(Based on Baddelely, 1990; Blakemore, 1988; Wearing, 2005.)

What the case of Clive Wearing shows is how fundamentally important memory (in particular, EM) is to our very sense of who we are (our self–identity) and our ability to function in society. As Blakemore (1988) says:

> Without memory we would be servants of the moment, with nothing but our innate reflexes to help us to deal with the world. There could be no language, no art, no science, no culture. Civilisation itself is the distillation of human memory.

(p. 43)

Memory, fiction, and religion

The concept of MTT helps explain the fragility of EM, which is more important for helping us construct future scenarios than providing a detailed record of the past (which it does very poorly). EM is itself a construction (as demonstrated by Bartlett's (1932) classic experiments: see Gross, 2015): 'Remembering is not like playing back a tape or looking at a picture, it is more like telling a story' (Neisser, 2008, p. 88). It's a process of establishing our own identities, often in defiance of the facts.

This leads to *fiction* itself, which is produced through the same linguistic processes that allow us to reconstruct the past and construct possible futures (such as *symbolic representation* and *displacement*: using symbols to refer to objects, actions, events, people, etc., that aren't physically present – or that could never actually exist!)

> We humans are addicted to folktales, legends, novels, movies, plays, soap operas, and everyday gossip. It is the power of *recursion* that makes these things possible. Critical in all of them is language, the device that enables us to share our memories, future plans, and dreams.
>
> (Corballis, 2011, p. 111; emphasis added)

In our evolution, language and MTT seem to be linked: language may have evolved precisely to enable us to share our mental travels through time. As a species, we're unique in telling stories; indeed, there's a blurred dividing line between memory and fiction. Stories also tend to become institutionalised, 'Ensuring that shared information extends through large sections of the community, creating conformity and social cohesion' (Corballis, 2011, p. 124), as in the Bible, Koran, *Harry Potter*, and TV soaps.

Religious conviction derives less from doctrine than from stories (Boyd, 2009). Like other religious works, the Bible tells stories of such supernatural incidents as virgin birth, walking on water, and rising from the dead. Evolution will favour belief in a falsehood if it motivates more adaptive behaviour than does belief in truth; one falsehood that is perhaps encouraged by tales of the supernatural is life after death. More generally, supernatural stories can engender social cohesion by spreading through a culture (Corballis, 2011). (See Chapter 9).

Is EM uniquely human?

Suddendorf and Corballis (1997, 2007) believe that EM is unique to human beings. Wolfgang Köhler agrees: for all their improvisational skills and insight, chimps had little concern for past or future; only humans can flexibly anticipate their own future mental states of need and act in the present to satisfy them.

> In humans, at least, mental time travel implies the conscious acting out of episodes, whether past or future, which further suggests *recursion*...a conscious episode is embedded in present consciousness. This can proceed to deeper levels, as when I remember that yesterday I planned an

episode…for some date in the future. It may be this recursively embedded structure that differentiates our own time–governed behaviour from that of other species.

(Corballis, 2011, p. 106; emphasis added)

Time and the human condition

Perhaps the most fateful consequence of MTT is the understanding that we all die (see Chapter 8):

> The understanding of death…is of course an unpalatable aspect of the human condition, but it is moderated to some extent by the understanding that time continues beyond death. Our lives, perhaps, can be continued in those of our offspring.
>
> (Corballis, 2011, p. 108)

Religion provides belief in an after–life. We can trace something of the history of MTT through burial sites: there's some evidence that Neanderthals buried their dead (although this may have been more for practical than religious reasons). But in some early human burials, symbolic material is added, suggesting a notion of a spiritual life that continued beyond bodily death – but these were restricted to *Homo sapiens* (Pettit, 2002). (Cognitive predispositions to religious belief are discussed below.)

Theory of mind

As we noted in Chapter 3 when discussing mirror neurons, the term '*theory of mind* ' (ToM) was first used by Premack and Woodruff (1978) based on their work with chimps. We also noted that much of the subsequent research involving humans has focused on those on the autistic spectrum, who suffer from *mind-blindness* (Baron-Cohen, 1990): a severe impairment in their understanding of mental states (their own and others') and in their appreciation of how mental states govern behaviour (Baron-Cohen, 1993, 1995a, 1995b). This means that most of us are capable of *mind-reading*.

> Mind reading…is…a mental process, dependent on common situations, shared experience, and an understanding that other minds are like our own. Mind reading is critical to human co-operation, but may also underlie some of our more deceitful practices, such as lying, stealing, and cheating.
>
> (Corballis, 2011, p. 129)

Language depends crucially on ToM; indeed, it's one of the mechanisms we use to read others' minds. ToM is *recursive*: it involves inserting what you believe to be someone else's state of mind into your own. What are some of the naturalistic ways we do this?

Whether instinctive or learned, the human ability to infer others' mental states goes well beyond detection of emotion; for example, we can understand what another person can see through *perspective-taking*, literally seeing things from another's perspective. More complex still is the capacity to infer what others *believe*, specifically *false beliefs* (and hence how they'll *behave*). A classic way of testing this capacity is the 'Sally–Anne' test, described in Box 5.6.

BOX 5.6 THE SALLY-ANNE FALSE BELIEF TEST

- In Baron-Cohen *et al.*'s (1985) study, 20 autistic children (mean age 11.11 years), 14 with Down's syndrome (10.11), and 27 normal children (4.5) were shown two dolls, Sally and Anne.
- Sally places her marble in a basket, before she leaves the scene.
- While she's away, Anne transfers Sally's marble to a box.
- The child is then asked the crucial *belief* question: where will Sally look for her marble? The *correct answer* is 'in the basket' (where she put it before leaving).
- Sally returns – and looks in the basket for her marble.
- While most of the normal and Down's children passed (i.e. they attributed Sally with a *false belief*) most of the autistic children failed (i.e. they answered 'in the box', where the marble actually was).

According to Baron-Cohen (1995a), 'mindreading' comprises four modules: (i) the *intentionality detector* (ID); (ii) the *eye-direction detector* (EDD); (iii) *shared-attention mechanism* (SAM); and (iv) *theory of mind mechanism* (ToMM). ToMM is innately determined and begins to mature from about 12–18 months to four years; it processes information in the form of *metarepresentations* ('beliefs about beliefs') (Leslie, 1987, 1994; Leslie and Roth, 1993). Southgate *et al.* (2007) found evidence that even two-year-olds may understand false beliefs.

Dennett (1983) refers to mind reading as the *intentional stance* (i.e. we tend to treat people as having intentional states, including beliefs, desires, hopes, etc., as well as intentions to act in a particular way). We interact with others according to what we think is going on in their minds, rather than in terms of their physical attributes. The *recursive* nature of ToM is captured by *different orders of intentionality:*

- *Zero-order:* actions or behaviours that imply no subjective state (as in reflex/automatic acts).
- *First-order:* a single subjective term (e.g. *Alice wants Fred to go away*).

- *Second-order:* two such terms (*Ted thinks Alice wants Fred to go away*); ToM begins at this level.
- *Third-order: Alice believes that Fred thinks she wants him to go away.*

Recursion kicks in once we get beyond first order.

For Corballis (2011), while chimps may have some capacity to discern what other individuals can feel, see, and perhaps know, this is *first-order recursion* at best; what they probably lack is *higher-order recursion* (see below). However, the difference is one of *degree* – not kind.

(For a discussion of why ToM evolved, and its biological advantages, see Chapter 4.)

ToM, lies, and deception

Survival during the Pleistocene, when our ancestors competed with dangerous carnivores, required co-operation and social intelligence (see Chapter 9). But there's a dark side to social intelligence, namely, *freeloading.* Evolutionary psychologists refer to a 'cheater-detection module' in the brain (Cosmides and Tooby, 1992), but the cheats have developed more sophisticated ways of escaping detection, producing a 'cognitive arms race' (Trivers, 1974; Barkow *et al.* 1992).

The ability to take advantage of others through such recursive thinking (cheater detection leads to cheater-detection detection) is known as *Machiavellian intelligence,* i.e. the use of social strategies to outwit or deceive our fellow human beings. Whether or not chimps have ToM, 'it seems that we humans are supreme in our ability to lie, cheat, and deceive, while also maintaining outward respectability' (Corballis, 2011, Note 12, p. 243).

Deception is widespread in nature (as, for example, in camouflage), but *tactical deception* (TD) involves the deceiver appreciating what the deceived is actually thinking or what it can see (i.e. an implied intentional stance). *Telling lies* is the most obvious form of TD. There's little evidence of TD among common chimps, bonobos, gorillas, or orang-utans (Whiten and Byrne, 1988).

According to Mitchell (1997):

> Possessing an understanding of mind is not just a superfluous intellectual gift that we are blessed with for no good reason, but is vital for ensuring that we thrive as humans…our aptitude for misleading other people… pervades much human interaction.
>
> (p. 150)

Mitchell believes that humans aren't easily duped and are frequently on guard in anticipation of being misled. But at the same time, we're hardwired to trust what others tell us – without this implicit trust, we'd be paralyzed as individuals and social relationships would break down. We don't (usually) expect or look for lies. But perhaps we're growing more suspicious as we become more aware of all the scams, etc., via the Internet.

Indeed, research by psychologists and neuroscientists suggests that our tendency to deceive others – and our vulnerability to being deceived – are especially consequential in the age of social media: our ability as a society to separate truth from lies is under unprecedented threat. However, lying is also a normal part of development – children become better at lying as they get older, reflecting development of ToM and as their language skills increase. Also fundamental to lying is the brain's *executive function* (i.e. planning, attention, and self-control). As expected, children on the autistic spectrum aren't very good liars (see above).

Bhattacharjee (2017) observes that the history of humankind is strewn with crafty and seasoned liars, including politicians who lie to gain power or cling to it (e.g. Richard Nixon, 1974: 'I am not a crook'; Bill Clinton, 1998: 'I did not have sexual relations with that woman'). Some lie in order to inflate their public image (such as Donald Trump's demonstrably false assertion that his Inauguration crowd was bigger than Obama's first one). Even scientists are sometimes guilty of 'cooking their books': famously, Cyril Burt's alleged invention of data from separated twins in his studies of intelligence.

However, such notorious liars aren't as exceptional as we might think; indeed, our capacity for dishonesty is as fundamental as our need to trust others: 'Being deceitful is woven into our very fabric, so much so that it would be truthful to say that to lie is human' (Bhattacharjee, 2017, p. 38).

A study by Garrett *et al.* (2016) used fMRI to scan the brains of participants as they told lies. To the extent that participants engaged in self-serving dishonesty (lies that would be to their advantage), the signal from the amygdala (which responds to stressful/emotionally arousing situations: see Chapter 3) became progressively weaker with each successive lie. Telling one lie made it easier to tell subsequent – and 'bigger' – lies: the brain seems to adapt to the stress of lying.

Are we naturally prejudiced?

According to Buchanan (2007), many researchers argue that prejudice (in all its forms) is part of human nature; only by facing up to our authentic nature can we gain real insight into the forces that drive group conflict, and learn how we might manage and defuse such urges.

Are stereotypes inherently bad?

Stereotypes constitute the cognitive component of attitudes, of which prejudice is an extreme example. Traditionally, stereotypes have been condemned for being both false and illogical – and potentially dangerous; people who use them have been regarded as prejudiced and even pathological.

However, Gordon Allport (in his classic *The Nature of Prejudice,* 1954) argued that most stereotypes do contain a 'kernel of truth'. Walter Lippman (1922), who first used the term in relation to prejudice, had acknowledged the categorisation processes involved in stereotyping as an important aspect of general cognitive functioning. According to Brislin (1993):

> Stereotypes should not be viewed as a sign of abnormality. Rather, they reflect people's need to organise, remember, and retrieve information that might be useful to them as they attempt to achieve their goals and meet life's demands.

(p. 171)

Time for reflection ...

- What do you think is meant by the term '*cognitive miser*'?

According to the concept of the *cognitive miser* (Fiske and Taylor, 1991), stereotypes are resource-saving devices; they simplify the processing of information about other people. They are both (i) basic human tendencies inherent within our cognitive architecture; and (ii) potentially damaging belief systems, depending on the power of the situation (Operario and Fiske, 2004).

Time for reflection ...

- Is it possible to think of oneself as without prejudice and at the same time to display *implicit* (unconscious) prejudice?

Unconscious prejudice and the brain

Most people would (strongly) deny that they are racist, sexist, or in any other way prejudiced and what they probably understand by this claim is 'old-fashioned', *explicit*, overt, crude racism, etc. (which now falls under the heading of 'hate crime', at least in the UK). Similarly, studies using the Modern Racism Scale (MRS) (McConahay, 1986), which explores racial attitudes by asking participants how much they agree or disagree with a number of race-related statements, tend to confirm people's low self-perceived racist attitudes.

But what about *modern* (McConahy, 1986), *symbolic* (Sears and Henry, 2003), or *aversive racism* (Gaertner *et al.*, 2005)? These terms describe the attitudes of the political liberal, who openly endorses egalitarianism but who harbours *unconscious* negative feelings or beliefs that are expressed in subtle, indirect, *implicit* ways (Dovidio *et al.,* 2016). Is it possible for individuals to display little bias on the MRS and at the same time for their behaviour and brain scans to reveal such (*unconscious*) bias? According to Greenwald *et al.* (2009), while a majority of US whites appear non-prejudiced on self-report (*explicit*) measures, a significant percentage typically show evidence of bias on implicit measures. One study that reports such a discrepancy is described in Box 5.7.

BOX 5.7 IMPLICIT RACIAL PREJUDICE AND THE BRAIN

- In a study by Phelps *et al.* (2000), white participants reported very low self-perceived racial bias on the MRS.
- While in a fMRI scanner, and before completing the MRS, they were shown pictures of either black or white male faces (all strangers and with neutral facial expressions), one at a time; they had to decide whether it was the same face as the last or a different one.
- The researchers' focus was on the *amygdala*, implicated in processing threat and detecting socially important stimuli (see Chapter 3).
- Participants were also given the Implicit Association Test (IAT); this is presented on a computer and comprises several stages: (i) 'black/bad' would appear in the top left corner of the screen, and 'white/good' in top right corner; (ii) single names (e.g. 'Temeka') are then presented in the centre of the screen: the participant has to decide whether to categorise the name as 'black' or white'; similarly, whether words (e.g. 'wonderful') are 'good' or 'bad'; (iii) the categories are then reversed: 'black/good' and 'white/bad'.
- The main measure ('dependent variable') is *reaction time*: if participants classify 'wonderful' as good faster with 'white/good' than with 'black/good' on the screen, then they're displaying an implicit negative bias against blacks (or positive white bias). This was, indeed, what was found.
- When these IAT results were compared with the imaging data, the higher the pro-white bias, the greater the amygdala activation to black versus white faces.
- Interestingly, this pro-white bias disappeared when participants were shown faces of famous people (including Muhammad Ali, Denzel Washington, Harrison Ford, and John F. Kennedy).

Time for reflection …
- How might you account for the IAT findings?

The reasoning behind the IAT findings is that, if you have a pre-existing association between 'white people' and 'good', then the 'white/good' pairing will be much easier to use; the 'black/good' pairing feels less 'right' and so will take longer to process.

Time for reflection ...

- But how can we explain the different activation levels of the amygdala in response to the black/white faces?

In another study, Terbeck *et al.* (2012) gave one group of participants propranolol (a beta blocker used to treat high blood pressure and anxiety) and a second group a placebo (sugar pill) before undergoing the IAT. The medication had no effect on explicit racial prejudice or mood, but it significantly reduced the implicit racial bias: fear and threat-processing seem to play an important role in racial bias (Sahakian and Gottwald, 2017).

Heuristics in decision-making

If stereotypes represent an in-built device for simplifying the world and helping us to manage the overwhelming amount of information that we have to deal with at every moment, then the *heuristics* used in decision-making (DM) represent another.

Clearly, important decisions should be approached rationally and systematically. But it's not always easy to make rational decisions: (i) we often don't have access to all the required information to make rational choices; (ii) we may simply not have the time to engage in rational DM given the sheer number of decisions that we have to make daily; and (iii) despite our highly evolved brains, human beings have only a limited capacity for reasoning according to formal logic and probability theory (Evans and Over, 1996). As a result, we often rely on *heuristics,* rules of thumb, guidelines, or short-cuts for selecting actions that will help us attain our goal (or solve a problem) – although it cannot guarantee it (DM is a form of problem-solving). Some of the more commonly used heuristics are described in Table 5.2.

The first two heuristics in Table 5.2 were first described by Tversky and Kahneman (1973, 1974). In *Thinking Fast and Slow* (2013), Kahneman distinguished between two kinds of systems in the mind:

- *System 1* is based on instinct and intuition and is where the representativeness and other heuristics belong. It works in a reflex way, using a limited amount of information to reach a conclusion quickly and in a shallow way. The 'solution' seems obvious, but we cannot explain how we arrived at it. It can triumph in situations where being slow and deliberate can be 'fatal'.

Table 5.2 Some commonly used heuristics in decision-making

Availability heuristic: making decisions on the basis of whatever information is most readily available in long-term memory. It's based on the assumption that an event's probability is directly related to the frequency with which it has occurred in the past and that more frequent events are usually easier to remember than less frequent ones.

Representativeness heuristic: judging the likelihood of something by intuitively comparing it with preconceived ideas of a few defining characteristics of a particular category (i.e. *stereotypes*).

Gambler's fallacy: the belief that the probability of winning will increase with the length of an ongoing sequence of losses.

Illusion of control: an expectancy of success which isn't warranted by objective probability.

Flexible attribution: The tendency to attribute success to personal skill and failure to external influence. (This corresponds to the *self-enhancing bias* and *self-protective bias*, respectively.)

- *System 2* thinks deeply, logically, and slowly, taking everything into account (the 'professor'). It can triumph where avoiding error is paramount and when we're trying to solve problems that require deliberation and reasoning.

However, these two Systems aren't mutually exclusive. Our minds are biased and flawed – but in a systematic way: human behaviour is irrational but predictably so (Lawton, 2013).

The cognitive basis of religious belief

As the discussion of prejudice and heuristics demonstrates, our minds aren't passive receptacles; they work in biased ways, which constrain the forms that cultural evolution is most likely to take. These biases extend to religions, as in belief in salvation, redemption, immortality, and the 'magical' powers of an all-powerful being. Why do religions often take these particular forms? Ironically, the answer might lie in the nature of our minds as organs designed by natural selection to understand the world (Pagel, 2012).

According to Bloom (2007), children are natural *dualists:* they're predisposed to allow that things like rocks, trees, sky, waterfalls, even clouds, can have minds, and if minds can exist independently of a body, then it can also wander alone as a disembodied spirit. (See Chapter 2.) We're also predisposed to see *purpose* in things (i.e. we have a taste for *teleology:* the expectation that things happen or exist for a reason). For example, seven-to-eight-year-old children overwhelmingly prefer *teleo-functional* explanations (such as mountains exist 'to give animals a place to climb') over mechanistic, or physical, causal explanations ('because volcanoes cooled into lumps'); it's only around the age of nine that children begin to give more scientifically accurate accounts (Bering, 2010).

In turn, this preference for teleological accounts makes us *creationists* at heart: if things have a purpose, our natural dualistic minds consider that something – a *creator* perhaps – gave them that purpose. In the adult mind, these tendencies turn into an appetite for religious explanations of what can otherwise be an inscrutable world. According to Barnes (2008), religions were the first great inventions of the fiction writers; they provided a plausible explanation of the world for understandably confused minds. Or, as Voltaire put it, 'If God did not exist, it would be necessary to invent him' (Pagel, 2012).

Time for reflection ...

- How can we so easily and uncritically accept religious beliefs that seem to fly in the face of basic laws of biology and physics (such as belief in immortality)?

Many religions require us to do things that resemble the behaviour of Skinner's pigeons reinforced randomly (see Chapter 6); if they happened to be turning to the right when a food reward was presented, they were more likely to continue turning to the right. Human counterparts include the strange rituals of bowing, genuflecting (bending knee in prayer), burning incense, chanting, singing in special buildings, all in hope of bringing about things we want to happen – but which are totally out of our control (like Skinner's pigeons?).

Language makes false beliefs even more likely to develop: we don't even have to witness an event to know about it. Widely publicising miracles and beatifying or even granting sainthood to people are ways of reinforcing the connection between beliefs and outcomes.

Early religion would have provided causal explanations of the world that are now provided by science, a sophisticated model of the cosmos, 'Giving a rationale for people to behave one way as opposed to another, in an arbitrary, dangerous, capricious, and unpredictable world' (Pagel, 2012, p. 147). But are things so different now for most people? Indeed:

> Nature taunts us to appeal to something stronger than our rational human best, and for animals with our brains this has often meant looking to supernatural powers.
>
> (Pagel, 2012, p. 148)

Religion provides answers to basic existential questions (such as how we got here and our place in the universe). Our minds may search for answers to such questions because they give us hope and direction (which are useful in themselves). Given our minds' predisposition to believe in gods, those gods might provide as useful an explanation for what happens in our lives as any other set of beliefs. Perhaps more importantly, belief in an afterlife (as most religions describe) provides protection from our fear of death – perhaps the ultimate existential issue that human beings have had to contend with since their time-travelling brains recognised that every individual's future will, ultimately, reach the same conclusion. (See Chapter 7.)

Summary and conclusions: meta–representation and metaphor

While Hauser doesn't explicitly use the term 'meta-representation', much of what he says regarding humaniqueness could be summarised using that concept. If, as Leslie (1987) claims, meta-representation lies at the heart of mind–reading, could it perhaps also be a central feature of human thought in general?

In a similar way, much of our use of language involves meta-representation: the use of words in a *non-literal* (meta-representational) way, based on their literal (primary representational) meaning. A major example of this non–literal use of language is *metaphor*, arguably a crucial aspect of what it means to be a symbolic creature.

Although we make the important distinction between literal and meta-phorical use of language, there may be something essentially metaphorical about *all* language, in the sense that, by definition, symbols (such as words) bear no intrinsic, inherent relationship to what they represent/stand for: but our thinking becomes so 'saturated' (there's another metaphor!) with the particular symbols we happen to use in our native language, that they appear to take on a concrete, literal reality that, in truth, they don't have. Perhaps this helps explain why it's so difficult to learn a second language (at least, as an adult): another language is like a meta-representation of our own beliefs about the world derived from all the years of thinking in our native tongue. Maybe *all* language use is metaphorical – but some uses are more metaphori-cal than others!

According to Langer (1951), thought starts out as metaphor before becoming more literal: at least as far as new ideas are concerned, the meta-representational *precedes* the primary representational:

> Metaphor is our most striking evidence of *abstractive seeing*, of the power of the human mind to use presentational symbols. Every new experi-ence, or new idea about things, evokes first of all some metaphorical expression. As the idea becomes familiar, this expression 'fades' to a new literal use of the once metaphorical predicate, a more general use than it had before…The use of metaphor can hardly be called a conscious device. It is the power whereby language, even with a small vocabu-lary, manages to embrace a multimillion things; whereby new words are born and merely analogical meanings become stereotyped into literal definitions.
>
> (Langer, 1951, p. 125)

Perhaps what this demonstrates is that we can only understand something new in terms of what we already know and understand. While this begs fundamental questions as to how we acquire understanding of *anything* in the first place, there's little doubt that language is the major symbolic tool that humans use for understanding the world.

Suggested further reading

Corballis, M.C. (2011) *The Recursive Mind: The Origins of Human Language, Thought, and Civilization*. Princeton, NJ: Princeton University Press.

De Wall, F. (2016) *Are We Smart Enough to Know How Smart Animals Are?* London: Granta.

Evans, V. (2014) *The Language Myth: Why Language Is Not an Instinct*. Cambridge: Cambridge University Press.

Goodall, J. (1988) *In the Shadow of Man* (revised edition). London: Phoenix.

Jackendoff, R. (1993) *Patterns in the Mind: Language and Human Nature*. Hemel Hempstead: Harvester-Wheatsheaf.

Savage-Rumbaugh, S. and Lewin, R. (1994) *The Ape at the Brink of the Human Mind*. New York: John Wiley.

6 Behaviourist and psychodynamic accounts

People as driven by forces beyond their control

Key questions

- What are the basic processes involved in Pavlovian/classical conditioning?
- What's stated by Thorndike's 'Law of Effect'?
- Why is the 'Little Albert' experiment of such significance in the history of behaviourism?
- What's meant by Watson's 'radical environmentalism'?
- How did Skinner modify the Law of Effect and why did he distinguish between respondent and operant behaviour?
- What's meant by the 'ABC of operant conditioning'?
- In what sense was Skinner a radical behaviourist?
- How did Tolman's cognitive behaviourism and Bandura's Social (or Cognitive) Learning Theory challenge Skinner's 'empty organism' view of learning?
- How are Freud's psychoanalytic theory and (other) psychodynamic theories related?
- What are the three levels of consciousness described by Freud and how do they relate to the psychic apparatus?
- How does Jung's account of the unconscious differ from Freud's?
- How does Erikson's psychosocial theory differ from Freud's psychosexual theory?
- Was Freud an instinct theorist?
- What are the main features of Adler's individual psychology?
- How did Skinner and Freud explain the illusory nature of free will?

Different psychologists make different assumptions about the particular aspects of human nature that are worthy of study, reflecting an underlying model or image of what people are like; in turn, this model or image determines preferred methods of investigation, a view of development and of the nature of psychological normality and abnormality, and the preferred methods and goals of treatment for abnormal behaviour.

A number of theoretical approaches or perspectives can be identified within psychology's history as a distinct scientific discipline (arguably dating from about 1860: see Gross, 2018). This chapter is devoted to two of the earliest approaches, the behaviourist and psychodynamic, whose influence is still felt within psychology (even if it is to *deny* their continuing influence).

In many ways, these two approaches are fundamentally opposed; however, they share two major views regarding human nature which make it appropriate to bring them together within the same chapter:

1   They are both *deterministic*. According to behaviourist psychologists (such as Watson, its founder), human behaviour is the product of external forces (stimuli) over which the individual has little or no control. Sometimes behaviour is seen as being automatically *triggered* (or *elicited*), making it *involuntary,* sometimes it is *voluntary* (it's *emitted* by the person); in the latter case, the *consequences* of the emitted behaviour determine the likelihood of it being repeated.

For psychodynamic psychologists, the causes of behaviour are *internal*, in particular *unconscious* memories, ideas, and wishes. In both cases – behaviourist and psychodynamic – the individual is *driven*, passively responding to, or at the mercy of, unknown or unknowable forces.

2   Both approaches reject the widely held belief in free will, albeit for very different theoretical reasons.

Within both these approaches there are two or more distinguishable strands or theories, both/all sharing certain basic principles and assumptions which give them a distinct 'flavour' or identity.

The behaviourist approach

John B. Watson first coined the term 'behaviourism' in 1913, arguing that all human and non-human animal behaviour can be explained in terms of *classical conditioning*. Behaviourism (at least in its Watsonian form) has its roots in associationism (a philosophical theory), physiology (in particular Pavlov's study of digestion in dogs), and two earlier forms of psychology, namely, functionalism (beginning with William James) and animal psychology (including Watson's own pre-1913 research with rats).

Pavlov's physiological research: psychic secretions

Pavlov was interested in the physiology of digestion. One of his innovations was to surgically create openings (*fistulas*) in different parts of the digestive tracts of dogs, such as the salivary ducts and isolated areas of the stomach. An incidental observation was that dogs which were used to the laboratory routine and apparatus would start salivating while merely being placed in the apparatus. Pavlov called these 'psychic secretions'; they were clearly *learned* (a result of the dog's experience), while salivation in response to a drop of acid placed on the dog's tongue is an innate, *unlearned*, involuntary reflex. (Pavlov was awarded the Nobel Prize for physiology in 1904.)

Conditioned reflexes

Having determined that 'psychic secretions' are the product of experience (more the domain of psychology than physiology), Pavlov re-read Sechenov's (1965/1863) *Reflexes of the Brain,* which tried to account for all behaviour – including such 'higher cognitive functions' as thinking, willing, and judging – in terms of an expanded concept of the reflex. Pavlov now decided that his dogs' psychic secretions could be redefined in purely *physiological* terms relating to the reflex.

> **Time for reflection …**
>
> - How could you characterise Sechenov's account of higher cognitive functions in terms of brain-related reflexes?
> - In principle, do you agree or disagree – with him and Pavlov – that *all* behaviour can be explained this way, giving your reasons?

If the drop of acid is presented enough times with another *neutral* stimulus (such as a ringing bell or ticking metronome) which *doesn't* naturally trigger salivation, the bell or metronome *on its own* will trigger salivation. This can be restated as follows: the bell or metronome will come to trigger salivation *on condition* that it is presented simultaneously with the acid. In other words:

- The acid is an *unconditional* (or, more commonly, *unconditioned*) *stimulus/*UCS).
- Salivation triggered by the acid is an *unconditional/unconditioned response* (UCR).
- A bell or metronome that, *on its own*, triggers salivation after being paired with the acid is a *conditional/conditioned stimulus* (CS).
- Salivation triggered by a bell or metronome *alone* is a *conditional/conditioned response* (CR).

Classical conditioning

What we have just described is the basic process of *classical* (*Pavlovian* or *respondent*) conditioning (Pavlov, 1927). 'Respondent' denotes the automatic nature of the response (conditioned or unconditioned). This is summarised in Figure 6.1.

Pavlov also discovered that there's much more involved in this type of learning than what we've described so far, including *higher order conditioning, generalisation and discrimination,* and *extinction and spontaneous recovery* (see Gross, 2018).

Acid on tongue → Salivation   [Before learning]
   (UCS)   (UCR)
Bell + Acid on tongue → Salivation [During learning]
(CS)   (UCS)   (UCR)
Bell → Salivation   [After learning]
(CS)   (CR)

Figure 6.1 The basic procedure involved in classical conditioning.

Functionalism and the study of animal behaviour

Functionalism was the first recognised school of American psychology and this largely reflects the influence of evolutionary theory and a practical ('pioneering') spirit. (William James, one of the two great pioneers of 'modern' (experimental) psychology, is usually described as a functionalist.)

Thorndike and the Law of Effect

One of the pioneers of functionalism, Edward Thorndike, is also regarded as a pioneering *associationist*; arguably, this makes his impact on behaviourism, specifically Skinner's work on operant conditioning, on a par with Pavlov's.

Thorndike saw psychology as primarily the study of stimulus-response *connections* (or bonds), but his understanding of 'stimulus' and 'response' was far broader than how the terms are commonly understood – and certainly far broader than the discrete 'events' studied by Pavlov and on which Watson's behaviourism was based (see below).

BOX 6.1 THORNDIKE'S (1898) LAW OF EFFECT

- Thorndike was impressed by animals' gradual learning of the correct response (e.g. with cats, operating the latch which would automatically release the flap so they could escape) and gradual elimination of incorrect ones. *Accidental* (i.e. chance/random) *success* played a large part in this process, which has come to be called *trial-and-error learning.*
- What was being learned was a *connection* between the stimulus (the manipulative components of the box) and the response (the behaviour that resulted in escape). Further, the S–R connection is 'stamped in' when pleasure results (e.g. a piece of fish waiting for the cat outside the box) and 'stamped out' when it doesn't.
- This is the *law of effect* and represents a crucial way of distinguishing between classical and operant conditioning, which Skinner was to do 40 years later (see text below).

Watson and classical conditioning

Conditioned emotional reactions

Watson (see Figure 6.2) was the first psychologist to apply Pavlovian/classical conditioning to human behaviour, both as an *explanatory* device and in an experimental setting. The latter involved an 11-month-old baby, Albert B. (better known as 'Little Albert'), destined to become one of the most famous children in the entire psychological literature. The study clinched Watson's fame as the father of behaviourism (Simpson, 2000) and is described in Box 6.2.

BOX 6.2 CONDITIONED EMOTIONAL REACTIONS (WATSON AND RAYNER, 1920)

- The aim of the study was to provide an empirical demonstration of the claim that various kinds of emotional response can be conditioned, in this particular case, *fear*.
- Albert was described as 'healthy from birth' and 'on the whole, stolid and unemotional'. When he was about nine months old, Watson and Rayner tested his reactions to various stimuli – a white rat, a rabbit, a dog, a monkey, masks with and without hair, cotton wool, burning newspapers, and a hammer striking a four-foot steel bar just behind his head. Only the last of these frightened him, and so was designated the UCS (and fear the UCR). The other stimuli were *neutral* with regard to fear.
- The experiment began when Albert was just over 11 months old. The rat and UCS were paired: as Albert reached out to stroke the rat, Watson crept up behind him and brought the hammer crashing down on the steel bar.
- This occurred seven times in total over the next seven weeks. By this time, the rat (the CS) produced a fear response (CR) without the need for Watson's 'intervention'. Watson and Rayner had succeeded in deliberately producing a rat phobia in a baby.

Time for reflection ...

- Watson (1931) believed that the child's UCRs (fear, rage, and love) to simple stimuli are merely the starting points in building up those 'complicated habit patterns' (or *conditioned emotional responses/* CERs) that we later call our emotions. For example, jealousy is a rage response to a (conditioned) love stimulus (manifested as reddening of the face, exaggerated breathing, etc.).

Figure 6.2 John B. Watson (1878–1956), founder of behaviourism. (Permission granted by Alamy.)

- To what extent would you agree with Watson's analysis of emotion?
- Watson also proposed that as children grow up, their behaviour becomes increasingly complex, but is basically the *same kind of behaviour* as it was earlier on (i.e. a series of CERs that become added and recombined).
- How could you characterise this view of developmental change and how might it be contrasted with theories such as those of Freud and Erikson (see below) (see Gross, 2015)?

Watson and the nature–nurture debate

Given Watson's views regarding fear, rage, and love as the only unconditioned (i.e. unlearned/innate) responses involved in human emotion, and his emphasis on classical conditioning in general, it's perhaps not too surprising that he adopted a *radical environmentalist* position in relation to behaviour as a whole.

Watson denied the existence of 'capacity, talent, temperament, mental constitution and characteristics', and, perhaps most famously, he claimed that the systematic application of conditioning principles could give caretakers almost total control over their children's development:

> Give me a dozen healthy infants, well-formed, and my own specified world to bring them up in and I'll guarantee to take any one at random and train him to become any type of specialist I might select – doctor, lawyer, merchant-chief and yes, even beggar-man and thief, regardless of his talents, penchants, tendencies, abilities, vocations, and race of his ancestors.
>
> (Watson, 1931, p. 104)

Beyond making psychology relevant to solving everyday problems, Watson also had had a utopian vision (Morawski, 1982): behaviourism could actually make the world a better place. This isn't as well-known as Skinner's vision (as depicted in his 1948 utopian novel, *Walden Two*: see below).

Skinner and operant conditioning

Skinner (1938) (see Figure 6.3) made a fundamental distinction between:

(i)   *Respondents* (or *respondent behaviour*), which are triggered automatically or *elicited* – by particular environmental stimuli; and
(ii) *Operants* (or *operant behaviour*), which are essentially voluntary – or *emitted* by the organism.

These are related to *classical/Pavlovian* (or *respondent*) *conditioning* and *instrumental/Skinnerian* (or *operant*) *conditioning*, respectively.

Figure 6.3 B.F. Skinner (1904–90), radical behaviourist. (Alamy.)

In making these distinctions, Skinner wasn't rejecting Pavlov's and Watson's ideas and research achievements. Rather, he was interested in how animals *operate* on their environment, and how this operant behaviour is *instrumental* in bringing about certain *consequences*; these consequences, in turn, determine the probability of that behaviour being repeated. Compared with Pavlov or Watson, Skinner's learner is much more *active*.

Just as Watson's ideas were based on the earlier work of Pavlov, so Skinner's operant conditioning grew out of the earlier work of Thorndike (see Box 6.1). Skinner devised a form of puzzle box (what he described as an 'automated operant chamber', but commonly referred to as a 'Skinner box'), designed for a rat or pigeon to *do* things in (press a lever or peck at an illuminated disc), rather than to escape from. The experimenter decides exactly what the relationship shall be between pressing the lever/pecking the disc and the delivery of a food pellet, providing total *control* of the animal's environment – but it's the animal that has to do the work.

Skinner's behaviour analysis

In Thorndike's *Law of Effect*, 'stamping in' refers to the effect that a piece of fish has on the cat's successful escape from the puzzle box. But for Skinner, this term was too mentalistic; like Watson, the mind was to have no place in a scientific explanation of behaviour (a feature of his radical behaviourism: see below). Instead, he used the term 'strengthen', which he deemed more objective and descriptive. Regardless of the term, the idea is that certain consequences of operant behaviour make that behaviour *more likely* to occur again. Similarly, other, *aversive* (literally, 'painful') consequences (such as electric shock) 'stamp out' the behaviour they follow or 'weaken' it. In Skinner's terminology, those consequences act as either *positive reinforcers* or *punishers*, respectively. *Negative reinforcers* also strengthen the behaviour they follow, but work in a different way: when behaviour results in the *removal* of, or *escape* from, some aversive state of affairs, the behaviour is being negatively reinforced.

According to Skinners's version of the Law of Effect, behaviour is shaped and maintained by its consequences. Behaviour analysis can be summarised as the 'ABC of operant conditioning' (Blackman, 1980), as summarised in Box 6.3.

BOX 6.3 THE ABC OF OPERANT CONDITIONING

The analysis of behaviour requires an accurate but neutral representation of the relationships (or *contingencies*) between:

- *Antecedents:* the *stimulus conditions* (such as the lever, the click of the food dispenser, a light that may go on when the lever is pressed).
- *Behaviours:* operants (such as lever pressing or disc pecking).
- *Consequences:* what happens as a result of the operant behaviour (*positive reinforcement, negative reinforcement,* or *punishment*).

(Based on Blackman, 1980)

Skinner's radical behaviourism

Skinner maintained that cognitions are *covert behaviours* ('within the skin') that should be studied by psychologists along with overt behaviours (capable of being observed by two/more people). He was *not* 'against cognitions', but argued that so-called mental activities are 'metaphors or explanatory fictions'; behaviour attributed to them can be more effectively explained in other ways.

For Skinner, these more effective explanations of behaviour come in the form of the principles of reinforcement. What's 'radical' about radical behaviourism is the claim that thoughts, feelings, sensations, and other private events cannot be used to explain behaviour but are to *be explained* through *behaviour analysis*.

Another feature of Skinner's radical behaviourism is his 'empty organism' view of the learner (human or non-human): there's nothing 'going on' inside the individual person or animal – either cognitive or physiological – that makes any difference to its emitted behaviour – either before or after learning. For Skinner, only an empty organism view was compatible with a 'science of behaviour'.

Alternatives to Skinner's 'empty organism' view

Challenges to Skinner's 'empty organism' view from within behaviourism have come in several different forms. Two noteworthy examples are Tolman's *Cognitive behaviourism* (see Box 6.4) and Bandura's *Social Learning Theory* (see Box 6.5).

BOX 6.4 TOLMAN'S COGNITIVE BEHAVIOURISM

- In *Purposive Behaviour in Animals and Man* (1932), Tolman presented evidence which he believed demonstrated conclusively that no adequate account of learning in rats could omit reference to their *goals* in solving a problem: a rat put in a maze wasn't a mere machine that, having by chance found its way to the goal-box, then mechanically repeated the movements that got it there.

- Rats form a '*cognitive map*' of the maze, a symbolic representation of the whole (or most of the) maze; the maze constitutes what Tolman called a *sign-gestalt* for the rat which leads to the development of 'means-end-readiness' or a plan to navigate the maze in order to repeat the pleasurable experience of obtaining the food reward (Tolman, 1948).

- Cognitive maps represent *expectations* regarding which part of the maze will be followed by which other part, an understanding of its spatial relationships.

- Indirect support for the cognitive map explanation comes from a famous experiment which demonstrated *latent learning* (Tolman and Honzig,1930). This demonstrated that reinforcement may be important in relation to *performance* (rats' ability to find their way to the goal-box) but *isn't* necessary for the learning itself (i.e. knowing where the goal-box is located and how to get there). (See Gross, 2015).

The very cognitive notion of 'expectations' has subsequently been used to explain what is taking place in classical conditioning (the most 'un-cognitive' account of learning!). Conditioning cannot be reduced to the strengthening of S–R associations by the automatic process called reinforcement. It's more appropriate to think of it as a matter of detecting and learning about *relations between events:* animals typically discover what signals or causes events that are important to them (such as food, water, danger, or safety). Salivation (as in classical conditioning) or lever pressing (as in operant conditioning) are simply convenient *indices* (or measures) of what the animal has learned (i.e. environmental relationships) (Mackintosh, 1978, see also Gross, 2018).

BOX 6.5 BANDURA'S SOCIAL LEARNING THEORY (SLT)

- Unlike Skinner and Tolman, Bandura was interested in *human social behaviour* and conducted several famous experimental studies of children's aggression during the 1960s and 1970s.
- While not denying the role of operant conditioning, Bandura (1965) argued that far more important with regard to human social behaviour is *observational learning*, i.e. learning merely through being exposed to a model's behaviour – and without any reinforcement having to take place.
- However, as with Tolman's demonstration of latent learning in rats, whether the model's behaviour is actually reproduced (i.e. *imitated*) depends partly on the *consequences* of the behaviour – for both model and learner; in other words, reinforcement is important only in as much as it affects *performance* (not the learning itself).
- For Bandura, thought *intervenes* (or *mediates*) between behaviour and its consequences. Whereas Skinner claims that reinforcements and punishments *automatically* strengthen and weaken behaviour, for Bandura they serve primarily to provide *information* about the likely consequences of certain behaviour under certain conditions: it improves our ability to predict whether a given action will lead

to pleasant (reinforcement) or unpleasant (punishment) outcomes *in the future.*

- Reinforcements and punishments also *motivate* us by causing us to anticipate future outcomes. Our present behaviours are largely governed by the outcomes we *expect* them to have and we're more likely to try to learn the modelled behaviour if we value its consequences. (The importance of social learning in the evolution and maintenance of *culture* is discussed in Chapter 9.)
- The importance of cognitive mediating variables in social learning is reflected in Bandura's (1986, 1989) renaming of SLT as *social cognitive theory* (SCT).

Time for reflection ...

- One of the strengths of Bandura's SLT/SCT (and other versions, such as that of Mischel, 1973) is the claim that behaviour can only be understood by taking the actor's *self-concept, self-monitoring,* and *self-efficacy* into account.
- What do you understand by these terms?
- How does their inclusion make SLT/SCT a more valid way of understanding human behaviour than Skinner's account?

These 'self' terms makes the theory far less *mechanistic* than Skinner's for example, which focuses exclusively on *external* events.

According to *reciprocal determinism* (Bandura, 1977a; 1986), people are both producers and products of their environment (a view echoed in discussion of *cultural evolution*: see Chapter 9). There's an ongoing, *two-way,* mutual influence between behaviour and the environment.

The psychodynamic approach

For many non-psychologists, 'psychology = Freud' and 'Freud = sex(uality) and the unconscious mind'. Freud (see Figure 6.4) regarded himself as a scientist, having originally wanted to pursue a career in physiological research, but (for practical and cultural reasons) trained as a doctor, specialising in neurology (disorders of the nervous system). He's probably best known as the founder of *psychoanalysis,* at the time (early 1900s) a revolutionary way of treating people with psychological disorders (psychoneuroses); this represents the original form of *psychotherapy* from which all subsequent methods have developed (see Gross, 2015).

Freud's psychoanalytic methods evolved alongside the associated explanations of what lay at the root of his patients' problems, namely unresolved

Figure 6.4 Sigmund Freud (1856–1939), founder of psychoanalysis; 1906 (aged 50). (Permission granted by Mary Evans Library.)

unconscious conflicts, often stemming from childhood trauma. His *psychoanalytic theory* as a whole included his *meta-psychology*, his account of the structure of the psyche, or a general model of the mind (both conscious and unconscious). The impact of his ideas is reflected in the number of 'Freudian' concepts used in everyday language in Western cultures (most of the time not being recognised as such); these have become part of our common-sense (or folk) psychology (Harré, 2006).

> *Time for reflection ...*
>
> • How many 'Freudian' and other psychodynamic terms and concepts can you name that are commonly used in everyday language?

Defining 'psychodynamic'

The term 'psychodynamic' denotes the active forces within the personality that motivate behaviour, and the inner causes of behaviour (in particular, the *unconscious conflict* between the *id, ego,* and *superego* that comprise the 'psychic apparatus' or the personality as a whole). While Freud's psychoanalytic theory (sometimes 'psychoanalysis', denoting both his meta-psychology and his psychotherapeutic methods) was the original psychodynamic theory, the psychodynamic approach as a whole includes all those theories and approaches to therapy based on his ideas; major examples include:

- *Ego psychology* (e.g. Freud's daughter, Anna (1895–1982)).
- *Psychosocial theory* (Erik Erikson (1902–94)).
- *Analytical psychology* (Carl Gustav Jung (1875–1961)).
- *Individual psychology* (Alfred Adler (1870–1937)).
- *Object relations school* (e.g. Fairbairn (1889–1964), Klein (1882–1960), Winnicot (1896–1971), Bowlby (1907–90)).

So, while Freud's psychoanalysis is psychodynamic, all the other approaches listed above are psychodynamic but *not* psychoanalytic (i.e. the two terms aren't synonymous). In this chapter, we'll focus on Freud's ideas, but compare them with those of Adler, Jung, and Erikson as a way of offering some evaluation of psychoanalytic theory.

The concept of the unconscious mind

According to Harré (2006):

> Freud likens the 'discovery' of the role of the unconscious as the main force in our mental lives to the Copernican revolution in astronomy and Darwin's proof of the descent of human beings from the animal kingdom. It is the third blow to human self-esteem. We are not in absolute control of our thoughts, feelings and actions.
>
> (p. 276)

The belief that Freud 'discovered the unconscious', or coined the concept, or was the first to explore it in any systematic way, are all myths. All we can say for sure, is that Freud discovered the *Freudian* unconscious (see below).

As Moghaddam (2005) points out, the notion of an unconscious has historical roots dating back to Plato (see Chapter 2). There is a long tradition of scholarship about how people can be mistaken in their beliefs about the world and themselves: we're often unaware of what we do and don't know, and so we often act on the basis of mistaken beliefs (Moghaddam, 2005).

A common thread running through disparate accounts of the unconscious is the idea that there's much more going on within our minds than we can possibly know at any one time: you don't have to be a Freudian (or any other kind of psychodynamic theorist) to believe in the conscious-mind-as-the-tip-of-an-iceberg metaphor. It could be argued that this belief has become part of our common-sense understanding of our own and others' psychology; in itself, there's nothing especially contentious about this description of the unconscious. So, what's different – and possibly contentious – about Freud's account?

The Freudian unconscious

To appreciate the distinctive character of Freud's account, we need to consider most other parts of his *meta-psychology*, as well as how his therapeutic methods helped to clarify for him the nature and content of the unconscious.

Freud identified three *levels of consciousness*, which, in turn, are interrelated with the three components of the 'psychic apparatus' (the *id, ego,* and *superego*):

(i) The *conscious mind* refers to those thoughts, feelings, wishes, memories, and so on that are *currently accessible* (i.e. we are fully aware of them). The *ego* represents the conscious part of the mind, together with some aspects of the *superego* (see below), namely, those moral rules and values that we're able to express in words.

(ii) The ego also controls the *preconscious,* a kind of 'ante-room', an extension of the conscious, whereby thoughts, etc., that we're not fully aware of at this moment could become so quite easily if we direct our attention to them (e.g. you suddenly notice a ticking clock that's been ticking away all the time). The pre-conscious also processes ill-defined *id* urges or impulses into perceptible images, and part of the superego also functions at a pre-conscious level.

(iii) The *unconscious* comprises (i) id urges/impulses; (ii) all *repressed* material (see below); (iii) the unconscious part of the ego (the part involved in *dream work, neurotic symptoms,* and *defence mechanisms*); and (iv) part of the superego (such as vague feelings of guilt or shame which we find difficult to explain, and 'finding yourself' behaving in ways that seem to reflect parental values).

(iv) Unconscious material can only become conscious through the use of special techniques, in particular *free association, dream interpretation,* and *transference*; these are the basic methods that Freud used in his psychoanalytic therapy, all designed to 'make the unconscious conscious'. Others include (the interpretation of) *resistance* and *parapraxes* ('Freudian slips', which constitute the 'psychopathology of everyday life'). (See Gross, 2015).

Time for reflection …

• To what extent (if at all) does Freud's levels of consciousness account correspond to our common sense use of these terms?

Repression

If there's one feature of the Freudian unconscious that makes it distinctive from all other accounts, it's the part played by *repression*. According to Jacobs (1992), this arguably represents the single most important theoretical concept, and Freud himself singled it out as a special corner-stone 'on which the whole structure of psychoanalysis rests. It is the most essential part of it' (Freud, 1914a, page 73). Repression is needed by virtue of the inherent *conflict* within the psychic apparatus (see below).

Freud first used the term in an initial publication co-authored with Joseph Breuer; this later formed the first chapter of *Studies of Hysteria* (1895). There, repression described a phenomenon whereby unacceptable feelings are 'removed' from conscious thought and 'forced' to stay in the unconscious; however, this isn't always successful, and the feelings can manifest as (are *converted* into) physical/bodily symptoms (such as blindness, deafness, paralysis, headaches). In the absence of any physical disease or injury, these symptoms were described as 'hysterical'.

According to Jacobs (1992), such an account uses a 'mechanistic, quasi-hydraulic image' (p. 37): feelings and ideas are damned up, but under growing pressure find an alternative route back into consciousness ('the return of the repressed'). Not only is repression highly individual, it's also an *ongoing process* (rather than a one-off event); this requires a great deal of *psychic energy* (see below).

Repression can be thought of as the 'master' *ego defence mechanism,* often just the 'first step' in keeping threatening or forbidden thoughts or feelings out of consciousness; a second line of defence involves the use of one or more of several others (such as displacement, denial, isolation, reaction formation, projection, regression, rationalisation, and sublimation). Many of these were originally proposed (or implied) by Freud, and later elaborated by his daughter, Anna Freud (1936).

The cognitive unconscious

According to Bargh (2014), contemporary cognitive psychologists have recast the Freudian worldview, adopting a more pragmatic view of what defines our unconscious self. For example, Kahneman (2013) has described the modern distinction between *automatic* and *controlled* thought processes (corresponding to unconscious and conscious, respectively: see Chapter 5). Automatic thought processes represent one facet of the *cognitive unconscious* (Kihlstrom, 1987); others include:

- *Blindsight* (Weiskrantz, 1986, 2007) (see Chapter four).
- *Prosopagnosia* (e.g. McNeil and Warrington, 1993; Ramachandran, 1998), a form of 'face blindness', the inability to consciously perceive faces (including those of familiar people: see Gross, 2015).

In both cases, loss of *explicit conscious recognition* is combined with the capacity for *implicit behavioural recognition*. It's now widely believed that most of the processing undertaken by the brain occurs without our awareness (Velmans, 1991). Nisbett and Wilson (1977) famously argue that we don't have direct access to cognitive processes at all; instead, we have access only to the ideas and inferences that are the *outputs* of those processes: our common sense, intuitive belief that we can accurately account for our own behaviour is *illusory* and what really guides our behaviour is unavailable to consciousness. (This, of course, is consistent with Freud's claim that the most important reasons for our actions ['the' reasons] are unconscious, although there may be accompanying conscious reasons ['our' reasons]: see below.)

The structure of the personality

As Jacobs (1992) observes, this represents one of the more hypothetical/speculative aspects of Freud's theorising: rather than trying to explain the direct observations of himself and his patients, the id, ego, and superego (Freud's *meta-psychology*) are *hypothetical constructs* designed to make sense of the unobservable.

The id

> It is the dark, inaccessible part of our personality ... It is filled with energy reaching it from the instincts, but it has no organization ... but only a striving to bring about the satisfaction of instinctual needs subject to the observance of the *pleasure principle*.
>
> (Freud, 1933, pp. 73–4, emphasis added)

Time for reflection ...

- The pleasure principle (PP) refers to seeking pleasure and avoiding pain.
- What in Skinner's account of operant conditioning corresponds to the PP?

The laws of logic don't apply within the id, so that (as in dreams), ideas can sit side-by-side which elsewhere would be considered contradictory; also, there's no recognition of the passage of time. Again:

> It contains everything that is inherited, that is present at birth – above all, therefore, the instincts.
>
> (Freud, 1940, pp. 145)

The kind of energy needed to fuel or operate the psychic apparatus is *psychic energy*, which performs 'psychological work'. The id is the source of psychic energy. Since the id is in closer touch with the body than with the outside world, and since it's unaffected by logic or reason, it can be thought of as the *infantile, pre-socialised* part of the personality.

The id retains its infantile character throughout our lives: whenever we act on impulse, selfishly, or demand "I want it and I want it now!", it's our id that's in control (the 'spoiled child' of the personality). The only real development that occurs within the id is the *primary process*: a form of thinking in which an image of the object needed to reduce tension is formed. However, the id is incapable of distinguishing between the subjective memory–image and the real thing; that's left to the ego.

The ego

> [T]he ego seeks to bring the influence of the external world to bear upon the id and its tendencies, and endeavours to substitute the *reality principle* for the pleasure principle … The ego represents what may be called reason and common sense, in contrast to the id, which contains the passions.
>
> (Freud, 1923, p. 25, emphasis added)

The ego gradually develops (starting at a few months after birth) as psychic energy is 'borrowed' from the id and directed outwards towards external reality. It can be described as the 'executive' of the personality, the planning, decision-making, rational, and logical part; these functions are made possible by *secondary process thinking*, roughly equivalent to the cognitive processes of attention, perception, remembering, reasoning, problem–solving, and so on (see Chapter 5). It enables us to distinguish between a wish and reality, inside and outside, subjective from objective, and so on (through the *reality principle*).

While the ego enables us to postpone the satisfaction of our needs until an appropriate time and place (*deferred gratification*), its priority is the *consequences* of our actions rather than whether they are (inherently) good or bad, right or wrong. So, like the id, the ego is *amoral,* although other people are taken into account (but for reasons of expediency rather than morals).

The superego

> The long period of childhood, during which the growing human being lives in dependence on his parents, leaves behind it as a precipitate the formation in his ego of a special agency in which this parental influence is prolonged. It has received the name of super-ego …
>
> This parental influence of course includes … not only the personalities of the actual parents but also the family, racial and national traditions handed on through them, as well as the demands of the immediate social *milieu* which they represent.
>
> (Freud, 1940, pp. 146–7)

Only when the superego has developed (at age five to six when the child's Oedipal conflict is resolved: see below) can a person be described as a moral being. The superego represents the *internalisation* or *introjection* of a set of moral values which determine that certain behaviour is right or wrong. While moral judgements often involve the belief that particular actions are *inherently* good or bad, these judgements are actually *culturally determined* and *culturally relative;* in other words, cultural (and sub-cultural) rules and values determine how individual members perceive the rightness or wrongness of particular behaviour without consciously linking it to those rules and values. Internalisation of these values occurs, according to Freud, through *identification* with the same-sex parent (See Box 6.7).

The superego represents the 'judicial' branch of the personality and comprises two components: (i) the *conscience,* which threatens the ego with punishment (in the form of guilt) for wrongdoing; and (ii) the *ego-ideal,* which promises the ego with rewards (in the form of pride and high self-esteem) for good, socially positive behaviour.

Several critics of Freud have argued that terms like 'id', 'ego', and 'super-ego' are bad metaphors: they don't correspond to any aspect of psychology or neurophysiology, and they encourage *reification* (treating metaphorical terms, or hypothetical constructs, as if they were 'things' or entities). However, in *Freud and Man's Soul* (1983), Bruno Bettelheim defends Freud and criticises his translators (see Box 6.6).

BOX 6.6 THE MIS-TRANSLATION OF FREUD

- According to Bettelheim (1983), much of Freud's terminology was *mistranslated,* which has led to a misrepresentation of those parts of his theory.

- For example, Freud himself never used the Latin words, *id, ego,* and *superego;* instead, he used the German *das Es* ('the it'), *das Ich* ('the I'), and *das Über-Ich* ('the over-I'), which were meant to capture how the individual relates to different aspects of the self.

- The Latin terms tend to *depersonalise* Freud's use of ordinary, familiar language, giving the impression they describe different 'selves' which we all possess!

- The Latin words (preferred by his American translators to lend greater scientific credibility to the theory) turn the concepts into cold, technical terms which arouse no personal associations: whereas the 'I' can only be studied from the *inside* (through introspection), the 'ego' can be studied from the *outside* (as behaviour observable by others).

- In translation, Freud's 'soul' became scientific psychology's 'psyche' or 'personality'.

No word has greater and more intimate connotation than the pronoun 'I' … If anything, the German *Ich* is invested with stronger and deeper personal meaning than the English 'I' … the translators present us with a term from a dead language that reeks of erudition precisely when it should emanate vitality.

(Bettelheim, 1983, pp. 53–5)

Freud's instinct theory and psychosexual development

Psychoanalytic theory is often described as an *instinct theory*. Based on the account of the id given above, it should be evident that for Freud personality is based on biological (mainly sexual and aggressive) drives that are rooted in the body with its unalterable hereditary constitution.

Psychosexual development is an integral part of personality development as a whole: the sexual instinct (libido) passes through a fixed sequence of biologically determined stages.

Oral stage (0–1 year): the nerve endings in the lips and mouth are particularly sensitive and the baby derives pleasure from sucking for its own sake (*non-nutritive sucking*). In the earlier *receptive* or *incorporative* sub-stage, the baby is passive and almost totally dependent; sucking, swallowing, and mouthing are the dominant oral activities. In the later *biting/aggressive* sub-stage, hardening gums and erupting teeth make biting and chewing important.

Anal stage (1–3): the most sensitive body areas are now the anal cavity, sphincter muscles of the lower bowel, and the muscles of the urinary system (hence, the 'anal-urethral stage'). In the earlier *expulsion* sub-stage, for the first time the child encounters external restrictions on its wish to defecate where and when it wishes (i.e. potty-training): parental love is no longer unconditional but depends on how the child *behaves* (parents are now seen as authority figures). In the later *retention* sub-stage, the child can retain faeces and urine at will; sensuous pleasure can be derived from holding onto these bodily 'productions' or 'creations'.

Phallic stage (3–5/6): sensitivity is now concentrated in the genitals and masturbation becomes a new source of pleasure (for both genders). The child becomes aware of anatomical sex differences, which sets in motion the conflict between erotic attraction, resentment, rivalry, jealousy, and fear as played out in the Oedipus Complex. (The term is derived from Sophocles' Greek tragedy, *Oedipus Rex;* Oedipus, King of Thebes, unknowingly kills his father and marries his mother.) This is described in Box 6.7.

BOX 6.7 THE OEDIPUS COMPLEX

- For boys (who, like girls, take the mother as their first love-object), beginning at about three, their love for their mother becomes increasingly passionate and they don't want to share her with anyone – least of all their father, who already 'possesses' her and whom they want 'dead' (i.e. out of the way). However, the father is bigger and stronger and the boy comes to fear his most prized possession, namely, his penis. This *fear of castration* derives partly from past punishment for masturbation and the boy's observation that girls don't have one ('have theirs already been cut off?').

- To resolve the dilemma, the boy represses his desire for his mother and jealousy of his father, and identifies with his father: he comes to think, feel, and act *as if* he were his father (*identification with the aggressor*).
- A girl's Oedipus Complex (originally termed the 'Electra Complex', after another character from Greek mythology who induced her brother to kill their mother) begins with the belief that she's already *been* castrated. Having taken the mother as her first love-object (as with boys), a girl then becomes erotically attracted to her father through *penis envy*: blaming her mother for her lack of a penis, she looks to her father to provide her with one. When she finally realizes that her wish for a penis is unrealistic, she replaces it with a wish for baby; this draws her back towards her mother. Freud also suggested that the girl identifies with her mother through fear of losing her love (*anaclitic identification*).

Latency stage (**5/6–puberty**): there are no new qualitative changes involved. The child becomes a victim of 'infantile amnesia', repressing the sexual preoccupations of the earlier stages and channelling much of its energy into social and intellectual development, acquiring new skills and knowledge.

Genital stage (**puberty–maturity**)

In relative terms, the balance between the id, ego, and superego is greater during latency than at any past or future time in the child's life; it's often depicted as the calm before the storm of puberty. The id begins to make powerful new demands in the form of heterosexual desires: members of the opposite sex are now needed to satisfy the libido.

As this account of the psychosexual stages demonstrates, Freud maintained that sexual pleasure isn't confined to adolescents and adults: it's evident from birth and changes qualitatively through childhood and beyond. Clearly, Freud doesn't equate 'sex(uality)' with 'sexual intercourse'; rather, it describes the desire for physical, sensuous pleasure of any kind, the rhythmical stroking or stimulation of virtually any part of the body; sexuality can be satisfied in a variety of ways and genital stimulation is just one of these.

Contrary to what many of his critics maintain, Freud wasn't exclusively concerned with the biologically determined nature of the psychosexual stages; he also stressed the influence of the reactions of significant others – especially parents – on the child's behaviour as it passes through the stages. Also, Freud's concept of 'instinct' was very different from how it was earlier understood, namely as an unlearned, largely automatic (pre-programmed) response to specific stimuli (based on the study of other species). Freud saw instincts as relatively undifferentiated energy, capable of almost infinite variation through experience; indeed, instead of using the German *Instinckt*, he used *Trieb*, which is most accurately translated as 'drive'.

In *Beyond the Pleasure Principle* (1920), Freud distinguished between the Life Instincts (*Eros*), which includes libido (sexual energy), and the Death Instincts (*Thanatos*), comprising, primarily, aggression. 'Libido' later came to refer to *all* kinds of psychic (drive) energy.

> *Time for reflection …*
>
> • Has this discussion of Freud's psychosexual theory changed your views as to what 'sex(uality)' means?
> • Do you (still) believe that 'Freud = sex(uality)'?

The unconscious: Freud and Jung compared

In terms of Jung's analytical psychology, repressed material that plays such a crucial role in the Freudian unconscious represents only one kind of unconscious content. For Jung (see Figure 6.5), the Freudian unconscious is predominantly 'personal', composed of the individual's particular and unique experiences. The personal unconscious also includes things we've forgotten, as well as all those things we think of as being 'stored in memory' and which could be consciously remembered without too much effort (Freud's *preconscious*).

Figure 6.5 Carl Gustav Jung (1875–1961), founder of analytical psychology. (Permission granted by Alamy.)

Associated groups of feelings, thoughts, and memories may cluster together to form a *complex*, a quite autonomous and powerful 'mini-personality' within the total psyche; an example would be Freud's Oedipus complex. Jung looked for the origin of complexes in the *collective* (or *racial*) *unconscious*, which is arguably what most distinguishes his theory from Freud's.

While Freud's id is part of each individual's personal unconscious and represents our biological inheritance (see above), for Jung the mind (through the brain) has inherited characteristics which determine how a person will react to life experiences, and what type of experiences these will be. Our *evolutionary history as a species* is all-important as far as the collective unconscious is concerned (see Chapter 9).

The collective unconscious can be thought of as a reservoir of *latent* (or *primordial*) images (or *archetypes* – a prototype or 'original model or pattern'). They relate to the 'first ' or 'original' development of the psyche, stemming from our ancestral past, human, pre-human, and animal (Hall and Nordby, 1973) and constitute *predispositions* or *potentialities* for experiencing and responding to the world in the same way as our ancestors (e.g. we're naturally predisposed to fear the dark or snakes). Jung identified a large number of archetypes, including birth, rebirth, death, power, magic, the hero, the child, the trickster, God, the demon, the wise old man, earth mother, and the giant. He gave special attention to the *persona,* the *anima/animus,* the *shadow*, and the *self* (see Gross, 2015).

Adler's individual psychology

Jung broke ranks with Freud in 1913, two years later than Adler (see Figure 6.6), Freud's other original 'disciple'. While both Adler and Jung agreed with Freud regarding the importance of the unconscious, they both rejected Freud's emphasis on sexuality as the major influence on the personality. For Adler, people are motivated primarily by the drive towards self-affirmation, self-preservation, and the *will to power* (or striving for superiority) (see the discussion of Nietzsche's philosophy in Chapter 2).

Adler was more interested than Freud in the *social* nature of human beings and, like Jung, saw the individual as an indivisible unity: if we're to understand any event properly, it must be considered in the light of the its effect on the *whole person* (see Chapter 7).

Adler was impressed by the body's capacity to compensate for organic damage, as when an intact area of the brain may take over the role usually performed by a damaged area. Similar compensatory processes could be observed in the psychological realm: artists with imperfect vision, deaf musicians and composers, might be compensating for their biological defect in such a way that their inferiority actually becomes transformed into superiority.

Figure 6.6 Alfred Adler (1870-1937), founder of individual psychology (Permission granted by Mary Evans Library.)

The origins of inferiority

Every child spends its early years in a state of dependence on others, experiencing a range of desires which cannot be satisfied; by comparison, adults seem happier and have more power. Consequently, children come to experience their dependence and powerlessness as a state of *inferiority* relative to adults; in reaction to this, an unconscious drive emerges towards its opposite – the *will to power*.

Time for reflection ...

- In addition to this natural – and inevitable – sense of inferiority, Adler identified several factors which could influence the degree to which an individual experiences it (by *increasing* it).
- Before reading Box 6.9, try to identify some of these additional factors.

**BOX 6.8 FACTORS CONTRIBUTING TO
A SENSE OF INFERIORITY**

- Any kind of physical *disability/deformity*, in so far as it's experienced *psychologically.*
- Adler recognised the existence of *gender inequality*: the stereotypical equation between 'masculine' and 'strong and superior' and 'feminine' and 'weak and inferior' is made at an early age. However, some boys may be unable to live up to these gender role expectations, especially if their fathers attribute them with masculine qualities they don't actually possess. This may be at the root of homosexuality and other sexual 'deviations'. Women may try to compensate by wishing to be like a man (the 'masculine protest') or by exploiting their 'weakness' and their feminine charms.
- *Birth order*, the family's *socio-economic status*, and *length* and *quality of education.*
- *How adults – in particular parents – react to the child's successes and failures.* Pressure to succeed may be unrealistic and a child's failures may actually increase that pressure.
- *Being a neglected, spoilt, or hated child.*Very low self-esteem is the likely outcome.

Erikson's psychosocial theory

Erikson, having undergone psychoanalytic training with Anna Freud, accepted many fundamental aspects of Freud's theory, including the stages of psychosexual development. However, for Erikson they didn't go far enough: he saw development as proceeding throughout the life–cycle, with the genital stage constituting the pre-adult (adolescent) stage, with a subsequent three stages spanning early, middle, and late adulthood. The resulting 'Eight Ages of Man' (1950) are listed in Table 6.1. (See Gross, 1987; 2015 for detailed accounts of the stages.)

Table 6.1 Erikson's 'Eight Ages of Man'

Basic trust vs. basic mistrust (0–1)
Autonomy vs. shame and doubt (1–3)
Initiative vs. guilt (3–5/6)
Industry vs. inferiority (7–12/so)
Identity vs. role confusion (12–18: adolescence)
Intimacy vs. isolation (20s: early adulthood)
Generativity vs. stagnation (late 20s–50s: middle adulthood)
Ego integrity vs. despair (50s and beyond: late adulthood)

Erikson, like many other *neo*-Freudians, argued that Freud under–emphasised the role of socialisation, in particular the various patterns of behaviour that are thought desirable in different cultures. The interaction between the individual and the socio-cultural environment produces psycho*social* (rather than psycho*sexual*) stages, each of which is centred around a developmental *crisis*; this involves a struggle between two opposing or conflicting personality characteristics (hence, 'identity *versus* role confusion', for example). For positive mental health (of much more concern to Erikson than to Freud), there needs to be an appropriate *balance* between the two opposing characteristics (e.g. more identity than role confusion): it's not 'either–or'.

Erikson believes that it's human nature to pass through these pre–determined psychosocial stages, based on his *epigenetic principle* (EP). Based on embryology, the EP states that the entire pattern of development is governed by a genetic structure common to all human beings: the genes dictate a timetable for growth of each part of the unborn baby. He extended the EP to social and psychological growth, proposing that at each predetermined step of personality development, the human organism is driven toward, aware of, and interacts with a widening radius of significant others and institutions. The socio-cultural environment has a significant influence on (i) the *psychosocial modalities* (dominant modes of acting and being) with which this interaction takes place; and (ii) the nature of the crisis/conflict that arises at each stage.

Summary and conclusions: Skinner and Freud on free will

As we noted earlier, in two otherwise diametrically opposed theoretical approaches, what's striking is the convergence between Skinner and Freud regarding free will.

Radical behaviourism and the free will illusion

Radical behaviourism probably represents the most outspoken expression among psychologists of the view that people are not free: in *Beyond Freedom and Dignity* (1971), Skinner argues that *behavioural freedom* is an illusion.

Radical behaviourists argue that their view of behaviour is the most scientific, because it provides an account in terms of *material causes*; these can all be objectively defined and measured. Free will is one of those 'explanatory fictions' that are *effects* – not, as commonly understood, causes.

Skinner claims that the illusion (or myth) of free will survives because the causes of human behaviour are often hidden from us in the environment. When what we do is dictated by force or punishment – or by their threat (i.e. negative reinforcement) – it's obvious to everyone that we're not acting freely (as in crimes punishable by imprisonment); in these cases, we know what the environmental causes of our behaviour are. Similarly, it's often obvious what positive reinforcements ('incentives' or 'carrots') are shaping or maintaining our behaviour.

However, most of the time we're *unaware* of the environmental causes of our behaviour, so it *looks* (and *feels*) as if we're behaving freely. Doing what we 'want' (i.e. behaving 'freely') is simply doing what we've previously been positively reinforced for doing. When we perceive others as behaving freely, we're simply ignorant of their reinforcement histories.

Strictly, Skinner argues that behaviour is merely *shaped* and *modified* by reinforcements and punishments; this is more consistent with his emphasis on operant behaviour (which, remember, is *emitted* by the active organism, rather than *elicited* in a passive organism by environmental stimuli). Indeed, Skinner (e.g. 1974) states that intention and purpose are what operant behaviour is all about, being found in the contingencies of reinforcement (the present circumstances and past consequences) – *not* inside the person. Operant behaviour is also purposive in the sense that its function is to change the environment and produce particular consequences. However, according to O'Donohue and Ferguson (2001), purposive behaviour doesn't imply that that the individual has free will, or that behaviour isn't determined, because all behaviour is determined. (This argument, in turn, rests on the assumption that 'free' and 'determined' are opposites. But the real opposite of determined is 'random': see Gross, 2014.)

Morality and 'autonomous man'

In *Beyond Freedom and Dignity* (1971), Skinner claims that what we call good or bad behaviour more or less equates to how others reinforce it: 'good' is what benefits others (what's positively reinforced) and 'bad' is what harms others (what's punished). This removes morality from human behaviour, either within the individual or within society. If we could arrange reinforcement appropriately, so that there was only mutually beneficial behaviour, we'd have created utopia. But in Skinner's utopia (as described in *Walden Two*), how can the planners plan? You must be free in the first place in order to be able to plan. For Skinner, 'oughts' are *not* 'moral imperatives' reflecting *moral* rules and guidelines; rather, they offer *practical* rules and guidelines (Morea, 1990).

Rather than portraying a utopian society, as was Skinner's intention, Carl Rogers (see Chapter 7) likened *Walden Two* to Orwell's *Nineteen Eighty-Four,* a nightmarish *dystopia,* which warns against a punitive society where people are treated as automata by those in power (O'Donohue and Ferguson, 2001). Many critics saw him as a totalitarian, fascist, evil scientist, with his denial of free will ('autonomous man') at the heart of the condemnation. Skinner believed that only a technology of behaviour could rescue mankind: since social ills are caused by behaviour, it follows that the remedy is to change the variables that control behaviour. While his critics claimed that any attempt to try controlling behaviour is an infringement of personal liberty, for Skinner, freedom versus control (or *behavioural engineering*) is a *false dichotomy:* all behaviour is controlled all of the time.

Time for reflection ...

- To what extent do you agree with Skinner's claim that behaviour is controlled all of the time?

Psychic determinism and free will

According to James Strachey, one of the American translators and editor of the 'Standard Edition' of Freud's collected works:

> Behind all of Freud's work ... we should posit his belief in the universal validity of the law of determinism ... Freud extended the belief [derived from physical phenomena] uncompromisingly to the field of mental phenomena.
>
> (1962, p. 17)

Similarly, Sulloway (1979) states that central to Freud's entire life's work was the conviction that all vital phenomena, including psychical ones, are rigidly and lawfully determined by the principle of cause- and–effect. For example, he chose the German word '*Einfall*' to convey an incontrollable 'intrusion' by pre-conscious ideas into consciousness. But it was translated as '*free association*', implying almost the complete opposite; in other words, while the German word is perfectly consistent with the idea of thoughts being determined beyond the person's control, the English translation is perfectly consistent with the idea of free will. In turn, this pre-conscious material reflected *unconscious* ideas, wishes, and memories, which was what Freud was really interested in: here lay the principal causes(s) of his patients' neurotic problems (Sulloway, 1979).

Ironically, the fact that the causes of our thoughts, actions, and (apparent) choices are unconscious (mostly *actively repressed*) is what accounts for the *illusion* that we are free: we *believe* we have free will because we are (by definition) unaware of the true, unconscious causes of our actions.

Time for reflection ...

- How does Skinner express this essentially identical explanation of why we believe we have free will?

The application of this general philosophical belief in causation to mental phenomena is called *psychic determinism*. Freud's aim was to establish a 'scientific psychology' through applying to the human mind the same principles of causality as were in his time considered valid in the natural sciences.

In his early studies of hysterical patients, Freud showed that their apparently irrational symptoms were in fact meaningful when seen in terms of painful, unconscious, memories; they weren't chance events and their causes could be revealed by psychoanalysis. The same reasoning was then applied to other seemingly random, irrational events, to parapraxes, and to dreams.

According to Gay (1988), a crucial feature of Freud's theory as a whole is that there are no accidents in the universe of the mind:

> To secure freedom from the grip of causality is among mankind's most cherished, and hence most tenacious, illusory wishes. But Freud sternly warned that psychoanalysis should offer such fantasies no comfort. Freud's theory of the mind is, therefore, strictly and frankly deterministic.
>
> (Gay, 1988, p. 119)

However, Gross (2014) suggests that Gay's conclusions need qualifying in the following ways:

1   Freud *didn't* deny that human choices are real and, indeed, one of the aims of therapy is to 'give the patient's ego freedom to decide one way or another' (Freud, in Gay, 1988). If we become aware of our previously unconscious memories, feelings, and so on, then we're freed of their stranglehold (although there's more to therapeutic success than simply 'remembering'). The whole of psychoanalysis is based on the belief that people *can* change. While change might be very limited (famously, he claimed that therapy aims at converting 'neurotic misery into everyday unhappiness') at least it is *possible*.

2   Freud acknowledged that sometimes, things happen beyond an individual's control which have nothing to do with his/her unconscious mind (such as being struck by lightning). However, an 'accident-prone' person is likely to be unconsciously helping to bring the event(s) about (and so these aren't true accidents).

3   Freud's concept of psychic determinism doesn't require that there's a one-to-one correspondence between cause and effect. One form of psychic determinism is *overdetermination*, according to which much of our behaviour (and thoughts and feelings) has *multiple* causes (some conscious, some unconscious). The conscious causes are what we normally take to be *the reasons* for our behaviour; but if the causes are also unconscious, then these reasons can never tell the whole story and for Freud, the latter are always the more important.

4   According to Rycroft (1966), the principle of psychic determinism remains an *assumption,* which Freud made out of scientific faith rather than on actual evidence. Freud denied more than once that it's possible to predict whether a person will develop a neurosis, or what kind it will be. Instead, he claimed that all we can do is ascertain the cause *retrospectively,* a process more in keeping with history than science (Rycroft, 1966).

While Skinner was a determinist through–and–through:

> Much of Freud's work was really *semantic* and ... he made a revolutionary discovery in semantics, viz. that neurotic symptoms are *meaningful* disguised communications, but ... owing to his scientific training and allegiance, he formulated his findings in the conceptual framework of the physical sciences.
>
> (Rycroft, 1966, p. 14, emphasis added)

Suggested further reading

Fancher, R.E. and Rutherford, A. (2012) *Pioneers of Psychology: A History* (4th edition). New York: W.W. Norton and Co. Inc. (Chapters 9 and 11).

Freidman, L.J. (1999) *A Biography of Erik H. Erikson*. London: Free Association Books.

Jones, E. (1964) *The Life and Work of Sigmund Freud* (abridged version: L. Trilling and S. Marcus). Harmondsworth: Penguin.

Leslie, J.C. (2002) *Essential Behaviour Analysis*. London: Arnold.

O'Donohue, W. and Ferguson, K.E. (2001) *The Psychology of B.F. Skinner*. Thousand Oaks, CA: Sage Publications.

Rycroft, C. (1985) *Psychoanalysis and Beyond*. (Edited and introduced by Peter Fuller). London: Chatto and Windus.

7 The humanistic-phenomenological approach

People as self-determining organisms

Key questions

- What are the essential differences between Eastern and Western psychology?
- In what ways has humanistic psychology been influenced by Eastern psychology and culture in general?
- What are the major features of humanistic psychology?
- How has Husserl's phenomenology influenced the ideas of humanistic psychologists?
- What does Maslow mean by claiming that humanistic psychology is the 'third force' within psychology?
- How does Maslow distinguish between D-motives and B-motives?
- How is this distinction related to his hierarchy of needs?
- How do Maslow and Rogers differ as regards 'self-actualisation'?
- What characteristics did Maslow identify as describing the self-actualised person?
- What other similarities and differences are there between Maslow and Rogers?
- How has humanistic psychology been influenced by existentialism?
- What are the major features of Frankl's logotherapy and Yalom's 'givens of existence'?
- How is Terror Management Theory (TMT) related to 'death terror'?
- How are humanistic psychology and positive psychology related?

During the 1950s, certain psychoanalysts and other psychotherapists encountered a puzzling phenomenon: social standards had become far more permissive than in Freud's day, especially with regard to sexuality. In theory, this more liberal attitude should have helped to *reduce* id–superego conflicts and the number of resulting neuroses (see Chapter 6). However, while hysterical neurosis and repression did seem to be less common than during the Victorian era, more people than ever were opting for psychotherapy:

> And they suffered from such new and unusual problems as an inability to enjoy the new freedom of self-expression (or…to feel much of anything), and an inner emptiness and self-estrangement. Rather than hoping to cure some manifest symptom, these patients desperately needed an answer to a

more philosophical question: how to remedy the apparent *meaninglessness* of their lives.

(Ewen, 1988, p. 369; emphasis added)

Some theorists approached this development from within a psychodynamic perspective (such as Erikson's *identity crisis* theory). Freud's insights may well have been brilliantly relevant to the Victorian mentality (sex was at the very least not meant to be pleasurable, especially for women). However, constructs such as psychic determinism and id, ego, and superego, together with Freud's pessimistic view of human nature, were now reinforcing the modern patient's apathy and depersonalisation by portraying personality as mechanical, fragmented, malignant, and totally pre-ordained by prior causes (Ewen, 1988).

Two of the better known and most outspoken critics of Freudian pessimism were Abraham Maslow, an academic psychologist, and Carl Rogers, a psychotherapist; they shared the view that human nature is inherently positive, healthy, and constructive. Both believed that we strive to fulfil our potential ((*self-*)*actualisation*) unless we're prevented from doing so by destructive external forces – which are all too common. Their respective 'solutions' to the changes within psychotherapy described above represented a major alternative to both the psychodynamic approach and to the application of behaviourist principles in behaviour therapy (or 'behavioural psychotherapy') (see Chapter 6).

Eastern and Western psychology compared

Whenever we refer to 'psychology' in this book, we're in fact referring to 'Western psychology', an empirical science that puts objectivity, measurement, cause-and-effect, experimentation, and so on above its subject-matter in importance ('method' before 'meaning').

The literal meaning of 'psychology' (from the Greek, *logos* = 'study' and *psyche* = 'soul') no longer (if, indeed, it ever did) reflects what takes place in its name within the Western 'version'. According to Graham (1986):

All knowledge is fundamentally *cosmology* inasmuch that it is an attempt by man to explore the universe in which he finds himself, and to understand thereby his own existence and nature. In the sense that personality, intellect, will and emotions comprise the human self, essence, or soul, man's attempts to understand himself constitute the study of the soul, or literally...psychology. Cosmology is thus intrinsic to psychology.

(Graham, 1986, p.11, emphasis added)

However, as Graham points out, cosmologies differ, often radically, between peoples and cultures; so, not surprisingly, 'psychology' differs according to the world view within which it's embedded.

In contrast to Western science's *positivism* (see Gross, 2018), Eastern culture and its institutions (including its religions, Buddhism, Taoism, and

Zen Buddhism) are traditionally *humanistic*: they're centred around the human potential for *self-transcendence* or *becoming* (i.e. to place value outside oneself, to pursue some higher purpose or cause: Batson and Stocks, 2004). Eastern psychology is rooted in the tradition of *mysticism*, with an emphasis on the *spiritual* (in the non-religious sense), the *subjective*, and the *individual*.

So, while Eastern Psychology's *dominant ethos* is humanistic, that of Western psychology is *mechanistic* and *impersonal*. As Fromm (1950) puts it:

> [In] trying to imitate the natural sciences–It [psychology] tried to understand those aspects of man which can be examined in the laboratory, and claimed that conscience, value judgements, and knowledge of good and evil are metaphysical concepts, outside the problems of psychology; it was often more concerned with insignificant problems which fitted the alleged scientific method than with devising new methods to study the significant problems of man. Psychology thus became a science lacking its main subject matter, the soul.
>
> (pp. 13–14)

As Graham (1986) puts it, 'Bereft of its soul or psyche, psychology became an empty or hollow discipline; study for its own sake' (p. 21).

Time for reflection ...

- Graham's comment raises the fundamental question: what should psychology's subject-matter be? (See Gross, 2018).
- Alternatively: what, *ultimately*, are we trying to find out about *ourselves* (i.e. human beings)?

According to Graham (1986), what's at issue here is the fundamental *perspective* adopted by each: psychology East and West represent the polar extremes of mystical *insight* and scientific *outlook*, respectively. This dichotomy can be seen as corresponding to the two aspects of mind as conceived by Indian thought: the *inward-looking* aspect directed towards the essential nature of human beings, and the *outward-looking* aspect directed towards the world of things and external appearances. In the Eastern tradition, both aspects are viewed as *complementary* facets of one whole or unity; virtue and harmony consist in maintaining a *dynamic balance* between them. However, humans tend to divide and separate, emphasising one or the other (what Ornstein, 1976, likens to blindness to half of the visual field/*hemianopia*).

In the pursuit of understanding innermost being the cultures of the East, most notably India, have tended to ignore the material world, developing their spiritual, poetic, artistic and mystical traditions and cultivating thereby an attitude to life quite alien to Western eyes. For in the West, with its reverence for the intellect and rationality, and the outward appearance of things, the inner man is neglected as science and technology progress apace.

(Graham, 1986, p. 21)

If Western science in general, and psychology in particular, is 'blind' to the 'inner' human being, then they may be 'missing the point' in terms of their ultimate aims (or, at least, missing half the point!).

Scientific method is implicitly *reductionist* (from the Latin *reduction* = 'to take away'). Mainstream psychology, in reducing the study of man to 'objective facts' (i.e. overt behaviour) and 'banning' study of experience, takes away what is 'essentially and fundamentally his humanness' (Graham, 1986, p. 25). This reduces people to mere things or objects; it's a small step from this to accepting the idea that man is a machine, and nothing but a machine (Heather, 1976).

Humanistic psychology: the 'Third Force'

As a reaction against such a mechanistic, *dehumanising* view of the person, and in an attempt to reconcile Eastern and Western perspectives, Maslow in particular (see Figure 7.1), along with other humanistic psychologists (including Rogers, Fromm, and May) emphasised the 'human' characteristics of human beings. (It seems 'obvious' that psychology would be concerned with subjective experience!).

Figure 7.1 Abraham Maslow (1908–70), humanistic psychologist. (Permission granted by Alamy.)

The term 'humanistic psychology', first coined by John Cohen, a British psychologist (in a 1958 book with that title), aimed at condemning 'ratomorphic robotic psychology' (see Chapter 6). But it was primarily in the US, and especially through the writings of Maslow, that humanistic psychology became popularised and influential, hailing it as a 'third force' (the other two being behaviourism and psychoanalytic theory). Rather than rejecting these two major approaches, Maslow hoped that his approach would act as a *unifying force*, integrating subjective and objective, the private and public aspects of the person, providing a complete, *holistic* psychology. He insisted that a truly scientific psychology must embrace a humanistic perspective, treating its subject matter as fully human. What does 'fully human' mean?

Major features of humanistic psychology

1 Humanistic psychology acknowledges individuals as perceivers and interpreters of themselves and their world, trying to understand the world from the perceiver's perspective, rather than from the position of a detached observer. This represents a *phenomenological* approach, which is described in Box 7.1.

BOX 7.1 PHENOMENOLOGY

- Husserl, the founder of phenomenology as a philosophical movement, aimed to provide a firm basis for *all* disciplines – sciences, arts, and humanities – by establishing the meaning of their most fundamental concepts (such as 'perception' in psychology) through providing a valid *method*.

- To achieve this, Husserl decided to begin with the problem of how objects and events appeared to consciousness: nothing could even be spoken about or witnessed if it didn't come through someone's consciousness (which included pre–conscious and unconscious processes).

- He advocated (1925/1977, 1931/1960, 1936/1970) a *return to the things themselves*, as experienced. His core philosophical belief was a rejection of the presupposition that there's something 'behind' or 'underlying' or 'more fundamental than' experience. Rather, we should begin our investigation with *what is experienced*, the thing itself *as it appears* (i.e. the 'phenomenon').

- Contrary to positivism, Husserl maintained that human experience in general is *not* a lawful response to the 'variables' assumed to be in operation. Rather, experience comprises a system of interrelated meanings (or *gestalten*) that's bound up in a totality (the 'life-world') (Husserl, 1936/1970): the human realm essentially entails embodied, conscious relatedness to a personal world of experience.

- The natural scientific approach is inappropriate: human meanings are the key to the study of lived experience, *not* causal variables.
- For phenomenology, then, the individual is a conscious agent, whose experience must be studied from the 'first-person' perspective. Experience is of a meaningful lifeworld.
- Because of the crucial influence of phenomenology, the approach of Maslow, Rogers, etc., is often referred to as the *humanistic-phenomenological approach*.

(Based on Ashworth, 2003; Giorgi and Giogi, 2003)

2 Humanistic psychology recognises that people help determine their own behaviour and aren't simply slaves to environmental contingencies (as proposed by Skinner) or to their past (as proposed by Freud). Probably the most well-developed account of free will within humanistic psychology is that of Rogers (see Figure 7.2). If we want to understand another person, experience is all-important; in particular, we need to understand his/her *self-concept*. Every experience is evaluated in terms of our self-concept, and most human behaviour can be regarded as an attempt to maintain consistency between our actions and our self-image (see Gross, 2018).

Figure 7.2 Carl Ransom Rogers (1902–87), founder of client-centred therapy. (Permission granted by Mary Evans Library.)

Understanding the self-concept is also central to Rogers' *client/person-centred therapy*. His experience over many years as a therapist convinced him that real change does occur in therapy: people *choose* to see themselves and their life situation differently. Therapy and life are about free human beings struggling to become *more* free. While personal experience is important, it doesn't imprison us; how we react to our experience is something we ourselves choose and decide (Morea, 1990).

However, we sometimes fail to acknowledge certain experiences, feelings, and behaviours if they conflict with our (conscious) self-image: they're *incongruent* precisely because they're not consistent with our view of ourselves, which makes them threatening. They're denied access to awareness (they remain *unsymbolised*) through actual denial, distortion, or blocking; these defence mechanisms prevent the self from growing and changing, and widen the gulf between our self-image and reality (our true feelings, and our actual behaviour). Defensiveness, lack of congruence, and an unrealistic self-concept can all be seen as a *lack of freedom*, which therapy is designed to restore.

Rogers' view of human beings as growth-oriented contrasts dramatically with Freud's 'savage beasts' view (in *Civilization and its Discontents*, 1930), whose aggressive tendencies and unpredictable sexuality can only be controlled by civilisation's structures. However, Rogers' deep and lasting trust in human nature didn't blind him to the reality of evil behaviour:

> In my experience, every person has the capacity for evil behaviour. I, and others, have had murderous and cruel impulses, desires to hurt, feelings of anger and rage, desires to impose our wills on others…Whether I, or anyone, will translate these impulses into behaviour depends…on: social conditioning and voluntary choice.
>
> (Rogers, 1982, in Thorne, 1992)

By distinguishing between 'human nature' and 'behaviour', Rogers manages to retain his optimistic view of human beings ('good people can behave badly'). But in *Freedom to Learn for the 80s* (1983), he states that science is making it clear that human beings are complex machines and their behaviour is *determined*. (See Chapter 8).

Time for reflection …

- How do you think Rogers might reconcile this belief in determinism with self-actualisation, psychological growth, and freedom to choose?
- (Are there different kinds of determinism?)

One proposed solution is a version of what James (1890) termed *soft determinism*. Unlike neurotic and incongruent people, whose defensiveness forces them to act in ways they'd prefer not to, the healthy, *fully functioning person chooses* to act and be the way he/she *has to*: it's the most fulfilling option (Rogers, 1983).

Humanistic psychologists regard the self, soul or psyche, personal responsibility and agency, choice and free will, as legitimate issues for psychology. Indeed, these in many ways *define* what it means to be human.

Maslow's contribution

Maslow is probably best known for his *hierarchy of human needs* (1954) and his study of *self-actualisers*.

Hierarchy of needs

According to Maslow, human beings are subject to two quite different sets of motivational states or forces:

- **Deficiency or D-motives** ensure *survival* by satisfying basic physical and psychological needs (physiological, safety, love and belongingness, and esteem needs); they're a means to an end, exceptions being sexual arousal, elimination, and sleep; and
- **Being or B-motives** promote *self-actualisation*, that is, realising one's potential, 'becoming everything that one is capable of becoming' (Maslow, 1970), especially in the intellectual and creative domains; they are *intrinsically* satisfying. Examples include being a good doctor or carpenter, playing the violin, the steady increase of understanding about the universe or about oneself, the development of creativeness in whatever field, and, most importantly, simply the goal of becoming a good human being (Maslow, 1968).

We share the need for food with all living creatures, the need for love with (perhaps) the higher apes, and the need for self-actualisation with *no* other species.

Traditionally, the hierarchy has been presented in textbooks as a triangle or pyramid, with physiological needs at the base and self-actualisation needs at the apex. According to Rowan (2001), Maslow himself never presented it in this form; he believes that it's much more logical to portray it as a simple ladder. Rowan also proposes that 'competence or mastery' should be inserted between 'safety' and 'love and belongingness'. He also distinguishes between 'self-esteem' needs and 'esteem from others' needs; these are two quite different things, as Maslow himself later observed (1965).

The hierarchy is often shown with cognitive needs immediately below self-actualisation. However, Maslow indicated that the needs to *know* and *understand* are active *throughout* the hierarchy, with their quality changing on the individual's 'journey' (Compton, 2018); in other words, cognitive needs shouldn't be allocated their own 'level' in the hierarchy.

However the hierarchy might be pictured, it was intended to emphasise the following points:

1   Needs lower down in the hierarchy must be satisfied before we can fully attend to needs at the next level up.

Time for reflection …

- Try to think of some specific examples of lower-level needs needing to be met before higher-level needs can be addressed.
- Try to think of an *exception* to this general rule.

However, Maslow pointed out that a need doesn't have to be fully (100 per cent) satisfied before the next need emerges. In fact, it's 'normal' for most members of our society to only be *partially* satisfied – and partially *unsatisfied* – in all their basic needs at the same time (Compton, 2018).

2   Higher-level needs are a later *evolutionary development* in the human species (*phylogenesis*); self-actualisation is a relatively recent need to have appeared. This applies equally to the development of individuals (*ontogenesis*): clearly, babies are more concerned with their bellies than their brains; however, this is always a *relative* preference (babies' brains need stimulation from birth, but this becomes *relatively more important* as they get older).

3   The higher up the hierarchy we go, the greater the need becomes linked to life experience, and the less its biological 'flavour'. Individuals will achieve self-actualisation in different ways, through different activities, and by different routes:

> Self-actualization is idiosyncratic, since every person is different … The individual [must do] what *he*, individually, is fitted for. A musician must make music, an artist must paint, a poet must write, if he is to be ultimately at peace with himself. What a man *can* be, he *must* be.
>
> (Maslow, 1968, pp. 7, 25)

4   Following 3, the higher up the hierarchy we go, the more difficult the need is to achieve: many human goals are remote and long-term, and can only be reached in a series of steps. This pursuit of ends that lie very much in the (sometimes quite distant) future is a unique feature of human motivation and individuals differ considerably in their ability to set and achieve such goals.

Maslow and Rogers compared

While Maslow put 'self-actualisation' at the top of his need hierarchy, Rogers preferred the term 'actualising' (or 'actualising tendency'); these relate to 'a psychology of *being*' and 'a psychology of *becoming*', respectively. According to Graham (1986):

> A danger inherent in any psychology of being such as that proposed by Maslow is that it has the tendency to be static and not account for movement, change, direction and growth, with the result that self-actualization or self-discovery comes to be viewed as an end in itself rather than as a process.
> (pp. 53–4)

Rogers, although taking a broadly similar view to Maslow, draws particular attention to the individual in the *process* of becoming a *fully functioning person*; this is central to his Self Theory (see Gross, 2018). However, they both recognise the fundamental pre-eminence of the subjective and the tendency toward *self-actualisation*; the latter is synonymous with psychological health and represents the realisation of the person's inherent capacities for growth and development (both of which are viewed as good or neutral).

Some other similarities and differences are outlined in Box 7.2.

BOX 7.2 MAJOR SIMILARITIES AND DIFFERENCES BETWEEN MASLOW AND ROGERS

- Their approach is essentially *holistic* (rather than reductionist): every individual is a unique totality, no aspect of which can be studied in isolation.
- While Maslow was fundamentally concerned with human *motivation* and the effects of goals and purposes on behaviour, Rogers was essentially concerned with *perception*: the primary object for psychological study is the person and the world *as viewed by that person him/herself*. So, for Rogers, the individual's *internal phenomenological* frame of reference constitutes the proper focus of psychology (see Box 7.1).
- As we noted earlier, Rogers was first and foremost a *therapist*. By emphasising the therapist's personal qualities (*genuineness/authenticity/congruence, unconditional positive regard*, and *empathic understanding*), he helped open up the provision of psychotherapy to non-medically qualified therapists ('lay therapy'), including psychologists. This is especially relevant in the US, where, until recently, only psychiatrists could practice psychoanalysis. Rogers originally used the term 'counselling' as a strategy for silencing psychiatrists who voiced their opposition to psychologists offering psychotherapy. In the UK, Rogers has helped facilitate the development of a counselling profession whose practitioners are drawn from a wide variety of disciplines (Thorne, 1992).

Maslow's study of self-actualisation

Although in theory we're all capable of achieving self-actualisation, most of us won't do so – or only to a limited degree. Maslow was particularly interested in the characteristics of people whom he considered to have achieved their potential as persons, including Albert Einstein, William James, Eleanor Roosevelt, Abraham Lincoln, Baruch Spinoza, Thomas Jefferson, and Walt Whitman. In *Motivation and Personality* (1954, 1970, 1987), he identified 19 characteristics of the self-actualised person, as shown in Table 7.1.

Table 7.1 Characteristics of the self-actualised person

1 **Perception of reality:** an unusual ability to detect the spurious, the fake, and the dishonest in personality, and in art. Also, not frightened by the unknown, and tolerant of ambiguity.
2 **Acceptance:** both self-acceptance and acceptance of others, a relative lack of overriding guilt, crippling shame and anxiety, and defensiveness.
3 **Spontaneity:** simplicity and naturalness, lack of artificiality or straining for effect, a superior awareness of their own desires, opinions, and subjective reactions in general.
4 **Problem-centring:** not ego-centred, usually having a mission in life, some problem outside themselves which enlists much of their energies.
5 **Solitude:** a liking for solitude and privacy, not needing other people in the ordinary sense – but still liking others' company.
6 **Autonomy:** self-contained/self-sufficient, able to maintain a relative calm in the midst of circumstances that would drive others to suicide.
7 **Fresh appreciation:** the ability to see familiar things in a new way ('through a child's eyes'), with awe, wonder, and even ecstasy.
8 **Peak experiences:** moments of ecstatic happiness and spontaneous mystical experience. (In fact, Maslow describes two types of self-actualising people: *peakers* and *non-peakers*; peakers are more likely to perceive sacredness in all things, are more drawn to awe and mystery, yet carry a 'cosmic-sadness' (Compton, 2018).)
9 **Human kinship:** a deep sense of identification, sympathy, and affection, and connection with others (as if we all belonged to a single family).
10 **Humility and respect:** a democratic character structure in the deepest sense; can learn from anyone who has something to teach them.
11 **Interpersonal relationships:** these can be profound.
12 **Ethics:** definite moral standards, although these may not always be conventional.
13 **Means and ends:** experiences and activities are valued for their own sake – not just as means to an end.
14 **Humour:** but this is never at other people's expense.
15 **Creativity:** they *are* creative (they *don't* 'have creativity').
16 **Resistance to enculturation:** maintain a certain detachment from the surrounding culture.
17 **Imperfections:** can be ruthless, absent-minded, impolite, stubborn, and irritating, and may experience internal conflicts.
18 **Values:** topmost portion of their value system is entirely unique.
19 **Resolution of dichotomies:** no conflict between head and heart, reason and instinct (they're *synergistic*).

(Based on Rowan, 2001)

Humanistic psychology as a science of human being

Whatever the empirical support or otherwise for Maslow's *idiographic* theory (i.e. focusing on the *uniqueness* of every individual), it undoubtedly represents an important counterbalance to the *nomothetic* ('law-like') approach of other personality theorists, such as Cattell and Eysenck (see Gross, 2015) by attempting to capture the richness of the personal experience of being human.

According to Compton (2018), self-actualisation has been found to be significantly related – in the expected direction – with a number of other psychological theories and research areas, including Rogers's theory of the fully functioning person (see above), Frankl's constructs of the meaning of life and self-transcendence (see below), Kohlberg's theory of moral development (see Gross, 2015), and Erikson's stages of psychosocial development (see Chapter 6).

Like Freud's theories, many of its concepts are difficult to test empirically and it cannot account for the origins of personality. Since it *describes* but doesn't *explain* personality, it's subject to the *nominal fallacy* (Carlson and Buskist, 1997).

However, also like Freud's theories, it shouldn't be condemned in its entirety. As we've seen, self-actualisation has been investigated empirically (and not just by Maslow) and Rogers was a prolific researcher, during the 1940s, 1950s, and 1960s, into his *client/person-centred therapy*. According to Thorne (1992), this body of research constituted the most intensive investigation of psychotherapy attempted anywhere in the world up to that time. Its major achievement was to establish beyond all question that psychotherapy could and should be subjected to rigorous scientific enquiry.

As we noted earlier, Maslow didn't reject behaviourism's mechanistic approach; rather he saw it as too narrow and limited to be able to provide a comprehensive understanding of human nature. He embraced science, but advocated that scientists should be more transparent, receptive, patient, empathic, caring, and open-minded (Compton, 2018). He saw his work as an attempt at *rehumanising* science (1969).

According to Rowan (2001):

> Humanistic Psychology is not just psychology. It is indebted to Eastern thought. And it is interested in science – not from the point of view of simply accepting the standard view of science as postulated in a myriad academic texts, but rather of creating a newer view of science as a human endeavour, which calls on the whole person rather than just on the intellect.
>
> (p. 21)

Rowan goes further: humanistic psychology has some claim to be the *only* true psychology. Most psychology, using 'empiric–analytic inquiry', makes the classic mistake of trying to study people by using the '*eye of flesh*' (Wilber, 1983), that is, how we perceive the external world of space, time, and objects; this 'isolates their behaviour – the observable actions they pursue in the world – and ignores most of what is actually relevant – their intentions, their meanings, their visions' (Rowan, 2001, p. 20).

By contrast, humanistic psychology is the classic way of using the *eye of the mind/reason*, by which we obtain knowledge of philosophy, logic, and the mind itself. While positivist science (including behaviourism and cognitive psychology) involves a *monologue* ('a symbolizing inquirer looks at a nonsymbolizing occasion'), humanistic psychology involves a *dialogue* ('a symbolizing inquirer looks at other symbolizing occasions') (Rowan, 2001, p. 22).

> The very field of humanistic inquiry is *communicative exchange* or inter-subjective and intersymbolic relationships (language and logic), and this approach depends in large measure on talking to and with the subject of investigation … any science that *talks* to its subject of investigation is not empirical but humanistic, not monologic but dialogic.
>
> (Rowan, 2001, p. 22)

Humanistic psychology is 'real psychology, proper psychology, the type of psychology that is genuinely applicable to human beings' (Rowan, 2001, p. 22).

Humanistic psychology and existentialism

So far, we've seen how both Eastern philosophy and religion, and Western philosophy (in the form of phenomenology) helped to shape humanistic psychology. One further major influence, again from Western philosophy, was *existentialism*, which, in turn, has helped generate the recent sub-discipline of *existential psychology*. While most existentialists are also phenomenologists, there are many phenomenologists who aren't existentialists. Box 7.3 describes some of the origins of existentialism.

BOX 7.3 SOME OF THE HISTORICAL ROOTS OF EXISTENTIALISM

- Existential thinking can be traced back to one of the oldest known written documents, the 4,000-year-old Babylonian *The Gilgamesh Epic*. In it, the hero, Gilgamesh, reflecting on the death of his friend, Endiju, expresses his fear of his own death; 'death terror' has become one of the core issues within existentialist philosophy and existential psychology (see text below).

- Consideration of existential issues can also be found in the work of the great thinkers of the Western classical era, such as Homer, Plato, Socrates, and Seneca, and continued through the work of theologians, such as Augustine and Aquinas (see Chapter 2).

- Existential issues were later explored in the work of European Renaissance poets and playwrights, such as Cervantes, Dante, Milton, Shakespeare, and Swift and nineteenth century Romantic poets (Byron, Shelley, and Keats), novelists (Balzac, Dostoyevsky, Hugo, and Tolstoy), and composers (Beethoven, Brahms, Bruckner, and Tchaikovsky).

- More recently, the plays of Beckett, O'Neill, and Ionesco, the classical music of Mahler and Cage, the rock music of John Lennon and the Doors, and the surrealist paintings of Dali, Ernst, Tanguy, and many others have explored fundamental issues relating to human being.

The expression of deep existential concerns may be the underlying commonality of all great artistic creation.

(Pyszczynski *et al.*, 2004, p. 5)

(Based on Pyszczynski *et al.*, 2004)

Defining existentialism

According to Blackham (1961):

> The peculiarity of existentialism … is that it deals with the separation of man from himself and from the world … existentialism goes back to the beginning of philosophy and appeals to all men to awaken from their dogmatic slumbers and discover what it means to become a human being.
>
> (pp. 151–2)

There cannot be any objective, universal answers to the question of what it means to be human: 'Man is and remains in his being a question, a personal choice' (p. 152) and is more than anything that can be said of him.

Because there's no common body of doctrine shared by all existentialists, Macquarrie (1972) prefers to describe existentialism as a 'style of philosophizing', rather than as 'a philosophy'. As such, it can lead to very different conclusions regarding the world and human beings' place in it. This is demonstrated by the three 'greats': Kierkegaard, Heidegger, and Sartre.

Despite the lack of 'doctrine', it's possible to identify some recurring existentialist themes, which distinguish it from other philosophical schools/approaches. These include *freedom, decision,* and *responsibility*, which constitute the core of personal being. The exercise of freedom and the ability to shape the future are what distinguish humans from all other creatures on the planet: it's through free and responsible decisions that we become authenti-cally ourselves. The focus has been very much on the individual, whose quest for authentic selfhood concerns the meaning of personal being; this implies a view of the person as an isolated, if not dislocated, creature. Other recurring themes include *finitude, guilt, alienation, despair,* and *death* (Macquarrie, 1972) (see below).

According to Pyszczynski *et al.* (2004), despite their differences, all the key existentialist thinkers addressed the questions of what it means to be a human being, how we humans relate to the physical and metaphysical world that surrounds us, and how we can find meaning given the realities of life and death.

> Most important, they considered the implications of how ordinary humans struggle with these questions for what happens in their daily lives. Thus, existential issues were ... conceived of as pressing issues with enormous impact on the lives of us all.
>
> (p. 6)

Viktor Frankl and logotherapy

Within psychology, a loosely defined existentialist movement began to emerge, initially as a reaction to orthodox Freudian theory. A number of European the-orists and therapists argued for the importance of basing our analyses of human behaviour in the phenomenological world of the subject.

Notable amongst these was Viktor Frankl (see Figure 7.3), founder of *logo-therapy* (what's come to be called the Third Viennese school of psychotherapy after Freud's psychoanalysis and Adler's Individual Psychology). Logotherapy, Frankl's own version of *existential psychotherapy*, is much less *retrospective* and *introspective* than psychoanalysis:

> Logotherapy focuses rather on the future ... on the meanings to be ful-filled by the patient in his future. (Logotherapy, indeed, is a meaning-centred psychotherapy.) ...
>
> In logotherapy, the patient is actually confronted with and reoriented toward the meaning of life. And to make him aware of this meaning can contribute much to his ability to overcome his neurosis.
>
> (Frankl, 2004, p. 104)

In 1945, shortly after his release from a Nazi concentration camp, he spent nine intensive days writing a psychological account of his three years in Auschwitz, Dachau, and other Nazi prison camps. The original German version bears no title on the cover because Frankl was initially committed to publishing an anonymous report that would never earn its author literary fame. The English version, expanded to include a short overview of logotherapy, first appeared as

Figure 7.3 Viktor Frankl (1905–97), left, with Martin Heidegger (1889–1976), circa 1960. (Permission granted by Mary Evans Library.)

From Death Camp to Existentialism, and finally under its well-known title, *Man's Search for Meaning* (1946/2004).

The book describes Frankl's harrowing experiences and his desperate efforts, and those of many fellow-inmates, to sustain hope in the face of unspeakable suffering. Those who lost meaning simply gave up and died at Auschwitz. But those who managed to retain some sense of purpose maintained at least some chance of survival. The human quest for meaning is a fundamental human tendency. His *existential psychology of meaning and purpose* was aimed at replacing psychoanalysis and behaviourism (Frankl, 2004; McAdams, 2012).

Otto Rank was perhaps the first theorist to incorporate existential concepts into a broad account of human behaviour: the twin fears of life and death play a critical role in the development of the child's self-concept and throughout the lifespan. Rank also discussed art and creativity, the soul, and the will, all to be found in later existential psychological theorising (Pyszczynski *et al.*, 2004).

Like Frankl and Rank, other major individuals with existential leanings weren't just influential theorists but practising psychiatrists, psychoanalysts, or both (including Horney and Fromm). More recent examples include R.D. Laing's involvement in the radical 'anti-psychiatry' movement during the 1960s and 1970s (see Gross, 2018), Ernest Becker's discussion of 'death terror' (in his classic *The Denial of Death,* 1973), and Ervin Yalom's 'givens of existence' (as discussed in *Existential Psychiatry* (1980) and *Staring at the Sun: Overcoming the Dread of Death* (2008)) (see Box 7.4).

Yalom's 'givens of existence'

BOX 7.4 THE 'GIVENS OF EXISTENCE' (YALOM, 1980)

- *Fear of death.* The inevitability of death is a simple fact of life of which we're all aware; this awareness in an animal that desperately wants to live creates a conflict that cannot be brushed aside. This is the most-studied of Yalom's four 'givens'.

- *Freedom.* The concern with freedom reflects the conflict between (i) a desire for self-determination/self-control; and (ii) the sense of groundlessness and ambiguity that results when we realise that much of what happens in our lives is really up to ourselves – and that there are few, if any, absolute rules to live by.

- *Existential isolation.* No matter how close each of us becomes to another, there remains a final, unbridgeable gap; we each enter life alone and must depart from it alone. This fundamental isolation is the inevitable consequence of the very personal, subjective, and individual nature of human experience that can never be fully shared with another being.

- *Meaninglessness.* This is a result of the first three givens. In a world where the only true certainty is death, where meaning and value are subjective human creations rather than absolute truths, and where one can never fully share one's experience with others, what meaning does life have? The very real possibility that human life *lacks* meaning lurks just behind the surface of our attempts to cling to whatever meaning we can find or create. According to Yalom, the crisis of meaninglessness stems from the dilemma of a meaning-seeking creature who finds itself in a universe that has no meaning.

Yalom acknowledged that these four concerns were by no means a complete list; others that have been (and are being) actively explored include: how we humans fit into the physical universe, how we relate to nature (see Chapter 9), and how we come to terms with the physical nature of our bodies, questions regarding beauty, spirituality, and nostalgia.

Time for reflection ...

- Does any one of the 'givens of existence' or other existential issues described above strike you as more fundamental – or have more personal significance for you – than the others?
- Try to identify the reasons for your choice.
- Are there any existential concerns that you think could/should be added to the list?

Another of these additional concerns is *identity*. We all feel the need to 'find ourselves' – to make sense of our diverse views and experiences of the world, and to integrate them into a coherent and consistent sense of who we are. Uncertainty about our identity can lead to defensive psychological moves, such as more zealous defence of our attitudes (McGregor, 2006).

> Work on the self has told us a great deal about the malleability and multiplicity of identities, their socially constructed nature, and the desire to sustain a coherent sense of self over the lifespan – a story about the self, or self-narrative.
>
> (Greenberg, in Jones, 2008)

In his classic text on existential psychotherapy, Yalom (1980) described existential thought as focused on human confrontation with the fundamentals of existence. He viewed existential psychology as rooted in Freudian psychodynamics, in the sense that it explored the motivational consequences of important human conflicts. However, the fundamental conflicts of concern to existentialists are very different from those emphasised by Freud (namely, those involving 'suppressed instinctual strivings' or 'internalised significant adults') (see Chapter 6); they focus on conflicts that flow from the individual's confrontation with the *givens of existence* (see Box 7.4). In other words, existential psychology attempts to explain how ordinary human beings come to terms with the basic facts of life that we all have to deal with; these are deep, potentially terrifying issues, and, consequently, people typically avoid confronting them directly. Indeed, many people claim that they *never* think about such things. Nevertheless, Yalom argues, these basic concerns affect us all – whether we realise it or not.

Terror management theory

As we noted in Box 7.4, fear of death is the most-studied of Yalom's 'givens of existence'. *Terror management theory* (TMT) (e.g. Solomon *et al.*, 1991a, 1991b, 2004) represents a broad theoretical account of how we cope with this fundamental fact of life.

According to TMT, human beings, like all forms of life, are the products of evolution by natural selection; over extremely long periods of time, they have acquired adaptations that enabled individual members of their species to successfully compete for resources needed for survival and reproduction in their respective environmental niches (see Chapter 9).

So, what are the distinctive human evolutionary adaptations? One answer relates to our highly *social* nature, linked, in turn, to our vast intelligence:

> These attributes fostered cooperation and division of labour and led to the invention of tools, agriculture…and a host of other very useful habits and devices that allowed our ancestral forbears to rapidly multiply from a

small band of hominids in a single neighbourhood in Africa to the huge population of *Homo sapiens* that currently occupy almost every habitable inch of the planet.

(Solomon *et al.*, 2004, p. 16)

A major aspect of human intelligence is *self-awareness* (see Chapter 4): we're alive and know we're alive and this sense of self enables us to reflect on the past and contemplate the future, which help us function effectively in the present (see Chapter 5). While knowing we're alive is tremendously uplifting and potentially joyous and awe-inspiring, we're also perpetually troubled by the knowledge that all living things, including ourselves, ultimately die: death can rarely be anticipated or controlled (Kierkegaard, 1944/1844). Human beings, therefore, by virtue of our awareness of death and our relative helplessness and vulnerability, are in constant danger of being overwhelmed by terror; this terror is compounded by our profound unease at being corporeal creatures (creatures with a body) (Rank, 1941/1958). Becker (1973) neatly captured this uniquely human existential dilemma like this:

> Man…is a creator with a mind that soars out to speculate about atoms and infinity…Yet at the same time, as the Eastern sages also knew, man is a worm and food for worms.
>
> (p. 26)

Homo sapiens solved this existential dilemma by developing *cultural worldviews*: humanly constructed beliefs about reality shared by individuals in a group that serve to reduce the potentially overwhelming terror resulting from death awareness.

> Culture reduces anxiety by providing its constituents with a sense that they are valuable members of a meaningful universe. Meaning is derived from cultural worldviews that offer an account of the origin of the universe, prescriptions of appropriate conduct, and guarantees of safety and security to those who adhere to such instructions – in this life and beyond, in the form of symbolic and/or literal immortality.
>
> (Solomon *et al.*, 2004, p. 16)

Time for reflection …

- What do you understand by 'symbolic immortality'?
- Give some examples.
- How can we achieve literal immortality?

Symbolic immortality can be achieved by perceiving oneself as part of a culture that endures beyond one's lifetime, or by creating visible testaments to one's existence in the form of great works of art or scientific achievements, impressive buildings or monuments, amassing vast wealth, or (simply) by having children. *Literal immortality* is achieved via the various afterlives promised by almost all organised world religions.

According to the *mortality salience hypothesis*, if cultural worldviews and self-esteem provide beliefs about the nature of reality that function to reduce anxiety associated with death awareness, then asking people to think about their own mortality (the *mortality salience paradigm*/MS paradigm) should *increase* the need for the protection provided by such beliefs. (For discussion of research using the MS paradigm and other research relating to the TMT, see Greenberg *et al.*, 2004.)

Summary and conclusions: humanistic psychology and positive psychology

According to Wilson *et al.* (1996), the humanistic approach doesn't constitute an elaborate or comprehensive theory, but rather should be seen as a set of uniquely personal theories of living created by humane people optimistic about human potential. It has wide appeal to those looking for an alternative to more mechanistic, deterministic theories.

Positive Psychology (PP) is about 'happiness' (Seligman, 2003). It can be defined as the scientific study of the positive aspects of human subjective experience, of positive individual traits, and of positive institutions. It can be understood as a reaction against psychology's almost exclusive emphasis on the negative side of human experience and behaviour, namely, mental illness, during the second half of the twentieth century.

Research into what we now call PP has been taking place for decades. In broad terms, PP has common interests with aspects of humanistic psychology, in particular the latter's emphasis on the fully functioning person (Rogers, 1951) and the study of healthy individuals (Maslow, 1968). More than 50 years ago, Maslow stated:

> The science of psychology has been far more successful on the negative than on the positive side. It has revealed to us much about man's shortcomings, his illness, his sins, but little about his potentialities, his virtues, his achievable aspirations, or his full psychological height. It is as if psychology has voluntarily restricted itself to only half its rightful jurisdiction, and that, the darker, meaner half.
>
> (Maslow, 1954, p. 354)

Maslow even talked specifically about a positive psychology, that is, a more exclusive focus on people at the extreme positive ends of the distribution, rather than what's understood today by PP. Nevertheless, in a broad sense, there's a strong convergence between the interests of humanistic psychology and modern PP (Linley, 2008).

Given the often contentious relationship between PP and humanistic psychology, Seligman *et al.*'s (2005) acknowledgement that PP has built on the earlier work of Rogers and Maslow represents quite a significant development (Joseph and Linley, 2006). While Rogers and Maslow and Positive Psychologists shared the aim of wanting to understand the full range of human experience, Rogers and Maslow were also vigorous critics of the *medical* (or disease) *model* as applied to psychology and it was their alternative view of human nature that made their positive psychology also a humanistic psychology (Joseph and Linley, 2006).

Suggested further reading

Becker, E. (1973) *The Denial of Death*. New York: Free Press.

Fancher, R.E. and Rutherford, A. (2012) *Pioneers of Psychology: A History* (4th edition). New York: W.W. Norton and Co. Inc. (Chapter 12).

Graham, H. (1986) *The Human Face of Psychology: Humanistic Psychology in its Historical and Social Context*. Milton Keynes: Open University Press.

Greenberg, J., Koole, S.L. and Pyszczynski, T. (eds.) *Handbook of Experimental Existential Psychology*. New York: The Guilford Press.

Maslow, A.H. (1971) *The Farther Reaches of Human Nature*. New York: The Viking Press.

Rogers, C.R. (1961) *On Becoming a Person: A Therapist's View of Psychotherapy*. London: Constable.

Rowan, J. (2001) *Ordinary Ecstasy: The Dialectics of Humanistic Psychology* (3rd edition). Hove: Brunner-Routledge.

Yalom, I.D. (2008) *Staring at the Sun: Overcoming the Dread of Death*. London: Piatkus Books.

8 The social psychology of good and evil

Key questions

- What do we mean by 'good' and 'evil'?
- How important is the intent to inflict harm on others as a criterion of evil?
- How important are (belief in) free will and moral responsibility to the creation and maintenance of culture?
- What's meant by 'dispositionism' and 'situationism'?
- What were the aims of the Stanford Prison Experiment (SPE) and what conclusions did Zimbardo *et al.* draw form it?
- How have their conclusions been challenged?
- What were the aims of Milgram's obedience experiments and what conclusions did he draw?
- How have his conclusions and explanations for his findings been challenged?
- How has the 'banality of evil' interpretation been supported and challenged?
- What's the role of *dehumanisation* in genocide and mass atrocities (GMA)?
- How has the Internet influenced the increase in terrorism in the 21st century?
- How have the Decision Model (DM) and Arousal Cost Reward model (ACR) helped explain prosocial behaviour?
- What are the conflicting claims of *universal egoism* and the *empathy–altruism hypothesis*?
- What are the underlying motives behind *volunteerism* and *heroism*?
- In what ways is heroism socially constructed?

Philosophical and religious views on good and evil

In examining the historical roots of the concepts of good and evil in Chapter 2, we came across a number of distinctions between the passions, appetites, or emotions, on the one hand, and reason or self-control on the other. Sometimes these have been regarded as different components of the soul (e.g. Plato), and at other times the 'good' soul has been seen as the controller of the inferior body (e.g. Descartes). Hobbes' hedonistic philosophy could be seen as opposed to Rousseau's view of people as intrinsically good, with society's institutions corrupting our human nature.

In relation to the Seven Deadly Sins, the question of freedom and personal responsibility inevitably arises; this is central to the debate within social psychology regarding the ultimate causes of behaviour judged to be 'evil'. More specifically, this debate has at times centred around how people can change from being 'good' to being 'evil' (and the related debate regarding 'good' and 'evil' *behaviour*). One of the major figures in this debate has been the American social psychologist, Philip Zimbardo, who describes the 'ultimate transformation of good into evil', the transformation of Lucifer into Satan (in *The Lucifer Effect*, 2007). His account, taken from Milton's (1667) *Paradise Lost,* is given in Box 8.1.

BOX 8.1 LUCIFER'S TRANSFORMATION INTO SATAN (BASED ON ZIMBARDO, 2007)

- Lucifer was God's favourite angel until he challenged God's authority; as punishment, he was thrown into Hell along with his band of fallen angels and was now God's enemy.
- Lucifer-Satan is assured that he cannot re-enter Heaven through any direct confrontation. However, Beelzebub, his statesman, proposes that to avenge themselves against God, they will corrupt God's greatest creation – humankind.
- Satan succeeds in tempting Adam and Eve to disobey God in the Garden of Eden by eating from the Tree of Knowledge. While God decrees that they will be saved in time, Satan will forevermore be allowed to enlist witches to tempt people to commit evil.

In *The Lucifer Effect,* Zimbardo attempts to understand the processes of transformation involved when good (or ordinary) people do bad or evil things ('what makes people go wrong?'). Rather than resorting to a traditional religious dualism of good *versus* evil, Zimbardo (2007) looks at:

> Real people engaged in life's daily tasks, enmeshed in doing their jobs, surviving within an often turbulent crucible of human nature. We will seek to understand the nature of their character transformations when they are faced with powerful situational forces.
>
> (p. 5)

It's this focus on situational (i.e. external) influences on people's behaviour that characterises a *social psychological* approach to explaining human behaviour.

What do we mean by 'good' and 'evil'?

Social psychology on good and evil

According to Miller (2016):

> From a social psychological perspective, good and evil are complex concepts. They seem to reside within individuals, in their very "natures" or their motives, but also in their actions and in the judgements and interpretations of those who observe their deeds.
>
> (p. 2)

Krueger and Funder (2004) identify a "negativity bias" within mainstream social psychology, according to which the research focus is on conformity, destructive obedience (as in Milgram's famous experiments, discussed in detail below), and bystander apathy (as in Latané and Darely's pioneering studies). We could add to this list Zimbardo's infamous Stanford Prison Experiment (SPE), which directly tested the impact of situational influences. (This is discussed in detail below.) Krueger and Funder (2004) advocate a more balanced social psychology, which would 'yield … a more positive view of human nature' (p. 317).

However, as Miller (2016) observes, isn't this advocacy of a more balanced view of human nature itself rather biased? 'Whether or not social psychology, as an academic discipline, should in fact promote a positive view of human nature is debatable' (p. 3). One could argue that the 'best' view is the one that most accurately reflects what people are *actually* like. But this, in turn, begs a number of fundamental questions regarding the difficulty of establishing the 'truth' about people (see the discussion of 'natural' and 'psychological' kinds in Chapter 2).

Defining good and evil

> **Time for reflection …**
>
> - What's your understanding of 'evil'?
> - Should we distinguish between 'evil people' and 'evil deeds'?

Zimbardo (2007) offers what he calls a simple, psychologically based definition:

> *Evil consists in intentionally behaving in ways that harm, abuse, demean, dehumanize, or destroy innocent others – or using one's authority and systemic power to encourage or permit others to do so on your behalf.* In short, it is "knowing better but doing worse."
>
> (p. 5)

Instead of offering definitions, we could give examples of acts that most people (at least within Western liberal democracies with a Judaeo-Christian tradition) would consider to be evil, including robbing, maiming, raping, torturing, and murdering (especially cold-blooded, pre-meditated murder). But some cold-blooded murders may be considered more evil than others: murder with malice, murder without provocation (as opposed to self-defence), murder of young defenceless individuals – especially children – serial murder, mass murder, and genocide (Duntley and Buss, 2016). We should add terrorism to this list.

According to Duntley and Buss, humans come second only to mosquitoes in the number of *conspecifics* (members of their own species) that they kill each year. Of the 5.8 million deaths from injuries that occur globally each year, about one in seven results from homicide or warfare (World Health Organisation/ WHO, 2008). Among 15–29-year-olds, homicide is the fourth leading cause of death (after traffic accidents, HIV/AIDS, and tuberculosis/TB) (WHO, 2008). Across all age groups, almost twice as many men as women die from injuries and violence. Of all causes of death, homicide is unique in there being a directly and recurrently identifiable causal agent, namely, another human being.

> Over evolutionary time, this trend would have contributed to the evolution of a perception of other humans as *potentially evil*. But … Uncertainty about the *intentions* of others also would have played an important role.
> (Duntley and Buss, 2016, p. 27; emphasis added)

Time for reflection …

- What makes intent to do harm such an integral part of the definition of evil?
- What does it tell us about free will?

Evil, free will, and moral responsibility

The intent to inflict harm on others can only be considered an inherent and critical feature of evil if it is possible – at least in principle – for the evil-doer to have chosen to act *otherwise*; in other words, the evil-doer has freely chosen to act in this way.

As we noted in Chapter 2, Descartes saw the possession of free will as a distinguishing feature of human beings as compared with (other) animals. Free will is also a major human characteristic according to humanistic psychology (see Chapter 7), in contrast with Freud's and Skinner's view of free will as an illusion (see Chapter 6).

Whether or not free will can be shown to exist, social – and legal – life proceeds on the assumption that it does: how else could people be held (morally and legally) *responsible* for their actions? And if no such responsibility was attributed to actors, we could only distinguish between good and evil *deeds* – and their *consequences*. But in the case of historical figures who personify evil, such as Hitler, Stalin, and Pol Pot, how can we separate the consequences of their actions from their intent: surely, it was the fact that they *meant* to commit mass murder or genocide *and* succeeded in doing so that makes them the hated figures they are? Even on the scale of a single murder, the same reasoning applies: cold-blooded murder of an innocent, often defenceless individual (such as the racially motivated murder of Stephen Lawrence in 1993) is an act of evil by virtue of being intended and planned.

Free will, morality, and culture

If belief in free will underlies moral and legal responsibility, there's also good reason to believe that free will was crucial for the evolution – and survival – of *culture*. According to Monroe *et al.* (2016):

> The emergence and functioning of free will must be placed in the context of a broad understanding of human nature ... free will can be understood as an advanced form of action control that evolved to enable people to function and thrive in cultural groups.
>
> (p. 41)

According to Baumeister (2005), humans were produced for culture by natural selection (i.e. living in culture is our natural state: see Chapter 9). If free will was a human adaptation for culture, it would have to confer benefits to survival and reproduction:

> People's belief in free will increases cultural fitness by promoting virtuous behaviour, including honesty, helping, restraining aggression, initiative, expressing gratitude, and upholding community standards by advocating punishment for rule breakers.
>
> (Monroe *et al.*, 2016, p. 42)

In other words, rewarding good behaviour and punishing wrongdoing (including evil acts) help cultures to evolve and survive; indeed, they're *necessary* for their survival.

Restraining aggression, the capacity for self-regulation and rational choice, the ability to inhibit one's impulses, and persistence in pursuing long-term goals are modern (psychology-based) versions of the philosophical and religious views of human nature outlined at the beginning of the chapter.

Situationism and dispositionism

If we are 'naturally' cultural creatures, and if free will evolved to facilitate the sense of self-regulation and personal responsibility necessary for living in culture, then it's almost as if (belief in) free will is our *default state*. (We're 'naturally good' in the sense that we are equipped with that form of action control that we call free will.) This means that we need to be able to explain *deviations* from that default state, from 'mere' abuse to mass murder and genocide; the latter, by definition, take place on a huge scale requiring the co-operation of hundreds/ thousands of individuals and involving massive organisational effort. We can start by focusing on much smaller-scale examples of how good people become evil.

The power of social situations: Zimbardo's Stanford Prison Experiment

Zimbardo was specifically interested in how ordinary people would respond to being put into the role of an authority figure: how easily would they assume the role and use the power that goes with it? He and his colleagues (Haney *et al.*, 1973; Zimbardo *et al.*, 1973) attempted to answer these questions in one of the best-known studies in the whole of Psychology, which is described in Box 8.2.

BOX 8.2 THE STANFORD PRISON EXPERIMENT (SPE)

- Male participants were recruited through newspaper advertisements asking for student volunteers for a two-week study of prison life.
- From 75 respondents, 24 were selected, being judged as physically healthy, emotionally stable, and 'normal to average' on personality tests. They had no history of psychiatric problems, had never been in trouble with the police, and constituted a relatively homogeneous sample of white, middle-class students from across the US. Participants were randomly assigned to the role of either 'prisoner' or 'prison guard'.
- The basement of Stanford University Psychology department was converted into a 'mock (simulated) prison', creating a prison-like environment that was as *psychologically* real as possible. The aim was to study how prison life impacts upon both prisoners and guards.

The basic aim of the study was to test the *dispositional hypothesis,* the claim that the deplorable conditions of the prison system and its dehumanising effects upon prisoners and guards is due to the nature of the people who run it (including guards) and who populate it (prisoners). They're 'bad' (sometimes 'evil') people: guards are naturally sadistic, uneducated, and insensitive (presumably why they're attracted to the job in the first place), while the antisocial attitudes and behaviour of prisoners will prevail whether they're living in the community or in prison. Force is needed to keep prisoners under control.

Zimbardo and his colleagues expected to find evidence that would allow them to *reject* the dispositional hypothesis in favour of the *situational hypothesis*: it's the conditions (physical, social, and psychological) of prison that are to blame, *not* the people in them.

After an initial rebellion had been crushed, the prisoners reacted passively as the guards stepped up their aggression daily, one making them clean the toilets out with their bare hands, and others expressing their enjoyment of this new-found power; this made the prisoners feel helpless and no longer in control of their lives. In less than 36 hours, one prisoner had to be released because of uncontrolled crying, fits of rage, disorganised thinking, and severe depression; three more with similar symptoms were released on successive days.

Having been planned to run for two weeks, the experiment was halted after just six days – because of the extreme behaviours of both prisoners and guards.

According to Zimbardo and Ruch (1977), the abnormal behaviour of both groups is best viewed as a product of transactions with an environment that supports such behaviour. Since they were randomly assigned their roles, showed no prior personality pathology, and received no training, how was it that the participants assumed their roles as readily and completely as they did? Zimbardo and Ruch propose two major explanations:

- Presumably, they'd all learned *stereotypes* of guard and prisoner from the media, as well as from social models of power and powerlessness (such as parent–child, teacher–student relationships). We draw on our knowledge and experience of other role relationships whenever we're faced with unfamiliar situations (as the mock prison was for both guards and prisoners).
- Environmental conditions facilitate *role-playing*: a brutalising atmosphere, like the mock prison, produces brutality. Had the roles been reversed, those who suffered as prisoners may just as easily have inflicted suffering on those randomly allocated to the role of guard; this suggests that we all have the *potential* for 'evil' (it's part of human nature) but this usually only manifests under certain environmental/situational conditions.

So, the findings of the SPE illustrate not only how a prison-like environment can turn ordinary, non-aggressive people (volunteer guards) into 'brutes' (who seemed to have no qualms about their treatment of the volunteer prisoners), but also how they have been socialised into behaving that way (i.e. through media representations and other stereotyped images of power and powerlessness).

But could this be an oversimplification? If the participants' stereotyped expectations *pre-dated* their participation in the experiment, this means that their behaviour cannot be wholly attributed to their actual experiences in their respective roles. This suggests that they were *merely* role-playing (Banuazzi and Mohavedi, 1975). Can role-playing ever constitute a 'real' experience and is it a valid means of testing the dispositional hypothesis? But at what point does 'mere' role-playing become a 'real' (authentic) experience? Ironically, the very reason for having to end the study prematurely is what appears to address this very question. According to Zimbardo (1971):

> At the end of only six days we had to close down our mock prison because what we saw was frightening. It was no longer apparent to us or most of the subjects where they ended and their roles began. The majority had

indeed *become* 'prisoners' or 'guards', no longer able to clearly differentiate between role-playing and self.

(p. 3; emphasis added)

This strongly suggests that even if they were 'merely' role-playing at the outset, they were very soon taking their roles very seriously indeed. (However, even if the role-playing argument has some validity in relation to the guards, can it be applied equally to the prisoner role: just how *are* prisoners meant to act? See Gross, 1994.)

Zimbardo has always maintained that he had nothing to do with the toxicity that led to the study's premature ending: the participants slipped 'naturally' – and perhaps unconsciously – into their roles as vicious guards or broken prisoners. But recently discovered video and audio tapes show that Zimbardo and his colleagues sought to ensure conformity amongst the guards (effectively treating them as research assistants) by making brutality appear necessary for the achievement of worthy goals, namely, prison reform (Reicher *et al.*, 2018).

In support of the dispositional account of evil rejected by the SPE, Tangney *et al.* (2016) point out that 15–20 per cent of the US prison inmate population can be thought of as evil – by virtue of having *psychopathic* personalities (selfish, callous, using others for their own ends, lacking empathy and guilt, etc.). While not all those who would be considered psychopathic end up in prison having committed serious crimes, those who do perhaps embody a widely held view of what evil means. However, the vast majority (80–85 per cent) or prisoners are *not* evil according to this definition.

Although Zimbardo's guards were screened for all major forms of abnormality and deviance, perhaps they were more vulnerable to his leadership influence than he's willing to admit (although this counts as a situational, rather than a dispositional, influence). This strongly suggests that we need to distinguish between evil *people* and evil *deeds* (Tangney *et al.*, 2016: see above).

According to Shaver (1987), the findings (in particular relating to the guards) can be interpreted in terms of *de-individuation* (e.g. Zimbardo, 1969): a loss of personal identity, associated with a lowering of inhibitions against behaving in socially undesirable ways and a decreased concern for social evaluation (either self-evaluation or evaluation of self by others). Possible influences on de-individuation include anonymity (provided by their role) and diffusion of responsibility (there were 12 of them).

Time for reflection ...

- The SPE itself has received a great deal of criticism regarding its *ethical status*.
- What kind of ethical issues do you think are raised by the SPE?

Savin (1973) argues that the benefits resulting from the experiment don't justify the distress, mistreatment, and degradation suffered by the prisoners: the end doesn't justify the means. However, Zimbardo (e.g. 1973) claims that the public outcry that the SPE caused was at least in part a result of its exposure of our ethical fragility: we're all much more easily manipulated by social situations – and much less morally 'robust' – than we'd like to believe.

Revisiting the SPE: The BBC Prison Study

The SPE seemed to show that human beings have an inherent tendency to act as the passive vehicles, indeed victims, of social structures and forces over which they have no control and which constrain their actions (Turner, 2006). However, this denies the capacity for human agency and choice. Bullies and tyrants come to be seen as victims who cannot be held accountable for their actions; in this way, psychological analysis easily ends up excusing the inexcusable (Haslam and Reicher, 2005).

Haslam and Reicher designed the BBC Prison Study (BPS) (conducted in 2001 and screened in 2002 as 'The Experiment') specifically in order to establish whether (i) oppression would be a product of blind conformity to role or else of active processes of social identification; and (ii) as well as being a basis for tyranny, social identification might also be a basis for *resistance*. (See Gross, 2012a, for a detailed summary of the BPS.)

The study challenged the received wisdom derived from the SPE. In particular, the guards didn't take on their roles uncritically and the prisoners didn't succumb passively to the guards' authority. Indeed, on day six of the study, the prisoners mounted a revolt that brought the guards' regime to a dramatic end; however, the study subsequently descended towards a tyranny similar to that of the SPE. Nevertheless, the BPS has challenged the conclusion derived from many classic studies in social psychology (including the SPE and Milgram's obedience studies: see below) that human beings' natural tendency to conform results inevitably in conflict, abuse, and tyranny. According to Haslam (2015), where these phenomena occur – and they're all too common – they don't result from zombie-like compliance, but from 'individuals' active identification and engagement with the groups of which they are part' (p. 457).

> Moreover, as much as these processes can lead us into the darkness, they can also take us into the light. Groups do not rob us of choice, they *give* us choices – not least because they are the principal means by which we can bring about social change.
>
> (Haslam, 2015, p. 457)

The power of social situations revisited: Milgram's obedience experiments

Milgram's obedience experiments have become the most famous in social psychology – if not the entire discipline of psychology (Reicher *et al.*, 2012). A brief account is provided in Box 8.3.

BOX 8.3 THE BASIC PROCEDURE USED IN MILGRAM'S OBEDIENCE EXPERIMENT

- Announcements were placed in local newspapers asking for people to participate in a study of memory and learning, to be held at Yale University; they were offered payment for an hour of their time.
- Upon arrival, the participants (initially all men) were introduced to the experimenter and Mr Wallace, another volunteer (both, in fact, actors and Milgram's accomplices).
- The experimenter explained that the study was in fact concerned with the effects of *punishment* on learning; this would take the form of the teacher delivering electric shock each time the learner made a mistake on a verbal learning task.
- The roles of teacher and learner were supposedly allocated randomly – but this was rigged so that the naive participant was always the teacher and Mr Wallace the learner.
- The teacher operated an authentic-looking shock generator (but which wasn't 'live'), with switches starting at 15 volts, and increasing in 15-volt increments up to 450 volts.
- Mr Wallace sat in an adjoining room (so couldn't be seen) and the teacher heard a series of pre-recorded responses to the increasing shock levels. (This basic procedure, the *remote-victim condition*, was used in the first of a large number of experiments, starting in 1961.)

The basic finding (from the initial, *remote-victim* experiment) was that every teacher continued giving shocks up to at least 300 volts (at which point Mr Wallace pounds loudly on the adjoining wall), with fully 62.5 per cent going all the way up to 450 volts. (After 315 volts, the pounding stopped and Mr Wallace gave no further answers.)

The real-world context of Milgram's research was the Holocaust. Specifically, he was testing one aspect of the Germans-are-different (GAD) hypothesis used by historians to explain the Nazis' systematic destruction of millions of Jews, Poles, and others during the 1930s and 1940s, namely: the Germans have a basic character defect, a readiness to obey authority without question regardless of the acts demanded by the authority figure. This readiness to obey provided Hitler with the co-operation he needed to put his evil plans into effect.

Based on this hypothesis, Milgram expected *very low* obedience rates (i.e. shocking up to 450 volts). The original experiment was, in fact, designed as a kind of pilot study, a 'dummy run' before conducting the research in Germany. In having to reject the GAD hypothesis, Milgram was forced to explore the situational determinants of what appeared to be a universal human tendency to obey authority figures: ordinary ('good') people, under certain conditions of authority, would be willing to inflict unexpectedly high levels of intolerable pain on an innocent, totally undeserving, protesting victim.

Time for reflection …

- How do you think you'd have acted if you'd been the 'teacher'?

Obedience research and the Holocaust: The banality of evil

Critics of Milgram have attacked the *ethics* of his experiments as much, if not more, than the explanations he offers of his findings. For example, Baumrind (1964) expressed concern for the welfare of his participants, questioning whether adequate measures were taken to protect them from the apparent stress and emotional conflict they experienced. In his defence, Milgram asks whether the criticism is based as much on the nature of the (unanticipated) findings as on the procedure itself. Aronson (1988) asks if we'd question the ethics if none of the participants had gone beyond 'moderate level' shocks (75–120 volts).

Could it be that underlying the criticisms is the shock and horror of the 'banality of evil' (the subtitle of Hannah Arendt's book on the Israeli trial of Adolf Eichmann, the Nazi war criminal (see Figure 8.1))? To believe that 'ordinary' people (like Milgram's American male participants) could do what Eichmann did is far less acceptable than believing that Eichmann was an inhuman monster – the

Figure 8.1 Eichmann on trial in Jerusalem. (Permission granted by Alamy.)

very personification of evil – or that experimental participants were exposed to immorally high levels of stress by an inhuman psychologist!

Time for reflection ...

- How valid – both practically and ethically – was Milgram's claim that there's a direct parallel between his experiments and the Holocaust?

Ross *et al.* (2010), in support of the banality of evil explanation, claim that most of the low-level Holocaust perpetrators were ordinary people who lived unexceptional lives before and after their infamous deeds, *not* self-selected psychopaths or sadists. However, there have always been critics of the 'banality of evil' view.

According to Lang (2014), when Milgram drew a direct parallel between the Holocaust and his obedience experiments (because the basic obedience process is essentially the same, regardless of context and situational details):

> He inadvertently deprived the Nazi genocide of its historical meaning and relegated perpetrator behaviour to a function of hierarchical social structures. The result, which continues to exert considerable influence both inside and outside ... social psychology, is an *ahistorical* explanation of perpetrator behaviour that eviscerates any forceful conception of *individual agency*, reduces political action to acts of submission, and finally calls into question the very idea of *personal responsibility*.
>
> (p. 665: emphasis added)

Similarly, Blass (2004) has criticised social psychology for glossing over the gratuitous brutality of the Holocaust; its preoccupation with Milgram's account diminishes the crucial role of its instigators and high-level planners.

The agentic state and moral responsibility

Relevant to Arendt's study of Eichmann is the recent publication (Kershner, 2016) of a previously unknown plea written by Eichmann to the Israeli Court. Having been convicted and sentenced to death, he pointed to the fact that he was a mere subordinate following orders – not issuing them! He described himself as a mere instrument in his leaders' hands, what Milgram called the *agentic state* (as opposed to the *autonomous state*, in which we see ourselves as in control of our actions and, thereby, *responsible*).

> The most far-reaching consequence of the agentic shift is that a man feels responsible *to* the authority directing him but feels no responsibility for the content of the actions that the authority prescribes.
>
> (Milgram, 1974; pp. 145–6)

In bureaucratic situations, such as the Holocaust, 'it is ethically easy to ignore responsibility when one is only an intermediate link in a chain of evil action but is far from the final consequence of the action' (Milgram, 1974, p. 11).

However, the obedience experiments provide no real evidence of any such agentic state: it doesn't tally with how participants actually behaved and it certainly cannot explain the differing obedience rates found in different experimental conditions (Reicher and Haslam, 2011). Similarly, Burger (2011) points out that few serious researchers talk about an agentic state these days; instead, they attribute participants' behaviour to situational variables embedded within the experimental setting, one of these being *diffused* or *missing responsibility* (see Box 8.4).

BOX 8.4 THE IMPORTANCE OF MORAL RESPONSIBILITY

- It was easy for Milgram's participants to *diffuse* (literally, 'spread') or *deny responsibility* for the consequences of their actions. If and when asked, the experimenter replied that *he* was responsible for any harm suffered by the learner (the question often prompted by Mr Wallace complaining that he had a heart condition, in the *voice feedback* experiment). So, at worst, participants could reason that they *shared* the responsibility with the experimenter; at best, and taking the experimenter at his word, they could deny it altogether.

- More generally, and an important and unintended consequence of the situationist explanation, the claim that good people perform bad deeds seems to soften the meaning of the harm those bad deeds bring about. For example, one implication is that these undesirable behaviours must be more common that we think: since most people aren't evil, most evil deeds must be carried out by ordinary people.

- Several social psychologists suggest that *any* attempt to understand a perpetrator's motives results in a more exonerating position (Miller, 2016), i.e. the behaviour is seen as 'less evil'.

- However, 'attempting to understand the situational and systemic contributions to any individual's behaviour *does not excuse the person or absolve him or her from responsibility* in engaging in immoral, illegal, or evil deeds' (Zimbardo, 2007a, p. xi; emphasis added).

- Finally:

  Auschwitz survivor Primo Levi warned against trying to understand the murderers 'because to understand is to justify'. Yet every murderer acted with free will and had no reason to fear punishment if he refused to commit murder. *No explanation can diminish the killer's terrible guilt.*

  (McMillan, 2014, p. viii; emphasis added)

Haslam and Reicher (2012) argue that 'It is time to reject the comforts of the obedience alibi. When people inflict harm to others, they *often do so wittingly and willingly*' (emphasis added). And again:

> To understand tyranny, we need to transcend the prevailing orthodoxy that this tyranny derives from something for which humans have a natural inclination, a 'Lucifer effect' to which they succumb thoughtlessly and helplessly (and for which, therefore, they cannot be held accountable.)
>
> (Haslam and Reicher, 2012)

The social psychology of genocide and mass atrocities

How useful is 'evil' in understanding genocide and mass atrocities?

According to Vollhardt and Campbell-Obaid (2016), 'Genocide and mass atrocities are commonly described as a particular evil, among the cruellest behaviours human beings engage in' (p. 159).

While much of the available social psychological research on genocide has focused on the Holocaust, other major examples include Darfur, Rwanda, and the Armenian genocide by the Turks (1915–17).

However, historical and social psychological scholarship reveals that the full picture of genocide and mass atrocities (GMA) is often more complicated than the popular understanding suggests. For example, as we noted when describing the 'GAD' hypothesis above, no individual, however evil, can commit GMA on his/her own. On the other side of the GMA coin, there are always also heroic rescuers among the perpetrator group; there is increasing recognition of resistance groups in the Holocaust and other cases of GMA (e.g. Haslam and Reicher, 2012). Conversely, some members of the victim group collaborate in order to ensure their survival (e.g. Frankl, 1946/2004).

So, the distinction between 'good' and 'evil' isn't always clear-cut; indeed, 'this very process of labelling people and groups as good and evil in itself contributes to support for mass atrocities and killing' (Vollhardt and Campbell-Obaid, 2016, p. 160). How might this happen? (See Box 8.5.)

BOX 8.5 SOME SOCIAL PSYCHOLOGICAL CONSEQUENCES OF USING THE TERM 'EVIL'

- People want to understand genocide as the product of 'purely evil people' in order to distance themselves from the possibility of committing such evil actions (Waller, 2001).
- Similarly, Baumeister (1997) argues that the 'myth of pure evil' is always a false image that is imposed or projected onto the perpetrator in order to distance ourselves from the possibility of evil. This helps us to see good and evil as oppositional forces and ourselves on the side of good; this, in turn, legitimises violence as a means of removing the evil ('redemptive violence': Wink, 1992).
- Evil individuals are perceived as 'monsters', something not quite human and also more threatening and powerful. This is also a form of ego defence: monsters are few in number and so we're unlikely to encounter them directly ourselves. Also, they may be more powerful than us – but they're also less rational and intelligent!
- Vollhardt and Campbell-Obaid (2016) quote from Barack Obama's Nobel Peace Prize acceptance speech: 'Evil exists in the world. A nonviolent movement could not have halted Hitler's armies. Negotiations cannot convince Al Qaeda's leaders to lay down their arms'. 'Evil' has also been used when discussing the Islamic State of Iraq and Syria (ISIS) and the Islamic State of Iraq and the Levant (ISIL).
- The belief that some people are 'just evil' predicted stronger support for violent intergroup positions, such as the death penalty for Muslim shooters in the US, continued possession of nuclear weapons, the use of enhanced interrogation techniques at Guantanamo Bay (Campbell and Vollhardt, 2014) and torture (Webster and Saucier, 2013), and criminal rehabilitation (Miller, 2016).

The role of dehumanisation in GMA

According to Hirsch (1995), many of the greatest crimes against humanity are committed in the name of obedience. Genocide tends to occur under conditions created by three social processes:

1 *Authorisation* relates to the agentic state, i.e. obeying orders because of where they come from.
2 *Routinisation* refers to massacre becoming a matter of routine, a mechanical and highly programmed operation.

3   *Dehumanisation* involves reducing victims to something less than human, allowing the perpetrators to suspend their usual moral prohibition on killing. Examples include the Nazis likening Jews to lice and rats, and Tutsis in Rwanda being branded as cockroaches. This 'reduction' of people to non-human animals (Jews weren't just seen as *like* vermin – they *were* vermin) facilitates violence towards these out-groups as a means of eliminating them. Most people are less morally concerned about doing harm to such creatures than to other human beings: they're not just less-than-human, they're also a *threat*.

In the above examples, language is being used as a weapon to define a group that is to become a potential target of violence and other forms of harm. Other language-based weapons include *dehumanising stereotypes* (distinct from the 'vermin' example: see Chapter 5) and *ideologies* (general belief systems that promote dehumanising perceptions of out-groups). Outside the context of GMA, groups stereotyped as low in both warmth and competence (such as drug addicts, prostitutes, and the homeless) are particularly likely to be dehumanised; they fail to elicit activation of brain regions typically associated with perceiving people (including the medial prefrontal cortex) (Harris and Fiske, 2006: see Chapter 3).

Modern forms of evil: terrorism

According to Moghaddam *et al.* (2016), 'There is widespread agreement that terrorism is evil, but little agreement as to why it has increased in the 21st century' (p. 415).

> **Time for reflection …**
>
> - Do you agree with Moghaddam?
> - Why do you think terrorism has increased this century?

It's clear that *globalisation* has played a crucial role:

> 21st – century globalization is, in important ways, new and central to the macro, collective processes shaping terrorism … [these] and not the personality of individuals are the major factor leading to the rise of terrorism.
> (Moghaddam *et al.*, 2016, p. 415)

Following the 9/11 terrorist attacks in the US (2001), information about terrorist individuals and networks rapidly increased; however, integrating and interpreting this information proved more challenging. One major attempt to plug this theoretical hole is Moghaddam's (2005) *staircase model*, which provides guidelines for adapting counter-terrorist measures to match the level of the metaphorical staircase the radicalised individual has reached.

At each level, the fundamentally important feature of the situation is how people *perceive* the building, spaces, and doors on each floor; as individuals climb, choices become fewer and fewer, and obedience and conformity increase, until destruction of life remains the only possible outcome. The model is described in Box 8.6.

BOX 8.6 THE STAIRCASE MODEL OF TERRORISM (MOGHADDAM, 2005)

- On the *ground floor*, perceptions of fairness and identity aspirations – and threats to identity – are key.
- On the *first floor*, individuals seek ways to get ahead and achieve social mobility. When this is blocked, some climb to the *second floor*, where frustration is intensified and aggression channelled towards particular targets.
- Some individuals keep climbing: on the *third floor* they experience a shift in moral thinking, adopting a moral code according to which the ends justify the means: terrorist violence is now justifiable.
- On the *fourth floor*, categorical thinking is accentuated, as is individuals' sense of legitimacy. Finally
- On the *fifth floor*, individuals take action to sidestep inhibitory mechanisms that, in most human beings, prevent killing fellow human beings.
- Longer-term policies are needed to tackle terrorism on the first four floors, while rapid, short-term intervention is required to deal with individuals who have reached the fifth floor.

At each floor, the context (including extremist narratives that are aggressively broadcast across the globe) is the most powerful factor shaping behaviour. In this sense, the staircase model gives priority to *collective* as opposed to individual processes; however, some individuals are more likely than others to climb the staircase. While *descent* is possible, the higher the individual has climbed, the more difficult it becomes for him or her to reintegrate into mainstream society: de-radicalisation *doesn't* involve retracing the same steps down the staircase (Moghaddam, 2009).

Terrorism and the Internet

As Moghaddam *et al.* (2016) point out, 'contemporary globalization is driven primarily by powerful technological and economic factors' (p. 417). Central to the technological side of this equation is the Internet; Amichai-Hamburger (2017) identifies what he calls the 'Magnificent Seven' factors which collectively explain the Internet's power to create a unique psychological space. These are listed in Box 8.7.

BOX 8.7 THE 'MAGNIFICENT SEVEN' FEATURES OF THE INTERNET (AMICHAI-HAMBURGER, 2017)

1 Feeling of anonymity.
2 Control over level of physical exposure.
3 High control over communications (between ourselves and our social contacts and the content of the messages we'd like to make known).
4 Ease of locating like-minded people.
5 Accessibility and availability at all times and places.
6 Feeling of equality.
7 Fun of web-surfing.

Regarding anonymity and control over physical exposure, perpetrators believe that no one will be able to identify them no matter what they do, and so they'll go unpunished; at the same time, the victim is unlikely to have any countermeasures available. Perpetrators may operate initially within a non-violent community or may exist as an organised community of aggressors who seek out particular victim groups (based on race, sexual orientation, religion, etc.) Even if a violent site is removed (such as a race–hate group), the perpetrators can always find another server somewhere in the world where they can upload the same offensive content (Amichai–Hamburger, 2017).

Perpetrators' high degree of control over their communications makes them feel empowered, while the victim feels helpless and vulnerable. The sense of control derives partly from the *remote* nature of their aggression (i.e. not face-to-face); this, combined with their anonymity, removes inhibitions against aggression, which may become increasingly extreme (Haslam *et al.*, 2008). Victims may be *dehumanised* (see above). Increasingly extreme behaviour may also occur as a means of strengthening the sense of belonging and loyalty to the online group.

The Internet can be thought of as an endless series of constantly active violent environments. For people with aggressive tendencies, it provides endless opportunities for expressing them and learning new forms of violence.

Frustrated, marginalised individuals can find themselves metaphorically rubbing shoulders with others whom they'd never approach offline. Chatrooms and forums are 'completely hate-centred environments wrapped in fun, interactive ribbons; for example, a Nazi-friendly site (www.americannaziparty.com) offers computer games whose goal is to kill as many Jews as possible!' (Amichai–Hamburger, 2017, p. 74).

Does the Internet turn good people bad?

Amichai-Hamburger's answer is 'no'. Rather, it frees people from social restraints, which can sometimes result in the unleashing of previously suppressed belligerent tendencies. The Internet allows aggressors to ignore social norms and escape their usual identities ('discard their masks').

> In that sense, it seems that the Internet has created paradise on earth for violent people. In this paradise, there are any number of ways to express violent tendencies: paedophilia, invasion of privacy, information theft, racial and religious incitement, intellectual property violation, and terrorism.
>
> (Amichai-Hamburger, 2017, pp. 75–6)

The Internet doesn't change people's nature but provides an environment in which those with strong violent tendencies will behave in ways that are most natural to them. Perhaps the closest that the Internet comes to turning 'good' people 'bad' is that it may actually serve as a school for modelling violence to non-aggressive people (i.e. showing *how to be violent*). While the more naturally aggressive are more likely to seek out the violent aspects of the Internet, naive, vulnerable, previously non-aggressive individuals may also fall prey to its spell of violence.

Prosocial behaviour: the 'good' side of human nature

So far in this chapter, the focus has been very much on how ordinary, 'good', 'moral', law-abiding people can be influenced to behave in antisocial, immoral, 'bad' ways. While Hitler, Stalin, Pol Pot, and a few select others are stand-out examples of people whom we tend to see as 'evil through-and-through', in the case of suicide bombers and other terrorists, we're still likely to judge them as evil based on their evil acts. Following this logic, those who act in prosocial ways are judged to be 'good' people. But is this necessarily always the case?

According to Schroeder *et al.* (1995), *prosocial behaviour* includes behaviour intended to benefit others, such as helping, comforting, sharing, cooperating, reassuring, defending, showing concern, and donating to charity. (We can add *volunteerism* and *heroism*: see below.) It follows that acts that *unintentionally* (i.e. fortuitously) benefit others *don't* count as prosocial, while unsuccessful attempts at intentionally benefiting others *do*.

Starting in the 1960s, social psychologists began to study prosocial behaviour largely in the form of helping, specifically, *bystander intervention* (e.g. Darley and Latané, 1968; Piliavin *et al.*, 1969). The focus of this early research was on 'emergency situations', staged situations in which strangers, often in public places, need others to intervene by coming to their assistance (for example, because they'd collapsed, or were bleeding, or were having an epileptic seizure: see Gross, 2015).

Explaining prosocial behaviour

Early explanations of *bystander apathy* – the tendency for people *not* to go to the aid of someone in need – include the *decision model* (DM) (Latané and Darley, 1970) and the *arousal–cost–reward* (ACR) *model* (e.g. Piliavin *et al.*, 1981).

According to the DM, before someone helps another, he/she must go through a logical sequence of steps: (i) notice that something is wrong; (ii) define it as a situation requiring help (an 'emergency'); (iii) decide whether to take personal responsibility; (iv) decide what kind of help to give; and (v) implement the decision to intervene. A negative response at any one step means that *that* bystander won't intervene.

The ACR represents a kind of 'fine-tuning' of the DM, identifying a number of critical situational and bystander variables which can help predict how likely it is that intervention will take place under any particular set of circumstances. Research has concentrated on the *cost–reward analysis:* before we go to someone's aid, we will have weighed up all the costs *and* rewards of helping *and* of not–helping. Based on this cost–reward analysis, we reach a decision that produces the best outcome – *for ourselves.*

Universal egoism versus empathy–altruism

> **Time for reflection …**
>
> * Do you believe it's possible to be truly altruistic (i.e. to do something aimed primarily at benefiting *someone else*)?

Underlying the ACR – and the cost–reward analysis in particular – is an *economic* view of human behaviour: people are motivated to maximise rewards and minimise costs (Dovidio *et al.*, 1991). (This echoes Hobbes' *hedonistic* philosophy: Chapter 2.) In turn, this economic view is one form of *universal egoism:* everything we do, no matter how noble and beneficial to others, is really directed towards the ultimate goal of *self-benefit.*

Another form of universal egoism relates to the *arousal* component of the ACR model. According to the *negative state relief* model (Cialdini *et al.*, 1987), harming another person, or witnessing another person being harmed, can induce negative feelings (such as discomfort, anxiety, and other *self-oriented* emotions); this motivates the perpetrator or witness to reduce these feelings. Through socialisation and life experience, we learn that this can be achieved through the good feelings derived from helping, making *us* feel better: this is the *universal egoism* account of helping behaviour.

Those who advocate the *empathy–altruism hypothesis* (EAH) (such as Batson, 1991; Batson *et al.*, 2016) don't deny that much of our behaviour (including helping others) is egoistic, but under certain circumstances, we're capable of a qualitatively different form of motivation: our ultimate goal is to *benefit others*. *Empathic emotions* (such as sympathy, compassion, and tenderness) give rise to *empathic concern*, an other-orientated emotion elicited by, and compatible with, the perceived welfare of someone in need. When we're motivated to help another out of empathic concern, we're demonstrating *altruism, 'a motivational state with the ultimate goal of increasing another's welfare'* (Batson *et al.*, 2016, p. 444).

> Increasing the welfare of a person in need by providing help can either be an *ultimate goal* (altruistic motivation) or an *instrumental means* to benefit oneself (egoistic motivation).
>
> > (Batson *et al.*, 2016, p. 444; emphasis added)

Volunteerism

Themes of benevolence and self-sacrifice can be found within the sacred texts of most of the world's religions, in philosophy, and in stories passed down in many cultures (Dovidio *et al.*, 2006) (see Chapter 2). Perhaps most famous in Western culture is the Christian parable of the Good Samaritan (Luke, 10: 29–37).

Volunteerism is an active, organised form of helping that involves giving (often considerable amounts of) one's time and energy, on an ongoing basis, to work on behalf of others and their communities, by engaging in a wide range of activities (from serving food at a homeless shelter to cleaning up the local environment) (Snyder *et al.*, 2016).

Consistent with the earlier distinction between self-oriented and empathic emotions, people's motives for volunteering can be more, or less, altruistic. For example, one of the most commonly identified motives is the expression of personal *values*, including *humanitarian concern for others* and other guiding convictions based on religious and spiritual values. However, more *self-orientated* motives include making new friends, an opportunity to use one's skills and knowledge, defending against feelings of guilt (about being better off than others), and enhancing self-esteem (Snyder *et al.*, 2016).

These different kinds of motives *aren't* mutually exclusive: if volunteers' primary, conscious focus is on helping others, then any benefits they derive from the activity merely serve to ensure they keep on giving. However, if a volunteer is driven primarily by egoistic needs, these are likely to interfere with, and reduce the effectiveness of, their help as far as the recipients are concerned.

Summary and conclusions: heroism

Just as when we think of 'evil' certain historical – or fictional – figures come to mind, so when we think of the ultimate in good behaviour we think of heroes. However, this may be to confound 'hero' and 'acts of heroism'.

Heroism and altruism

> **Time for reflection ...**
>
> • What do you understand by 'heroism'?
> • Are there different kinds of heroism (associated with gender, for example)?

Spontaneous acts of selfless heroism receive considerable media attention; they often involve making split-second decisions and putting the hero's own life in danger in trying to save another's. Such heroic deeds have been described as illustrating *biological* (or *evolutionary*) *altruism,* something we have in common with other species: in extreme situations, such as natural disasters or terrorist attacks, people often display *impulsive, reflexive helping*.

However, unlike other species, humans are also capable of *psychological* (or *vernacular*) *altruism* (Sober, 1992); the latter is what most of the social psychological research has been concerned with.

Although altruism doesn't tell the whole story of heroism (Franco *et al.*, 2011), it's an important component, with some describing heroism as an *extreme extension* of altruism (Monin *et al.*, 2008; Oliner and Oliner, 1988; Staub, 1991). Feigin *et al.* (2014) distinguish between *pseudo-altruism* (egoism in disguise) and *autonomous altruism* (true altruism). Just as with other examples of prosocial behaviour, heroic acts might sometimes appear more altruistic than they really are: self-oriented emotions, and (unconscious) motives relating to the 'rewards' of being a hero, as well as social expectations regarding how we should act in certain types of emergency situation, might limit our choices. However, this doesn't mean that biological altruists aren't celebrated as heroes.

Interestingly, biological altruism is stereotypically associated more with men (what Eagly, 1987, calls *agentic helping*). But are women actually *more* likely to act heroically in situations that typically fall within everyday activity domains involving mainly women (what Eagly calls *communal helping*, which doesn't involve obvious risk to the helper in an emergency situation)? Are these heroines hidden from our view – or simply uncelebrated? (Polster, 2014). According to Becker and Eagly (2004), actual acts of heroism, such as heroic rescue, are at least as frequently carried out by women as by men. Women more typically create and maintain social networks, which were key to saving the lives of thousands of Jewish children from certain death by helping them escape from the Warsaw Ghetto (Mayer, 2011).

Everyday heroism

Perhaps women's heroism doesn't make the headlines precisely because it is commonplace (mundane). Indeed, heroism is a fundamental aspect of human existence that *anyone* can display (Franco and Zimbardo, 2016). The idea of the "banality" of heroism (Franco and Zimbardo, 2007) as a counteracting force to Hannah Arendt's (1964) 'banality of evil' has important, far-reaching implications for reducing social injustice, for conflict resolution, and for accountability within social systems (Johnson and Friedman, 2014).

In contrast with the impulsive nature of biological altruism (what Boyd and Zimbardo, 2008, call *physical risk* heroes), *social risk* heroes generally engage in activities (such as whistle-blowing) that unfold over a period of time. This gives them the opportunity to consider the possible consequences and the sacrifices that might face them (such as loss of career), as well as the possible consequences of their *failure* to act; indeed, some Christians who helped Jews during the Holocaust reported that they imagined the guilt they'd experience in the future had they not done so (Zimbardo and Boyd, 2008).

The social construction of heroism

While heroic *actions* are fundamentally personal and internal, how they're interpreted, and labelling someone a hero, are fundamentally *socio-cultural* processes (Franco *et al.*, 2011):

> The mantle of heroism is rarely something that heroic actors assume for themselves … the title *hero* is … bestowed in a social context by eye witnesses, colleagues, agencies, governments … The relative merits of an act, the intent of the actor, and the outcomes … are all used by the social structures around the actor to make a determination as to whether the act met the criteria for heroism.
>
> (Franco and Zimbardo, 2016, p. 508)

Once the title has been bestowed, there's the danger, through the *halo effect* (Asch, 1946) of 'hero worship'. For example, there's a tendency to turning firefighters into 'mythic creatures – virtuous, courageous, modern-day messiahs who offer up their bodies as living sacrifices for us' (Desmond, 2008a, p. 58). Desmond claims that by doing this, we 'flatten their humanity' through a process of *dehumanisation*: while the dehumanisation involved in genocide strips people of all virtue (see above), in this case, firefighters are being cleansed of all *sin*.

This is wrong – morally and psychologically – because, as human beings, we're 'naturally sinful'; to be sin-free is as extreme a view as it is to view someone as thoroughly evil. While we're all *capable* of both evil acts and heroic deeds, the fact that most of us aren't described in either of these two ways implies that these two possibilities 'cancel each other out'. We rarely face extreme situations which 'demand' evil or heroism. If we acknowledge everyday heroism as a fundamental feature of human existence, then, for the sake of consistency, we must also acknowledge 'everyday evil' (sins of both omission and commission) that we're all allowed to make; we're only human (see Chapter 1).

According to Zimbardo (2007):

> Heroism focuses on what is right with human nature. We care about heroic stories because they serve as powerful reminders that people are capable of resisting evil, of not giving into temptations, of rising above mediocrity, and of heeding the call to action and to service when others fail to act.
>
> (p. 461)

> Heroes represent the ideal in human nature to which each of us can aspire.
>
> (Franco and Zimbardo, 2016, p. 516)

> We are all primed to become everyday heroes. It will require refashioning our old ideas of good and evil. It will require adopting the more nuanced view that situations and psychology and personality intersect in a complex dance over which we ultimately have control, but which, if we are caught unawares, can instead come to control us.
>
> (Zimbardo, 2018, p. 4)

Suggested further reading

Hirsch, H. (1995) *Genocide and the Politics of Memory*. Chapel Hill, NC: University of North Carolina Press.

Milgram, S. (1974) *Obedience to Authority*. New York: Harper Torchbooks.

Miller, A.G. (ed.) (2012) *The Social Psychology of Good and Evil*. New York: The Guilford Press.

Zimbardo, P. (2016) *The Lucifer Effect: How Good People Turn Evil*. London: Rider.

9   Culture and human nature

Key questions

- What do we mean by 'culture'?
- Is culture uniquely human? Is it a *human universal*?
- What claims have been made for culture in non-humans?
- Is *social learning* (SL) the key process involved in culture?
- How do we distinguish between SL and '*stimulus enhancement*'?
- How does this distinction relate to that between high and low fidelity SL?
- How does tool-making illustrate *cumulative cultural evolution* (CCE)?
- How might tool-making have influenced brain evolution?
- How does *creative collaboration* influence the evolution and maintenance of culture?
- What's special about human co-operation?
- Is it possible for human beings to exist outside of culture? Is it our natural habitat?

Culture – both its nature and its relationship to other contenders for what it is that makes us human – has been a theme running throughout this book. Dunbar (2007), along with many others, has claimed that it is in humans' capacity for culture, to live in a world constructed by ideas, that we really differ from the other apes. This capacity for culture, in turn, is one manifestation of our status as symbolic creatures, with language being the ultimate symbolic activity (Tattersall, 2007).

Language enables us to stand back from the real world and ask if it could have been otherwise than it is. Literature and science, both fundamental features of (Western) culture, are prominent demonstrations of mental time travel (MTT) and illustrate the human ability to imagine different worlds; religion is another example. As a cultural institution, religion may represent a major component of cultural worldviews, which provide beliefs about the nature of reality that function to reduce death-related anxiety (the mortality salience/MS hypothesis: see Chapter 7).

According to Baron-Cohen (2006), second-order (and other meta-) representations (i.e. thinking about possible, hypothetical, as opposed to actual, states of affairs) equip us with the ability to imagine and are essential for mind-reading or theory of mind (ToM) (see Chapters 3 and 5). In turn, ToM is essential for both face-to-face social interaction and, more broadly, the development and maintenance of culture.

Also in Chapter 5 we noted that the making and use of tools were once taken to be defining features of human behaviour. Oakley (1957) claimed that tool-making was the chief biological characteristic of human beings that drove the evolution of our powers of mental and bodily co-ordination. He argued that the key to toolmaking was the uniquely human ability to imagine different kinds of tools as a kind of mental template to be reproduced. As important as this imagining may be, Stout (2016) believes that knowing what you want to make is the 'easy' part: the difficulty lies in actually making it. (Toolmaking as a feature of culture is discussed further below.)

What do we mean by 'culture'?

Time for reflection ...

- What do you understand by the term 'culture'?
- Should we distinguish between narrow definitions – that would automatically exclude the possibility of non-human culture – and broader, more inclusive definitions – that would allow for it?

One early definition of culture as 'the human-made part of the environment' (Herskovits, 1955) is narrow and exclusive; while it was meant to contrast human beings' contribution to the environment with nature's, it implies that non-humans have no culture. The 'human-made' part can be subdivided into:

1 *Objective* aspects (such as tools, roads, and radio stations).
2 *Subjective* aspects (such as categorisations, associations, norms, roles, and values). Value systems have a significant impact on various other aspects of culture, including child-rearing techniques, patterns of socialisation, identity development, kinship networks, work and leisure, and religious beliefs and practices (Laungani, 2007).

While there's no evidence of any non-humans building roads or radio stations, that may (simply) reflect the fact that they don't *need* them: in turn, this may suggest that there's only a quantitative difference between human and non-human culture. Regarding subjective aspects, most of the examples given above are, without question, uniquely human behaviours (many of which are based, directly or indirectly, on language or other symbolic abilities); however, kinship networks are common to all social animals, human and non-human.

What these 'exceptions to the rule' suggest is that, rather than taking the possession of culture as an absolute (a species either has it or it doesn't), we need to specify which aspect(s) of culture we're interested in. Some, like religion, are indisputably uniquely human, while others, such as imitation and other forms of social learning (central to cultural transmission) are claimed to exist in chimpanzees and orang-utans as well as humans. These are all discussed in detail below.

Is culture unique to humans?

For Triandis (1994), culture is an unambiguously human characteristic: culture is to society what memory is to individuals (i.e. it comprises traditions that tell 'what has worked' in the past). While culture is made by humans, it also helps to 'make' them: humans have an interactive relationship with culture (Moghaddam *et al.*, 1993).

Rather dismissively, Pagel (2012) claims that not having culture (as humans know it) is why 'chimpanzees sit in the forest as they have for millions of years cracking the same old nuts with the same old stones' (p. 4). However, there are many examples of animal behaviour cited as demonstrating culture: (i) New Zealand chaffinches learn their songs from parents and thereby produce a surprising range of local dialects; (ii) some chimp troops have local traditions in styles of tools for termite fishing or stones for nut-cracking; and perhaps most famously, (iii) Japanese macaques potato-washing (see Box 9.1).

BOX 9.1 JAPANESE MACAQUE SWEET POTATO WASHING (KAWAI, 1965; KAWAMURA, 1959): CULTURE OR TRADITION?

- In 1953, an 18-month-old, female macaque (Imo) began to take sand-covered pieces of sweet potato (given to her and the rest of the Koshima troop by researchers) first to a stream, then to the ocean, and to wash the sand off the potato pieces before eating them. Most Japanese macaques brush sand off with their hands.
- About three months after this first happened, Imo's mother and two of her playmates (and then their mothers) began to do the same thing.
- During the next two years, seven other youngsters also began to wash their potatoes, and within three years of Imo's first potato washing, 40 per cent of the troop was doing it.
- By 1958, 14 of 15 juveniles and two of 11 adults in the Koshima troop had started washing potatoes (Itani and Nishimura, 1973; Nishida, 1987).

This spread of potato-washing behaviour is often explained in terms of naive monkeys observing Imo and others and then imitating them: sweet potato washing is cultural, so it's claimed (Galef, 1992).

Consistent with this interpretation is the fact that it was Imo's close associates who learned the behaviour first, and their associates directly after that. Also, it's intuitively improbable that so many monkeys could learn the behaviour independently of each other (Galef, 1992). However, many years later this was exactly what was claimed: each monkey acquired sweet potato-washing *on its own* without assistance from any other monkey. De Waal (2016) rejects this counter-explanation: the learning nicely tracked the network of social relationships and kinship ties.

However, it seems that sweet potato-washing is less unusual than originally thought; this implies that Imo wasn't the creative 'genius' that has been suggested by some. Also, in captivity, individuals of other monkey species learn quite quickly on their own to wash their food when presented with sandy foods and bowls of water (Visalberghi and Fragaszy, 1990).

Is social learning the key process involved in culture?

If potato-washing was 'discovered' independently by different monkeys among Imo's relatives and friends, then this, of course, detracts from the argument that they possess culture. Learning through and from fellow monkeys, chimps, or humans (i.e. *social learning* (SL), with *imitation* at its core) would seem to be at least a *necessary* or *minimal* requirement of calling something 'culture'.

According to Galef (1992), one sign of SL should be relatively rapid spread, but in fact the spread was 'painfully slow': the average time for acquisition by all the troop members that learned it was two years. Also, if imitation was the mechanism of transmission, we'd expect an increased rate as more demonstrators/models become available over time – but this didn't happen. The slow rate is more consistent with *individual*, rather than *imitative* learning (Galef, 1992; Tomasello, 1999).

What do we mean by 'imitation'?

According to De Waal (2016), resistance to examples like potato-washing rested on a much narrower definition of 'imitation' than what seemed to be involved: 'If it could be shown that human culture relies on distinct [learning] mechanisms, so the thinking went, we might be able to claim culture for ourselves' (p. 151).

True imitation requires that the individual *intentionally copies* another's specific technique to achieve a specific goal (Thorndike, 1898; Tomasello and Call, 1997): merely *duplicating* behaviour, such as one songbird learning another's song, wasn't enough anymore – it had to be done with insight and comprehension. While imitation is common in many species according to the old definition, true imitation is very rare.

According to De Waal, 'For culture to arise in a species, all that matters is that its members pick up habits from *one another*' (p. 152). He cites a decade-long research programme (Whiten *et al.* (2005); Horner *et al.* (2006); Bonnie *et al.* (2006); Horner & De Waal (2009)), which found that when given a chance to watch one another, chimps display incredible talents for imitation: they 'truly do ape, allowing behaviour to be faithfully transmitted within the group' (p. 154). Indeed, chimps turn out to be *conformists* (De Waal, 2016). De Waal cites similar findings among monkeys, dogs, corvids, parrots, and dolphins.

Social learning versus stimulus enhancement

Unlike true SL, learning from *social enhancement* (SE) doesn't seem to translate into new or purposeful behaviours that faithfully copy or pick up where others have left off (Pagel, 2012). Rather, it just makes use of old – or even hard-wired – behaviours already in animals' repertoires (even if sometimes in a slightly new context). So, for example, blue tits pecking at milk bottle tops might be more a case of SE than of SL.

> **Time for reflection …**
>
> - How might we choose between SL and SE?
> - What would we expect to happen to a particular behaviour over long periods of time?

Only with true SL would the behaviour become more refined and sophisticated; without it, each new generation will have to rely on trial-and-error, catalysed only by a little push of SE, to discover for themselves how to perform some action or tool use. For example, although chimp groups in different parts of the forest have about 30 different cultural traditions regarding ant/termite fishing or using stones to crack nuts, there's no evidence that they – or any other species – get better at these tasks. Instead, being surrounded by other chimps that use the tools this way seems to make it more likely that a naïve one will pick up a stick and poke or prod things with it – what they do anyway. Then, just by chance, this might result in acquiring a few termites and this reward seems to keep the behaviour going.

What this means for most species is that any new innovations or improvements seem limited almost entirely to what an individual can produce on its own: they don't seem to recognise and then acquire them from others the way we do:

> Lacking social learning, there is no real *cultural ratchet* that leads to improvement over time, no shared reservoir of accumulated ideas, skills, and technologies … were we to go away for a million years, upon our return the chimpanzees would probably still be using the same sorts of tools to fish termites from the ground.
>
> (Pagel, 2012, p. 41; emphasis added)

The crucial reason for this seems to be their lack of ToM (see Chapter 3).

The distinction between SL and SE corresponds to that between *high* and *low fidelity SL*, respectively. According to Boyd (2018a), while social cues make it more likely that certain behaviours will be learned (such as nut-cracking amongst chimps), in every case individuals are capable of learning them *on their own* (i.e. low-fidelity SL). By contrast, *cumulative cultural evolution* (CCE) is highly sensitive to the accuracy of SL. The ability to learn by observation (*true imitation* or high-fidelity SL) is essential for CCE and this is what humans are uniquely capable of (Boyd and Richerson, 1996).

CCE and tool-making

CCE is illustrated by the evolution of *tool-making* amongst early *Homo sapiens*. As shown in Figure 9.1., the Stone Age (the prehistoric period which ended somewhere between 8,700 and 2000 BCE with the advent of metal tools, etc.) can be divided into three major sub-periods: the Palaeolithic (PSA), Mesolithic

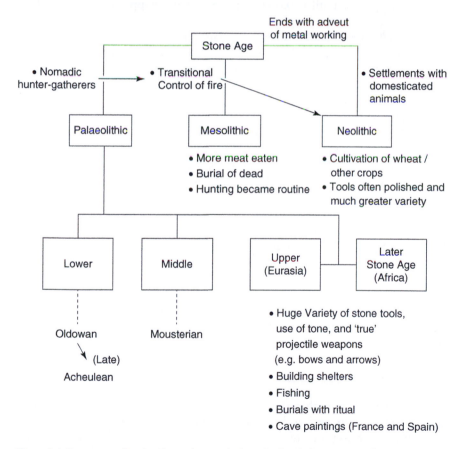

Figure 9.1 Summary of major Stone Age periods and related changes in tool technology.

(MSA), and the Neolithic (NSA). Each sub-period is characterised by different styles or ways of making stone tools and differences in broader lifestyles.

Figure 9.1 shows that the Palaeolithic can be sub-divided into *Lower, Middle,* and *Upper* (in Eurasia) or *Late Stone Age* (in Africa), corresponding to changes in types of stone tools 'technology' (see Box 9.2).

BOX 9.2 CHANGES IN LOWER AND MIDDLE STONE AGE TOOL TECHNOLOGY

- Crude stone (pebble) tools begin to appear around 2.5 million years ago and are referred to as *Oldowan* (first found in the Olduvai Gorge in Tanzania in the 1950s). They were found only in Africa and continued to be made for hundreds of thousands of years.
- *Acheulean* tools (from St. Acheul, France) were not confined to Africa. They were first found in Africa about 1.7 million years ago, and in Europe not until 600,000 years ago (then disappeared by 250,000 years ago).
- The characteristic Acheulean 'hand axe' was pointed/teardrop-shaped, flaked on both sides ('bifaces') and were much more refined than the Oldowan tools (but still large and chunky). Some were quite beautifully symmetrical. However, there was extreme conservatism in tool-making throughout this period, with very little invention or change.
- In the Middle Stone Age, similar *Mousterian* tools (originally found in the Le Mousterian Neanderthal site, SW France, and dating from about 250,000 years ago) were found in North Africa, Europe, and Western Asia. Tools seems to have been made by *Homo heidelbergensis* as well as by its (probable) daughter species, Neanderthal and *Homo sapiens*.
- Mousterian tools differ from Acheulean in that bifaces disappear; they're now often made from stones that have first been shaped into a tool blank ('prepared core') (although this was also used in Acheulean tools). There was also much more variation in both the finished tools and methods used to make them.
- Other Mousterian changes included collection of reddish, iron-rich rocks (perhaps as pigment); the first hearths appear, there was control of fire, more meat was being eaten, and humans started to bury the dead. Hunting, not just scavenging, became routine.

(Based on Roberts, 2009; Stout, 2016)

In the Upper Palaeolithic (Eurasia)/Later Stone Age (Africa) (dating from about 40,000 years ago), a huge and varied range of stone tools emerged; bone was also being used regularly. People were using 'true' projectile weapons (spear-throwers with darts or bow and arrows, as distinct from hand-cast spears), and building shelters, fishing, and burying the dead with a degree of

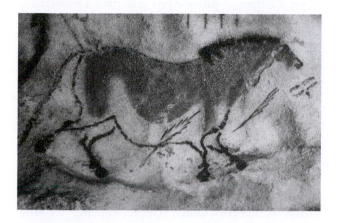

Figure 9.2 Horse (and arrows) detail of rock painting from ceiling of corridor, Lascaux Cave, Dordogne, France. (Permission granted by Mary Evans Library.)

ritual not seen before. This is also when the magnificent cave paintings found in France and Spain were made (see Figure 9.2).

What this brief account illustrates is precisely what distinguishes human from non-human tool manufacture: only in the former is there an evolution from the basic to the more advanced and sophisticated (a *history*).

Tool-making and evolution of the brain

According to Stout (2016), teaching and learning increasingly complex tool-making 'may even have posed a formidable enough challenge to our human ancestors that it spurred evolution of human language' (p. 31). In fact, many neuroscientists now believe that linguistic and manual skills rely on some of the *same* brain structures.

Stout has been conducting research over several years that involves trying to emulate the skills of Palaeolithic tool-makers. Participants are trained to make either Oldowan or Late Acheulean tools while their brains are scanned. During the Lower Palaeolithic period, hominin brains almost tripled in size: might this expansion in brain size have resulted from new demands placed on the brain by the development of these technologies?

Stout's research showed that making even the simplest stone tools (through *knapping* – the shaping of flint) requires not only precise control but carefully reasoned planning. Some of the same brain regions (such as visuomotor areas) are involved in both Oldowan and Acheulean knapping. However, Acheulean knapping also involves regions not involved in the former, including a specific region of the prefrontal cortex (PFC) called the *right inferior frontal gyrus;* this has been linked to the cognitive control needed to switch between different tasks and to suppress inappropriate responses (see Chapter 3). Stout also demonstrated – on a small scale – that practice in knapping actually enhanced neural re-wiring in this region: the more someone practiced, the greater the changes.

Brain changes ('plasticity': see Chapter 3) provide raw material for evolutionary change (*phenotypic accommodation*):

> Plasticity allows species the flexibility to try out new behaviours – to "push the envelope" of their current adaptation … toolmaking *could* actually have driven brain change through known evolutionary mechanisms [natural selection].
>
> (Stout, 2016, p. 34)

So, Palaeolithic tool-making 'helped to shape the modern mind' (Stout, p. 35).

However, knapping is extremely tedious and time-consuming; it requires (amongst other things) motivation in addition to the right kind of brain. One source of external motivation is a teacher; many researchers consider teaching to be the defining feature of human culture; 'faithful copying' (or true imitation) is the other side of this coin. It has also been shown that when teaching a skill (such as tool-making) involves using language instead of simply demonstrating it, learning is significantly enhanced (Morgan *et al.,* 2015).

This finding is supported by the recognition that most regions of the human brain perform basic computations related to a variety of different behaviours/abilities. For example, since the 1990s research has shown that Broca's area contributes not only to speech production (see Chapter 3), but also to music, maths, and the understanding of complex manual actions. Findings such as this have revived the long-standing claim that toolmaking, along with the human propensity to communicate through gestures, may have served as pivotal evolutionary precursors to language (e.g. Arbib, 2012).

Human culture, creativity, and co-operation

According to Fuentes (2017):

> Countless individuals' ability to think creatively is what led us to succeed as a species. At the same time, the initial condition of any creative act is collaboration.
>
> (p. 2)

Creativity is at the very root of how we evolved the way we did: it is 'our ability to move back and forth between the realms of "what is" and "what could be" that has enabled us to reach beyond being a successful species to become an exceptional one' (p. 2).

> We are neither entirely untethered from our biological nature nor slavishly yoked to it … We are, first and foremost, the species singularly distinguished and shaped by creativity. This is the new story of human evolution, of our past and current nature.
>
> (p. 2)

Fuentes identifies what he thinks are the four major misconceptions of human evolution (see Box 9.3).

**BOX 9.3 THE BIG FOUR MISCONCEPTIONS
OF HUMAN EVOLUTION**

1. We're stamped with a deep evolutionary history in which natural selection favoured more aggressive males; this produced a biological tendency towards violence and sexual coercion. Males are naturally selfish, aggressive, and competitive.
2. We're naturally caring, altruistic, and co-operative, distinguished early in our evolution by privileging the sharing of food and other resources, self-sacrifice, and service to the good of the group over self-interest. We're a species of supercooperators (see Chapter 8).
3. Our nature is shaped primarily by environmental challenges and opportunities. We're still better adapted to a traditional hunter-gatherer lifestyle than to modern, mechanised, urbanised, and technology-connected life. This disconnect with our evolutionary roots causes mental health issues and widespread dissatisfaction.
4. Our intelligence allowed us to transcend the boundaries of biological evolution, rising above the pressures and limits of the natural environment and moulding the world to serve our purposes – but at the planet's huge cost.

While each of these misconceptions has been instrumental in enhancing our understanding of human nature, each has also led to oversimplification and some serious misunderstandings …

> Perhaps most important, these popular accounts have obscured the wonderful story at the heart of our evolution – the story of how, from the days of our earliest, protohuman ancestors, we have survived and increasingly thrived because of our exceptional capacity for *creative collaboration*.
>
> (Fuentes, 2017, p. 4; emphasis added)

An extended evolutionary synthesis

According to Fuentes (2017), new findings in the fossil record and ancient DNA, together with theoretical shifts in evolutionary theory, have changed the basic story of humanity. An *extended evolutionary synthesis* (EES) (based on evolutionary biology, genetics, primatology, anthropology, archaeology, psychology, neuroscience, ecology, and even philosophy) shows that humans acquired a distinctive set of neurological, physiological, and social skills that enabled us to work together and think together in order to purposefully co-operate.

Using these skills, they started to help one another care for the young (biologically their own or not), began to share food for both nutritional and social reasons, and to co-ordinate activities beyond what was needed for survival. Acting in ways that benefited the whole group – not just the individual or family – became increasingly common. This creative co-operation transformed us into the beings that invented the technologies that supported large-scale societies and ultimately nations; it also drove the development of religious beliefs, ethical systems, and masterful artwork. While we're sadly capable of intense damage and cruelty, 'our tendency toward compassion plays a larger role in our evolutionary history' (Fuentes, 2017, p. 5).

As part of the EES, researchers have identified a range of different processes, beyond just natural selection (NS); these are central in explaining how and why all living things evolve. Some of these processes are described in Box 9.4.

BOX 9.4 SOME OF THE PROCESSES INVOLVED IN THE EES

- *Mutation* produces genetic variation, much of which can be passed between generations through reproduction/other forms of transmission and inheritance (see Chapter 3).
- *Natural selection* isn't about 'survival of the fittest', but is a filtering process that shapes variation in response to environmental constraints and pressures. Imagine a giant strainer with openings of a certain size, which vary as environmental conditions vary. Organisms – which come in various shapes and sizes – have to pass through the strainer in order to reproduce and leave offspring; those which successfully pass through will produce more offspring (who inherit that specific size and shape).
- *Genetic inheritance* (see Chapter 3).
- *Epigenetic variation:* differences between otherwise identical individuals, specifically, differences in the phenotypes of monozygotic (or identical) twins (MZs). A key process involved in epigenetic variation is *methylation*, which is described in Chapter 3.
- *Behavioural inheritance:* learning from older generations.
- *Symbolic inheritance:* the uniquely human passing down of ideas, symbols, and perceptions that influence how we live and use our bodies; these can potentially affect transmission of biological information from one generation to the next.
- *Niche construction* (NC): the process of responding to environmental challenges and conflicts by reshaping the very pressures the world

places on (each of) us. A *niche* is the sum total of an organism's ways of being in the world – its ecology, behaviour, and all other aspects (and organisms) that make up its surroundings. Many species 'do' NC: for example, beavers build dams, and worms change the chemical structure of the soil. However:

Humans are in a class of their own when it comes to niche construction. Towns, cities, domestic animals, agriculture – the list goes on. The co-operative and creative responses to the conflicts the world throws at us, and to those we create ourselves, reshape the world around us, which in turn reshapes our bodies and minds. We are the species that has a hand in making itself – niche constructors extraordinaire.

(Fuentes, 2017, p. 10)
(Based on Fuentes, 2017)

Humans have evolved to be *supercooperators:* it occurs within communities of ants, hunting dogs, meerkats, and baboons, but never as intensively or frequently as in humans. It's central to everyday human life. Many other species focus co-operative behaviour on those who share their genes. However, 'humans co-operate with friends, collaborators, strangers, other species, and even enemies upon occasion' (Fuentes, 2017, p. 9).

Biological and cultural evolution

Time for reflection …

- How might biological and cultural evolution be related?
- Are they opposed or complementary processes?

According to Pagel (2012), the invention of culture 160,000–200,000 years ago represented a competitor to the rule of genes. Humans had acquired the ability to learn from others, to imitate and improve their actions. This meant that elements of culture – ideas, language, art, music, technologies – could themselves act like genes, capable of being transmitted to others and reproduced. But unlike genes, they could 'jump directly – and very quickly – from one mind to another, shortcutting the normal genetic routes of transmission' (Pagel, 2012, p. 3). So, culture came to define a second great system of inheritance. While we take this cultural inheritance for granted, its invention irrevocably altered the course of evolution and our world.

> Having culture means that we are the only species that acquires the rules of its daily living from the accumulated knowledge of our ancestors rather than from the genes they pass to us. Our cultures and not our genes supply the solutions we use to survive and prosper in the society of our birth; they provide the instructions for what we eat, how we live, the gods we believe in, the tools we make and use, the language we speak, the people we cooperate with and marry, and whom we might fight and even kill in a war.
>
> (Pagel, 2012, p. 3)

But genetic and cultural evolution aren't opposites: instead of adapting to the demands of any single physical (geographical) environment, 'our genes have evolved to use the new social environment of human society to further their survival and reproduction. These are the adaptations that have wired our minds and bodies for culture' (Pagel, 2012, p. 7).

At the heart of this new social environment is the creative collaboration that we discussed above. To say we have an evolved social nature *doesn't* mean that our behaviours are determined by genes; rather, we have certain predilections or tendencies. This is very far from determinism, but still revealing of who we are and why we might have the tendencies to behave as we do (Pagel, 2012). (See Chapter 1.)

Are we wired for culture?

Time for reflection ...

- What do you think this question means?
- If you think we are, what is it that's actually hardwired?
- Can culture be a human universal without *particular* cultures being genetically determined?

Pagel asks if the 160,000–200,000 years we've been around is long enough for traits to have evolved in response to living in the social environment of our cultures. Has there been time enough to become 'wired for culture'?

Pagel's answer is to look at examples of *genetic adaptations* that have occurred since the exodus from Africa: these take much longer than socio-psychological adaptations. (See Box 9.5 and Chapter 3.)

BOX 9.5 HUMAN GENETIC ADAPTATIONS TO DIVERSE ENVIRONMENTS

- About 25,000 years ago, people began living above 12,000 feet in the high Tibetan plateau; they acquired physiological adaptations allowing them to cope with reduced oxygen at these altitudes. One of these adaptations was so advantageous that it might have spread to 90 per cent of all Tibetans in just 4,000 years.
- The Dinka tribespeople of Sudan are tall and slim, with unusually dark skin (which protects them from the sun); their spaghetti-like shape gives them large surface area for shedding heat.
- The Inuit people of North America are shorter, stockily built, with lighter skin (due to less melanin because less is needed); their more spheroid shape reduces their surface area to conserve heat.

The Tibet and Inuit examples are genetic adaptations acquired since humans left Africa. 'If this kind of rewiring of our genes and physiology can take place over such short periods of time, this tells us that other features of our nature, including our psychology and social behaviours, have had plenty of time to evolve since we acquired culture' (Pagel, 2012, p. 9).

As we noted in Chapter 1, the fact that cultures differ regarding both social norms, traditions, and individual psychology (quite apart from language, art, dress, food, etc.) *doesn't* mean that culture isn't a human universal; it indisputably is. To take advantage of culture meant evolving a new kind of mind, a cultural *tabula rasa*, designed to be programmed by and embrace the culture in which it happened to be born. We're *primed* to become cultural creatures – but not any particular culture (Pagel, 2012).

Is it possible for human beings to exist outside of culture?

Time for reflection ...

- If we define humans as cultural beings, then the answer has to be 'no'.
- Can we even imagine what 'being human' means *outside* culture?

Kemp (2015) describes a *thought experiment,* in which an amoral scientist put 100 babies (50 boys, 50 girls) on an uninhabited but fertile island. He provided them with the bare minimum to keep them alive (food, protection, etc.), but no culture (including education and language). He gradually fed and watered them less and less. After 20 years, what have they become? Would they have invented their own culture?

By Kemp's own account, many of our defining traits as humans – such as language, art, technology, storytelling, and cooking – are transmitted *culturally;* although products of our biology, they're not fully encoded by genes. Rather, they pass from generation to generation by social learning, evolving as they go.

So, by definition, 'Being human' =

> *biological humans* (*Homo sapiens*, with a specific genetic make-up, brain, anatomy, sensory capabilities, etc.) born into a human culture
>
> +
>
> *enculturation* (i.e. being raised within a particular set of behavioural norms, values, religious belief system, language, etc.)

While we may be predisposed to become a full member of any culture we happen to be born into, we cannot *logically* separate the two. This is why, to ask 'When humans grow up without culture, do they invent it anyway?', as Kemp does, makes no sense: if we're cultural creatures (it's part of our nature), then we'd only be *biologically* human in the above scenario. Human culture evolved over the course of thousands of years, but in the island scenario, it would have to be created from scratch! Indeed, would any of the 'participants' have survived? We cannot think of human beings independently of their (or some) culture or society.

Kemp asks: 'How much of our humanity is hardwired, and how much of it depends on the culture in which we are raised?' This is, of course, a way of asking the centuries-old 'nature/nurture' question; but as with that debate, doesn't Kemp's question rest on a *false dichotomy*? According to Pagel and others, it's our cultural interdependence with other human beings that's as hardwired as any of our biological or psychological attributes. Even if we believe in the innateness of certain abilities (language being the classic example), the child still needs a spectrum of different inputs in order for that ability to function properly (as even Chomsky acknowledges). ('Innate' here *doesn't* mean 'ready-made' or 'fully-formed'; rather, it means something like 'potential': see Chapter 1). These island-children would be like the proverbial 'fish out of water': as Pinker (1994) says, it's (more literally) like studying how fish swim by taking them out of water and watching them flopping around on the ground. Culture is our 'natural habitat'.

We rely more than any other species on the accumulated knowledge of our ancestors to survive and prosper; for the most part, we embrace our culture because it's our ticket to the future. Our dispositions for culture evolved because they were those that led to the greatest reproductive success. We seem programmed willingly to accept the culture of our birth: 'it is hard to adjust to a new cultural environment once the one we were born into has been installed into our minds' (Pagel, 2012, p. 27) – as evidenced by the resistance to stamping out culturally defined emotions, such as xenophobia and racism (see Chapter 5).

Culture and history

Harari (2011) defines *history* as the development of human cultures; once they appeared, they never ceased to change and develop. He identifies three major revolutions in human history: *Cognitive* (approximately 70,000 years ago); *Agricultural* (approximately 12,000 years ago); and the *Scientific* (500 years ago). (Here, we'll focus on just the first of these.)

The Cognitive Revolution is the point at which history:

> declared its independence from biology. Until the Cognitive Revolution, the doings of all human species belonged to the realm of biology, or … prehistory … From the Cognitive Revolution onwards, historical narratives replace biological theories as our primary means of explaining the development of *Homo sapiens*.
>
> (Harari, 2011, pp. 41–2)

To understand the rise of Christianity or the French Revolution, it's not enough to comprehend the interaction of genes, hormones, and organisms: we need to take into account 'the interaction of ideas, images and fantasies as well' (Harari, 2011, p. 42). This doesn't mean that *Homo sapiens* and human culture became exempt from biological laws: we're still animals, and our physical, emotional, and cognitive abilities are still shaped by our DNA (see Chapter 1):

> Our societies are built from the same building blocks as Neanderthal or chimpanzee societies, and the more we examine these building blocks – sensations, emotions, family ties – the less different we find between us and other apes.
>
> (Harari, 2011, p. 42)

(See Chapter 3.)

However, it's a mistake to look for the differences at the level of the individual or the family: significant differences begin to appear only when we cross the threshold of 150 individuals, and when we reach 1,000–2,000, the differences are astounding. If you tried to bunch together thousands of chimps into the United Nations HQ, there'd be pandemonium. But we regularly gather by the thousands in such places to create orderly patterns.

> The real difference between us and chimpanzees is the mythical glue that binds together large numbers of individuals, families and groups. This glue has made us the masters of creation.
>
> (Harari, 2011, p. 42)

Of course, we also needed other skills (such as tool-making and use) – but these are of little use unless we can combine them with co-operation with many others. Physiologically, there's been no significant improvement in our tool-making capacity over the last 30,000 years, but our capacity for co-operation has improved dramatically. In order to understand how Sapiens behave, we must describe the *historical evolution* of their actions (Harari, 2011).

Sex (biology) versus gender (culture)

Harari (2011) asks if the binary division into men and women is a natural division with deep biological roots, and, if so, whether there are also biological explanations for the preferences given to men over women. Some of the cultural, legal, and political disparities between men and women reflect the obvious biological differences (for example, men don't have wombs).

> Yet around this hard universal kernel, every society accumulated layer upon layer of cultural ideas and norms that have little to do with biology. Societies associate a host of attributes with masculinity and femininity that, for the most part, lack a firm biological basis.
>
> (Harari, 2011, p. 163)

Harari compares democratic Ancient Athens (5th century BCE) with modern Athens in terms of 'female' (a strictly biological category) and 'woman' (a cultural category). While 'female' hasn't changed between these two time periods, 'woman' has changed *fundamentally:* in Ancient Athens she *couldn't* vote, become a judge, hold government office, decide for herself who to marry, was typically illiterate, and was legally owned by her father or husband. 7,000 years later, she can do all those things, is typically literate, and is legally independent.

In trying to distinguish what is biologically determined from what people merely try to justify through biological myths, a good rule of thumb is 'Biology enables, culture forbids' (Harari, 2011, p. 164) (for example, biology *enables* women to have children, and some cultures *oblige* them to have them; homosexuality is another example). Culture tends to argue that it forbids only what is *unnatural*, but from a biological perspective, *nothing* is unnatural.

> A truly unnatural behaviour, one that goes against the laws of nature, simply cannot exist, so it would need no prohibition. No culture has ever bothered to forbid men to photosynthesise, women to run faster than the speed of light, or negatively charged electrons to be attracted to each other.
>
> (Harari, 2011, pp. 164–5)

> A man is not a Sapiens with particular biological qualities such as XY chromosomes, testicles and lots of testosterone. Rather, he fits into a particular slot in his society's imagined human order. His culture's myths assign him particular masculine roles (like engaging in politics), rights (like voting) and duties (like military service).
>
> (Harari, 2011, p. 166)

(This mirrors the 'equation', on page 196.)

Likewise, women. Not only have the meaning of 'manhood' and 'woman-hood' varied immensely from one society to another, but these are constantly changing within the same society.

Human culture as part of the natural world: revisiting nature–nurture

According to Boyd (Richerson and Boyd, 2005; Boyd, 2018a) culture is cru-cial for understanding human behaviour: we acquire beliefs and values from the people around us, and we cannot explain human behaviour without taking this reality into account. But the importance of culture isn't to the exclusion of the role of biology (this would represent a *false dichotomy*). Indeed, *culture is part of biology,* as much a part of human biology as walking upright; it is an evolving product of populations of human brains, which have been shaped by natural selection to learn and manage culture.

Culture-making brains are the product of more than two million years of more-or-less gradual increases in brain size and cultural complexity (see Chapter 3). During this period, culture must have increased the reproductive success of our ancestors – otherwise, the features of our brain that make culture possible wouldn't have evolved.

While it may seem obviously true that, like all human behaviour, culture must in some way be rooted in human biology, most economists, many psychologists, and many social scientists influenced by evolutionary biology place little empha-sis on the role of culture. By contrast, especially anthropologists, sociologists, and historians stress the importance of culture and social institutions in shaping human affairs. This is another example of the 'nature–nurture' debate, applied to human nature (rather than individual differences), that is, what we all have in common and what distinguishes us from other species (see Figure 9.3).

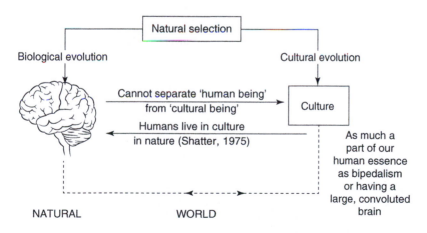

Figure 9.3 Relationship between biological and cultural evolution.

Culture as what makes humans exceptional

Boyd (2018a) compares humans with other species in terms of the same zoo-logical criteria we use to compare the ecological importance of other species, including (i) *species range* and (ii) *biomass*.

(i)   *Species range:* humans occupy every corner of the planet (*terrestrial habitat* or *geographical range*) – except Antarctica; we also occupy a greater set of habitats (*ecological range*). These are both useful measures of how adaptable a species is. By contrast, gorillas and bonobos are limited to moist forests in tropical Africa; chimps to forest or woodland in roughly the same parts of Africa. This dispersion of *Homo sapiens* had happened by 10,000 years ago.

(ii)   *Biomass* refers to the sum of the mass of all individual members of a species at any given time. Among vertebrates, human biomass is exceeded only by that of domesticated animals and pets and is many times that of all wild terrestrial species combined. It's partly the result of agricultural and industrial production.

'The key to this … is that people adapt culturally, gradually accumulating information crucial to survival' (Boyd, 2018a, p. 10). Different species have different adaptations that allow them to succeed in particular environments, including their social behaviours. By contrast, 'humans are *generalists*, able to adapt to a vast range of different environments and to develop local knowledge, specialized tools, and a wide variety of social arrangements' (Boyd, 2018a, p. 13; emphasis added).

Much human adaptation involves artefacts – but so too does that of other species (such as bird nests, beaver dams, and termite mounds) and the technological sophistication of some of these rivals anything made by humans until the last few thousand years. Boyd cites the example of the hanging nests of weaverbirds, which are beautifully designed and are at least as complex as thatched dwellings made by many foragers. But what makes humans special is the ability to make many different kinds of artefacts that are appropriate in many different habitats.

What makes humans so good at this is the *high fidelity imitation* of others discussed earlier. While weaver birds can produce these beautiful handing nests without ever having seen one being made, humans, as intelligent as we may be, 'are not nearly smart enough *as individuals* to solve the adaptive problems that confronted modern humans as they spread across the globe. The package of tools, foraging techniques, ecological knowledge, and social arrangements used by any group of foragers is far too complex for any individual to create' (Boyd, 2018a, p. 16). We're able to learn all the things we need to know in each of the diverse environments we occupy only because we acquire information from others; this refers to CCE discussed above. We don't have to reinvent everything for ourselves.

Norms and the puzzle of human co-operation

Co-operation in *larger groups* requires systems of *norms* enforced by sanctions imposed by third parties (including coercive institutions, such as police and courts). *Small-scale* co-operation in human societies is also typically regulated by shared norms enforced by third-party sanctions: individuals aren't free to make any bargain they want and deals are constrained by existing norms. These norms affect behaviour closely related to fitness: for example, most societies recognise 'marriage' as an institutionalised form of *pair-bonding*, associated with normative rights and obligations.

However, this doesn't mean that people are norm-following robots: they are actors with their own interests, and they make deals with others to further these interests. However, norms affect the kinds of deals that people make: first, people have to take into account the cost of violating norms, and second, people internalise their society's norms, which affects their preferences and thus the choices they make (Boyd, 2018b). Culturally evolved norms provide a *scaffold* to guide individual sharing decisions and limit the scope for conflict.

Co-operation and fair inequality

There's immense concern in liberal democracies about all kinds of inequality ('inequality aversion') – both in these countries and in other, non-democratic societies. The focus is typically on prejudice and discrimination with regards to gender, sexual orientation, religion, and ethnic background, perhaps reflecting the wired–in tendency towards unequal treatment of different groups within most cultures, both currently and historically (see Chapter 5). But we cannot defend prejudice and discrimination by claiming it's part of human nature, and the fight for gender, sexual, religious, and racial equality is, according to Sheskin (2018; Starmans *et al.*, 2017), *morally straightforward*.

However, the battle against *economic* inequality is rather more complicated. When people are surveyed about ideal distribution of wealth, they actually prefer *unequal* societies: they aren't bothered about inequality *per se* but with *economic unfairness*. Sheskin (2018; Starmans *et al.,* 2017) believes that human beings naturally favour *fair* distributions of wealth – not equal ones. When fairness and equality clash, people generally prefer *fair inequality* over *unfair equality*. So, for example, it's fair that someone with an exceptional talent, or who works much harder than most people, should earn more than the rest of us; conversely, it would be unfair if everyone was paid the same regardless of the hours they work, the skills or training required to do the job, etc.

This intuition for fairness seems to be deeply ingrained ('wired-in'); it's what allows humans to work together in large groups. Wouldn't you prefer to work with someone who puts in at least a fair share of the effort and takes at most a fair share of the reward, rather than someone who's lazy (a 'free-rider') or greedy (one of the Seven Deadly Sins: see Chapter 2)? Likewise, other people will prefer to work or interact with you if you have a reputation for fairness:

> Over our evolutionary history, individuals who cooperated fairly outcompeted those who didn't, and so evolution produced our modern, moral brains, with their focus on fairness.
>
> (Sheskin, 2018, p. 30)

Summary and conclusions: how are biological and cultural evolution related?

According to Boyd (2018b), culture *cannot* override biology:

> Culture is as much a part of human biology as our peculiar pelvis and the thick enamel that covers our molars. Four million years ago, culture likely played a minor role in the life of our ancestors. Today, we are culture-saturated creatures, completely dependent on information acquired from others. Culture allowed us to evolve complex, highly co-operative social arrangements unlike those of any other creature. But there is nothing unnatural or nonbiological about any of this. The morphological, physiological, and psychological changes that make human culture possible evolved over the last several million years as a consequence of the usual evolutionary processes. Culture has made us a very different kind of animal, but without doubt, we are still part of the natural world.
>
> (Boyd, 2018b, p. 122)

Even if we all agreed that modern humans represent the pinnacle of biological evolution, in this chapter we've considered the argument that what's distinctive or unique about us is that we're 'wired for culture'. If that is our 'natural' state, such that we exist in culture in nature (Shotter, 1975: see Chapter 1), while other (wild) animal species exist in nature only, then focus shifts from:

(i) how we evolved from other primates and other hominins to become modern humans; to
(ii) how we are continuing to evolve by means of applications of (certain aspects) of human culture.

The central driving force involved in (i) was natural selection, and the associated evolution was *biological/genetic*, which, by definition, is beyond the control of the organisms that are evolving. As we've seen in various points in this book, the most important 'legacy' of our biological evolution is the human brain, the most complex entity in the known universe. That product of biological evolution has, in turn, enabled us, its owners, to make discoveries and achieve understanding of the world, including ourselves, which can then be used deliberately to change aspects of our biological make-up and functioning. In other words, human biology is continuing to evolve through *cultural evolution*, rather than natural selection. (This is discussed further in Chapter 10.)

At the same time, (biological) evolution is no match for the speed and variety of modern life (Max, 2017); culture – and its 'weaponized cousin', technology – is the 'primary mover for reproductive success' (Max, 2017, p. 49) – and thus evolutionary change. As we noted above, the speed of cultural evolution far exceeds that of biological/genetic evolution, partly because it occurs deliberately and builds on already-acquired knowledge and skills (as Newton (1676) famously put it, 'If I have seen further it is by standing on the shoulders of giants').

Suggested further reading

Boyd, R. (2018) *A Different Kind of Animal: How Culture Transformed Our Species*. Princeton, NJ: Princeton University Press.

Fuentes, A. (2017) *The Creative Spark: How Imagination Made Humans Exceptional*. New York: Dutton.

Harari, Y.N. (2011) *Sapiens: A Brief History of Humankind*. London: Vintage Books.

Laland, K.N. (2017) *Darwin's Unfinished Symphony: How Culture Made the Human Mind*. Princeton, NJ: Princeton University Press.

Pagel, M. (2012) *Wired for Culture: The Natural History of Human Cooperation*. London: Penguin Books.

Roberts, A. (2009) *The Incredible Human Journey: The Story of How We Colonised the Planet*. London: Bloomsbury (by arrangement with the BBC).

10 The future of human evolution

From *Homo sapiens* to gods

In *Homo Deus* (2015), Harari claims that, in seeking perfect happiness and immortality, humans are in fact trying to upgrade themselves into gods. An increasing minority of scientists and thinkers is speaking more openly these days about defeating death and achieving eternal youth (such as gerontologist, Aubrey de Grey, and polymath and inventor, Ray Kurzweil). Kurzweil was appointed a director of engineering at Google (2012); in 2013, Google launched a sub-company (Calico), whose stated mission was 'to solve death'. Other Silicon Valley luminaries include PayPal co-founder, Peter Thiel, who aims to live forever.

Kurzweil and De Grey maintain that anyone with a healthy body and bank account in 2050 will have a serious shot at immortality by cheating death a decade at a time. Every ten years or so, we'll receive a makeover treatment that will not only cure illnesses, but will also regenerate decaying tissues, and upgrade hands, eyes, and brains. In between times, doctors will have invented a plethora of new medicines, upgrades, and gadgets.

Strictly, such 'creatures' will be *a-mortal* (rather than immortal): 'future superhumans' could still die from unnatural causes (such as accidents).

> If we ever have the power to engineer death and pain out of our system, that same power will probably be sufficient to engineer our system in almost any manner we like, and manipulate our organs, emotions and intelligence in myriad ways … Up till now increasing human power relied mainly on upgrading our external tools. In the future it may rely more on upgrading the human body and mind, or on merging directly with our tools.
>
> (Harari, 2015, pp. 49–50)

This upgrading may follow any of three paths: (i) biological engineering; (ii) cyborg engineering; and (iii) engineering of non-organic beings. In all three cases, cultural evolution trumps biological evolution. In the rest of this chapter, we'll focus on (i) and (ii).

Biological engineering

This starts from the insight that we're far from realising the full potential of organic bodies; there's no reason to believe that *Homo sapiens* is the pinnacle (see Chapter 3):

> Relatively small changes in genes, hormones and neurons were enough to transform *Homo erectus* – who could produce nothing more impressive than flint knives – into *Homo sapiens*, who produces spaceships and computers. Who knows what might be the outcome of a few more changes to our DNA, hormonal system or brain structure.
>
> (Harari, 2015, p. 50)

This has already begun, not perhaps with this grand aim of transforming the entire species into 'new godlings', as different from *Homo sapiens* as we are from *Homo erectus,* but more modestly – albeit just as ethically challenging – in an attempt to remove certain genetic diseases or determine a baby's sex or intelligence. A new technology – CRISPR-Cas9 – was first tried out in 2013; it refers to a procedure for snipping out a section of DNA sequence from a gene and replacing it with a different one – quickly and accurately.

No technology remotely as powerful has previously existed for manipulating the human genome. Max (2017) compares CRISPR with IVF: in the latter, you select the embryo you want from the ones nature has provided, hoping that it will possess the characteristics you wish the resulting baby to possess (based on what genes each parent has – randomly – contributed). Max quotes the (likely apocryphal) story involving the playwright, George Bernard Shaw and dancer, Isadora Duncan. When she suggested that they have a baby together so it would have her looks and his brains, he retorted, 'But what if it had your brain and my looks?' CRISPR would eliminate that risk: it allows researchers to insert a new genetic trait directly into the egg or sperm. But so far, experiments using CRISPR have only involved non-humans and there's an international moratorium on all therapies for making heritable changes in human genes until they're proved safe and effective – including CRISPR.

Compared with IVF, CRISPR is a vastly more powerful technology, carrying a far greater risk of abuse – including the temptation to try to engineer some sort of genetically perfect race. While the potential benefits are undeniable, who decides what enhancements should be made? However, as powerful as CRISPR may be, there are already over 2,000 gene therapy trials under way in relation to ageing and Alzheimer's disease. While society is unlikely to object to such research producing treatments for devastating (and extremely expensive) medical conditions such as Alzheimer's, those same treatments will probably also work for cognitive enhancement. The boundary between different uses of genetic engineering research was seriously blurred in 2016, when the UK's independent fertility regulator – the Human Fertility and Embryology Authority (HFEA) – granted permission to a research team to use CRISPR to explore the mechanism of miscarriage with human embryos (all of which will be destroyed).

Cyborg engineering

The term 'cyborg' (short for '*cyb*ernetic' '*org*anism') was first coined in 1960 by Manfred Clynes and Nathan Kline. Not to be confused with 'bionic' or 'android', a cyborg is a being (organism) with restored – or enhanced – functions and abilities due to the insertion or addition of some artificial (*biomechatronic*) body part(s) into its organic ('natural') body. While in 1960 the concept of a part human, part machine 'creature' was science-fiction (i.e. belonging to the realm of fantasy), in the early 21st century this has become reality. Some examples are described in Box 10.1 below.

BOX 10.1 SOME EXAMPLES OF CYBORG ENGINEERING

- Neil Harbisson is a real-life cyborg. He has a rare condition called *achromatopsia*, a form of colour-blindness which prevents him from perceiving any colour at all. In his early 20s, he found a surgeon willing to implant a device, a cybernetic enhancement, into his biological self; this enhancement takes the form of an antenna, which ends in a fibre–optic sensor that hovers right above his eyes. The sensor picks up the colours in front of him, and a microchip implanted in his skull converts their frequencies into vibrations on the back of his head; these become sound frequencies, turning his skull into a sort of third ear (Max, 2017).
- Another implant is a Bluetooth communication hub, allowing friends to send him colours via a smart phone. Over time, the input from the antenna has begun to feel neither like sight nor hearing but a different kind of (sixth) sense.
- Remarkably, Harbisson can also 'see' ultraviolet light (which humans naturally *cannot*); this represents a first step on the road to 'the vast expansion of human potential' (Kurzweil, in *The Singularity is Near*).
- Harbisson is the world's first *official* cyborg: he persuaded the British government to let him wear the antenna in his passport photo, arguing that it wasn't an electronic device, but an extension of his brain!
- Kurzweil – and other *transhumanists* – believes that we will transcend all the limitations of our biology; extending who we are is what it means to be human.
- Cochlear implants that enable deaf people to hear are now commonplace and the surgery is routine, but we don't normally refer to those who possess these implants as cyborgs.
- Other commonplace examples include heart pacemakers; 'brain pacemakers' for Parkinson's patients; and artificial retinas for some types of blindness.

Summary and conclusions

Human enhancements needn't confer superhuman powers. Starting in 1998, hundreds of people have had radio-frequency identification (RFID) devices embedded in their bodies that allow them to unlock their doors or log on to their computers without touching anything. As with most major technological innovations, what was once revolutionary – having started out as sci-fi – soon becomes normal and commonplace. As Max (2017) observes, virtual reality headsets are hugely popular as gamer toys (but are also being used as a therapy device).

> Our cars are our feet, our calculators are our minds, and Google is our memory. Our lives now are only partly biological, with no clear split between the organic and the technological, the carbon and the silicon.
>
> (Max, 2017, p. 63)

While for cyborgs the technology is internal and literally attached (usually implanted), for the rest of us (the majority) technology has become an extension of our body without being attached/implanted. If we equate 'natural' with 'biological'/'organic', then human nature, through the technological innovations that are a crucial feature of cultural evolution, is morphing increasingly into something 'unnatural' (i.e. manufactured). Given the rate of recent and current technological change, at some point in the future (perhaps just 50–100 years or so), *Homo cyborgalis* (or some such species) may look back at *Homo sapiens* and note differences that are as great as those between modern humans and their hominin ancestors.

Suggested further reading

Harari, Y.N. (2015) *Homo Deus: A Brief History of Tomorrow.* London: Vintage.
Max, D.T. (2017) Beyond Human. *National Geographic, 231*(4), 40–63.

References

Aitchison, J. (1983) *The Articulate Mammal* (2nd edition). London: Hutchinson.

Allen, C. and Bekoff, M. (2007) Animal consciousness. In M. Velmans and S. Schneider (eds.) *The Blackwell Companion to Consciousness*. Oxford: Blackwell Publishing.

Allport, G. (1954) *The Nature of Prejudice*. Reading, MA: Addison-Wesley.

Amichai-Hamburger, Y. (2017) *Internet Psychology: The Basics*. London: Routledge.

Annas, J.E. (1992) *Hellenistic Philosophy of Mind*. Berkeley, CA: University of California Press.

Arbib, M. A. (2012) *How the Brain Got Language: The Mirror System Hypothesis*. Oxford: Oxford University Press.

Arendt, H. (1964) *Eichmann in Jerusalem: A Report on the Banality of Evil*. New York: Viking Press.

Aronson, E. (1988) *The Social Animal* (5th edition). New York: W.H. Freeman & Co.

Asch, S.E. (1946) Forming impressions of personality. *Journal of Abnormal & Social Psychology, 41*, 258–290.

Ashworth, P. (2003) The origins of qualitative psychology. In J.A. Smith (ed.) *Qualitative Psychology: A Practical Guide to Research Methods*. London: Sage Publications.

Atance, C.M. and O'Neill, D.K. (2005) The emergence of episodic future thinking in humans. *Learning & Motivation, 36*, 126–144.

Aziz-Zadeh, L., Wilson, S.M., Rizzolatti, G. and Iacoboni, M. (2006) Congruent embodied representations for visually presented actions and linguistic phrases describing actions. *Current Biology, 16*, 1818–1823.

Baddeley, A.D. (1990) *Human Memory*. Hove: Lawrence Erlbaum Associates.

Bamshad, M.J. and Olson, S.E. (2003) Does race exist? *Scientific American, 289*(6), 78–85.

Bandura, A. (1965) Influence of model's reinforcement contingencies on the acquisition of imitative responses. *Journal of Personality & Social Psychology, 1*, 589–595.

Bandura, A. (1977) *Social Learning Theory* (2nd edition). Englewood Cliffs, NJ: Prentice-Hall.

Bandura, A. (1986) *Social Foundations of Thought and Action*. Englewood Cliffs, NJ: Prentice-Hall.

Bandura, A. (1989) Social cognitive theory. In R. Vasta (ed.) *Six Theories of Child Development*. Greenwich, CT: JAI Press.

Banks, W.P. and Pockett, S. (2007) Benjamin Libet's work on the Neuroscience of Free Will. In M. Velmans and S. Schneider (eds.) *The Blackwell Companion to Consciousness*. Oxford: Blackwell Publishing.

Banuazzi, A. and Mohavedi, S. (1975) Interpersonal dynamics in a simulated prison: A methodological analysis. *American Psychologist, 30*, 152–160.

Bargh, J.A. (2014) Our unconscious minds. *Scientific American, 310*(1), 20–27.

Barkow, J.H., Cosmides, L. and Tooby, J. (eds.) (1992) *The Adapted Mind: Evolutionary Psychology and the Generation of Culture*. Oxford: Oxford University Press.

Barnes, J. (2008) *Nothing to be Frightened of*. London: Vintage.

Baron-Cohen, S. (1990) Autism: A specific cognitive disorder of 'mindblindness'. *International Review of Psychiatry, 2*, 79–88.

Baron-Cohen, S. (1993) From attention-goal psychology to belief-desire psychology: The development of a theory of mind and its dysfunction. In S. Baron-Cohen, H. Tager-Flusberg and D.J. Cohen (eds.) *Understanding Other Minds: Perspectives from Autism*. Oxford: Oxford University Press.

Baron-Cohen, S. (1995a) *Mindblindness: An Essay on Autism and Theory of Mind*. Cambridge, MA: MIT Press.

Baron-Cohen, S. (1995b) Infantile Autism. In A.A. Lazarus and A.M. Colman (eds.) *Abnormal Psychology*. London: Longman.

Baron-Cohen, S. (2006) Mindreading: evidence for both innate and acquired factors. *Journal of Anthropological Psychology, 17*, 57–59.

Baron-Cohen, S., Leslie, A.M. and Frith, U. (1985) Does the autistic child have a 'theory of mind'? *Cognition, 21*, 37–46.

Barras, C. (2016) Scrapheap Challenge. *New Scientist, 231*(3084), 29–31.

Bartlett, F.C. (1932) *Remembering: A Study in Experimental and Social Psychology*. Cambridge: Cambridge University Press.

Batson, C.D. (1991) *The Altruism Question: Toward a Social Psychological Answer*. Hillsdale, NJ: Lawrence Erlbaum.

Batson, C.D., Ahmad, N.Y. and Stocks, E.L. (2016) Benefits and liabilities of empathy-induced altruism: a contemporary review. In A.G. Miller (ed.) *The Social Psychology of Good and Evil*. New York: The Guilford Press.

Batson, C.D. and Stocks, E.L. (2004) Religion: Its core psychological functions. In J. Greenberg, S.L. Koole and T. Pyszczynski (eds.) *Handbook of Experimental Existential Psychology*. New York: The Guilford Press.

Baumeister, R.F. (1997) *Evil: Inside Human Violence and Cruelty*. New York: Freeman Holt.

Baumeister, R.F. (2005) *The Cultural Animal; Human Nature, Meaning and Social Life*. New York: Oxford University Press.

Baumrind, D. (1964) Some thoughts on the ethics of research: After reading Milgram's behavioural study of obedience. *American Psychologist, 19*, 421–423.

Beck, B.B. (1980) *Animal Tool Behaviour: The Use and Manufacture of Tools by Animals*. New York: Garland STPM Press.

Becker, E. (1973) *The Denial of Death*. New York: Free Press.

Becker, S.W. and Eagly, A.H. (2004) The heroism of women and men. *American Psychologist, 59*(3), 163–178.

Bem, S. and Looren de Jong, H. (1997) *Theoretical Issues in Psychology: An Introduction*. London: Sage Publications.

Bering, J. (2010) The nonexistent purpose of people. *The Psychologist, 23*(4), 290–293.

Bettelheim, B. (1983) *Freud and Man's Soul*. London: Flamingo.

Bhattacharjee, Y. (2017) Why we lie. *National Geographic, 231*(6), 30–51.

Bishop, D.V.M. and Norbury, C.F. (2002) Exploring the borderlands of autistic disorder and specific language impairment: a study using standardised diagnostic instruments. *Journal of Child Psychology & Psychiatry, 43*(7), 917–929.

Blackham, H.J. (1961) *Six Existentialist Thinkers*. London: Routledge & Kegan Paul Ltd.

Blackman, D.E. (1980) Image of man in contemporary behaviourism. In A.J. Chapman & D.M. Jones (eds.) *Models of Man*. Leicester: British Psychological Society.

Blackmore, S. (2010) *Consciousness: An Introduction* (2nd edition). London: Hodder Education.

Blakemore, C. (1988) *The Mind Machine*. London: BBC Books.

Blass, T. (2004) *The Man Who Shocked the World: The Life and Legacy of Stanley Milgram*. New York: Basic Books.

Bloom, P. (2007) Religion is natural. *Developmental Science, 10*, 147–151.

Bodmer, W. (2007) Foreword. In C. Pasternak (ed.) *What Makes Us Human?* Oxford: Oneworld.

Bonnie, K.E. V., Horner, A., Whiten, A. and de Waal, F.B.M. (2006) Spread of arbitrary conventions among chimpanzees: A controlled experiment. *Proceedings of the Royal Society of London B 274*, 367–372.

Boyd, J.N. and Zimbardo, P.G. (2005) Time perspective, health, and risk taking. In A. Strathman and J. Joireman (eds.) *Understanding Behaviour in the Context of Time: Theory, Research, and Application*. Mahwah, NJ: Erlbaum.

Boyd, R. (2009) *The Origin of Stories: Evolution, Cognition and Fiction*. Cambridge, MA: Belnap Press of Harvard University Press.

Boyd, R. (2018a) Not by brains alone: The vital role of culture in human adaptation. In R. Boyd (ed.) *A Different Kind of Animal: How Culture Transformed Our Species*. Princeton, NJ: Princeton University Press.

Boyd, R. (2018b) Beyond kith and kin: Culture and the scale of human cooperation. In R. Boyd (ed.) *A Different Kind of Animal: How Culture Transformed Our Species*. Princeton, NJ: Princeton University Press.

Boyd, R. and Richerson, P.J. (1996) Why culture is common but cultural evolution is rare. *Proceedings of the British Academy, 88*, 73–93.

Brislin, R. (1993) *Understanding Culture's Influence on Behaviour*. Orlando, FL: Harcourt Brace Jovanovich.

Buchanan, M. (2007) Born prejudiced. *New Scientist, 193*(2595), 40–43.

Burger, J.M. (2011) Alive and well after all these years. *The Psychologist, 24*(9), 654–657.

Caldwell, R. (2006) How to be conscious: mind & matter revisited. *Philosophy Now, 54*, 26–29.

Callaway, E. (2010) Modern humans' Neanderthal origins. *New Scientist, 206*(2760), 8.

Campbell, M. and Vollhardt, J.R. (2014) Fighting the good fight: The relationship between belief in evil and support for violent policies. *Personality & Social Psychology Bulletin, 40*(1), 16–33.

Carlson, N.R. and Buskist, W. (1997) *Psychology: The Science of Behaviour* (5th edition). Needham Heights, MA: Allyn & Bacon.

Carroll, D.W. (1986) *Psychology of Language*. Monterey, CA: Brooks/Cole Publishing Co.

Carroll, J. (2006) Literature and evolution. In R. Headlam Wells and J. McFadden (eds.) *Human Nature: Fact and Fiction*. London: Continuum.

Cassirer, E. (1944) *An Essay on Man*. New Haven, CT: Yale University Press.

Chalmers, D. (2007) The hard problem of consciousness. In M. Velmans and S. Schneider (eds.) *The Blackwell Companion to Consciousness*. Oxford: Blackwell Publishing.

Chappell, J. and Kacelnik, A. (2002) Tool selectivity in a non-primate, the New Caledonian crow (*Corvus moneduloides*). *Animal cognition, 5*, 71–78.

Chomsky, N. (1957) *Syntactic Structures*. The Hague: Mouton.

Chomsky, N. (1979) *Language and Responsibility*. Sussex: Harvester Press.

Cialdini, R.B., Schaller, M., Houlihan, D. *et al.* (1987) Empathy-based helping: Is it selflessly or selfishly motivated? *Journal of Personality Social Psychology, 52*, 749–758.

Coghlan, A. (2011) Key to humanity is in missing DNA. *New Scientist, 209*(2803), 6–7.

Cohen, J. (1958) *Humanistic Psychology*. London: Allen and Unwin.

Compton, W.C. (2018) Self-actualization myths: What did Maslow really say? *Journal of Humanistic Psychology*, March. Doi:10.1177/0022167818761929.

Corballis, M.C. (2002) *From Hand to Mouth: The Origins of Language*. Princeton, NJ: Princeton University Press.

Corballis, M. and Suddendorf, T. (2007) Memory, time, and language. In C. Pasternak (ed.) *What Makes Us Human?* Oxford: Oneworld.

Corballis, M.C. (2011) *The Recursive Mind: The Origins of Human Language, Thought, and Civilization*. Princeton, NJ: Princeton University Press.

Cosmides, L. and Tooby, J. (1992) Cognitive adaptations for social exchange. In J. Barkow, L. Cosmides and J. Tooby (eds.) *The Adapted Mind: Evolutionary Psychology and the Generation of Culture*. New York: Oxford University Press.

Crusius, I. and Mussweiler, T. (2013) Untangling envy. *Scientific American, 24*(5), 34–37.

Danziger, K. (1997) *Naming the Mind: How Psychology Found its Language*. London: Sage.

Darley, J.M. and Latané, B. (1968) Bystander intervention in emergencies: Diffusion of responsibility. *Journal of Personality & Social Psychology, 8*, 377–383.

Darwin, C.R. (1871) *The Descent of Man and Selection in Relation to Sex*. London: John Murray.

De Waal, F. (2016) *Are We Smart Enough to Know How Smart Animals Are?* London: Granta.

Deacon, T. (1997) *The Symbolic Species: The Co-evolution of Language and the Human Brain*. London: Penguin.

Dennett, D. (1969) *Content and Consciousness*. London: RKP.

Dennett, D.C. (1983) Intentional systems in cognitive ethology: The "Panglossian paradigm" defended. *Behavioural & Brain Sciences, 6*, 343–390.

Dennett, D. (1997) *Kinds of Minds: Towards an Understanding of Consciousness*. New York: Basic Books.

Desmond, M. (2008) The lie of heroism. *Contexts, 7*(1), 56–58.

Dovidio, J.F., Piliavin, J.A., Schroeder, D.A. and Penner, L.A. (2006) *The Social Psychology of Prosocial Behaviour*. Mahwah, NJ: Erlbaum.

Dovidio, J.F., Gaertner, S.L. and Pearson, A.R. (2016) Racism among the well intentioned. In A.G. Miller (ed.) *The Social Psychology of Good and Evil* (2nd edition). New York: The Guilford Press.

Dovidio, J.F., Piliavin, J.A., Gaertner, S.L. *et al.* (1991) The arousal: cost-reward model and the process of intervention. In M.S. Clark (ed.) *Prosocial Behaviour: Review of Personality and Social Psychology*, Vol.12. Newbury Park, CA: Sage Publications.

Dunbar, R. (1993) Coevolution of neocortical size, group size, and language in humans. *Behavioural & Brain Sciences, 16*, 681–735.

Dunbar, R. (2004) Can you guess what I'm thinking? *New Scientist, 182*(2451), 44–45.

Dunbar, R. (2007) Why are humans not just great apes? In C. Pasternak (ed.) *What Makes Us Human?* Oxford: Oneworld.

Duntley, J.D. and Buss, D.M. (2016) The evolution of good and evil. In A.G. Miller (ed.) *The Social Psychology of Good and Evil*. New York: The Guilford Press.

Eagly, A.H. (1987) *Sex Differences in Social Behaviour: A Social-Role Interpretation*. Hillsdale, NJ: Lawrence Erlbaum.

Edelman, G. and Tononi, G. (2000) *A Universe of Consciousness: How Matter Becomes Imagination*. New York: Basic Books.

Edelman, G. (1992) *Bright Air, Brilliant Fire: On the Matter of the Mind*. Harmondsworth: Penguin.

Eiser, J.R. (1994) *Attitudes, Chaos and the Connectionist Mind*. Oxford: Blackwell.

Eliot, I. (1999) *Early Intelligence*. London: Penguin Books.

Enard, W., Przeworski, M., Fisher, S.E., Lai, C.S.L., Wiebe, V., Kitano, T., Monaco, A.P., and Paabo, S. (2002) Molecular evolution of FOXP2, a gene involved in speech and language. *Nature, 418*, 869–871.

Evans, J. St. B.T. and Over, D.E. (1996) *Rationality and Reasoning*. Hove: Psychology Press.

Ewen, R.B. (1988) *An Introduction to Theories of Personality* (3rd edition). Hillsdale, NJ: Lawrence Erlbaum.

Eysenck, H.J. (1985) *Decline and Fall of the Freudian Empire*. Harmondsworth: Penguin.

Fancher, R.E. and Rutherford, A. (2012) *Pioneers of Psychology* (4th edition). New York: W.W. Norton & Company Inc.

Feigin, S., Owens, G. and Goodyear-Smith, F. (2014) Theories of human altruism: A systematic review. *Annals of Neuroscience and Psychology, 1*(1), 1–9.

Fernando, S. (1991) *Mental Health, Race & Culture*. London: Macmillan Press in association with MIND Publications.

Fisher, S.E., Vargha-Khadem, F., Watkins, K.E., Monaco, A.P., and Pembrey, M.E. (1998) Localisation of a gene implicated in a severe speech and language disorder. *Nature, 18*, 168–170.

Fiske, S.T. and Taylor, S.E. (1991) *Social Cognition* (2nd edition). New York: McGraw-Hill.

Franco, Z., Blau, K. and Zimbardo, P.G. (2011) Heroism: A conceptual analysis and differentiation between heroic action and altruism. *Review of General Psychology, 15*(2), 99–113.

Franco, Z. and Zimbardo, P.G. (2007) The banality of heroism. *Greater Good* (Fall/Winter), 30–35.

Franco, Z. and Zimbardo, P.G. (2016) The psychology of heroism: extraordinary champions of humanity in an unforgiving world. In AG. Miller (ed.) *The Social Psychology of Good and Evil*. New York: The Guilford Press.

Frankl, V.E. (1946/2004) *Man's Search for Meaning*. London: Rider.

Freud, A. (1936) *The Ego and the Mechanisms of Defence*. London: Chatto & Windus.

Freud, S. (1914) *On the History of the Psychoanalytic Movement*. Pelican Freud Library (15). Harmondsworth: Penguin.

Freud, S. (1920/1984) *Beyond the Pleasure Principle*. Pelican Freud Library (11). Harmondsworth: *Penguin*.

Freud, S. (1923/1984) *The Ego and the Id*. Pelican Freud Library (11). Harmondsworth: Penguin.

Freud, S. (1933) *New Introductory Lectures on Psychoanalysis*. Standard Edition of the Complete Psychological Works of Sigmund Freud (Vol. 22). London: Hogarth Press.

Freud, S. (1940) *An Outline of Psychoanalysis*. Standard Edition of the Complete Psychological Works of Sigmund Freud (Vol. 23). London: Hogarth Press.

Freud, S. and Breuer, J. (1895) *Studies on Hysteria*. Pelican Freud Library (3). Harmondsworth: Penguin.

Frith, C. and Rees, G. (2007) A brief history of the scientific approach to the study of consciousness. In M. Velmans and S. Schneider (eds.) *The Blackwell Companion to Consciousness*. Oxford: Blackwell Publishing.

Fromm, E. (1950) *Psychoanalysis and Religion*. New Haven, CT: Yale University Press.

Fuentes, A. (2017) *The Creative Spark: How Imagination Made Humans Exceptional*. New York: Dutton.

Gaertner, S.L., Dovidio, J.F., Nier, J. *et al.* (2005) Aversive racism: Bias without intention. In L.B. Nielsen and R.L. Nelson (eds.) *Handbook of Employment Discrimination Research*. New York: Springer.

Galef, B.G. (1992) The question of animal culture. *Human Nature, 3*(2), 157–178.

Gallup, G.G. (1970) Chimpanzees: Self-recognition. *Science, 167*, 86–87.

Gallup, G.G. (1977) Self-recognition in primates. *American Psychologist, 32*, 329–338.

Gallup, G.G. (1998) Self-awareness and the evolution of social intelligence. *Behavioural Processes, 42*, 239–247.

Gallup, G.G., Anderson, J.R. and Shillito, D.J. (2002) The mirror test. In M. Bekoff, C. Allen and G.M. Burghardt (eds.) *The Cognitive Animal: Empirical and Theoretical Perspectives on Animal Cognition.* Cambridge, MA: MIT Press.

Gardner, R.A. and Gardner, B.T. (1969) Teaching sign language to a chimpanzee. *Science, 165*, 664–672.

Garrett, N., Lazzaro, S.C., Ariely, D. and Sharot, T. (2016) The brain adapts to dishonesty. *Nature Neuroscience, 19*, 1727–1732.

Gay, P. (1988) *Freud: A Life for our Time.* London: J.M. Dent & Sons.

Gelman, R. (1996) *Perceptual and Cognitive Development.* New York: Academic Press.

Gentilucci, M. and Corballis, M. (2007) The hominid that talked. In C. Pasternak (ed.) *What Makes Us Human?* Oxford: Oneworld.

Gerhardt, S. (2004) *Why Love Matters: How Affection Shapes a Baby's Brain.* London: Routledge.

Gergen, K. (2001) Psychology in a postmodern context. *American Psychologist, 56*, 803–813.

Giorgi, A. and Giorgi, B. (2003) Phenomenology. In J.A. Smith (ed.) *Qualitative Psychology: A Practical Guide to Research Methods.* London: Sage Publications.

Gokham, D., Lavi, E., Prufer, K. *et al.* (2014) Reconstructing the DNA methylation maps of the Neanderthal and the Denisovan. *Science, 344*(6183), 523–527.

Goodall, J. (1988) *In the Shadow of Man.* London: Orion Books Ltd.

Goodall, J. (2010) Jane of the jungle (interview by Kate Wong). *Scientific American, 303*(6), 62–63.

Gopnik, A. (2010) How babies think. *Scientific American, 303*(1), 56–61.

Graham, H. (1986) *The Human Face of Psychology: Humanistic Psychology in Historical, Social and Cultural Context.* Milton Keynes: Open University Press.

Gravotta, L. (2013) History of sin. *Scientific American, 24*(5), 42–43.

Green, R.E. *et al.* (2010) A draft sequence of the Neanderthal genome. *Science, 328*(5979), 710–722.

Greenwald, A.G., Poehlman, T.A., Uhlmann, E. and Banaji, M.R. (2009) Understanding and using the implicit association test: III. Meta-analysis of predictive validity. *Journal of Personality & Social Psychology, 97*, 17–41.

Gregory, R.L. (1981) *Mind in Science.* Hove: Lawrence Erlbaum.

Gross, R. (1987) *Psychology: The Science of Mind & Behaviour.* London: Edward Arnold.

Gross, R. (1994) *Key Studies in Psychology* (2nd edition). London: Hodder & Stoughton.

Gross, R. (2012a) *Being Human: Psychological and Philosophical Perspectives.* London: Routledge.

Gross, R. (2012b) *Key Studies in Psychology* (6th edition). London: Hodder Education.

Gross, R. (2012) *Being Human: Psychological and Philosophical Perspectives.* London: Routledge.

Gross, R. (2014) *Themes, Issues and Debates in Psychology* (4th edition). London: Hodder Education.

Gross, R. (2015) *Psychology: The Science of Mind & Behaviour* (7th edition). London: Hodder Education.

Gross, R. (2018) *Psychology in Historical Context: Theories and Debates.* London: Routledge.

Hall, C.S. and Nordby, V.J. (1973) *A Primer of Jungian Psychology.* New York: Mentor.

Harari, Y.N. (2014) *Sapiens: A Brief History of Humankind.* London: Vintage Books.

Harari, Y.N. (2017) *Homo Deus: A Brief History of Tomorrow.* London: Vintage.

Harré, R. (2006) *Key Thinkers in Psychology*. London: Sage.

Haney, C., Banks, C. and Zimbardo, P. (1973) A study of prisoners and guards in a simulated prison. *Naval Research Reviews, 30*(9), 4–17.

Harris, L.T. and Fiske, S. (2006) Dehumanizing the lowest of the low: Neuroimaging responses to extreme out-groups. *Psychological Science, 7*, 176–186.

Haslam, A. (2015) Social Identity and the positive psychology of groups. In R. Gross *Psychology: The Science of Mind and Behaviour* (7th edition). London: Hodder Education.

Haslam, S.A., Kashima, Y., Loughnan, S., Shi, J. and Suitner, C. (2008) Subhuman, inhuman, and superhuman: Contrasting humans with nonhumans in three cultures. *Social Cognition, 26*, 248–258.

Haslam, S.A. and Reicher, S.D. (2005) The psychology of tyranny. *Scientific American Mind, 16*(3), 44–51.

Haslam, S.A. and Reicher, S.D. (2012) Contesting the "nature" of conformity: What Milgram and Zimbardo's studies really show. *PLoS Biology, 10*(11), e1001426.

Haslam, S.A. and Reicher, S.D. (2015) Self-categorization theory. In J. Wright (ed.) *International Encyclopaedia of the Social and Behavioural Sciences* (2nd edition). New York: Elsevier.

Hauser, M.D. (2009) Origin of the mind. *Scientific American, 301*(3), 44–51.

Heather, N. (1976) *Radical Perspectives in Psychology*. London: Methuen.

Heather, N. and Segal, G. (2017) *Addiction and Choice: Rethinking the Relationship*. Oxford: Oxford University Press.

Heather, N. (2018) Rethinking addiction. *The Psychologist*, January, 24–28.

Hernando-Herraez, I., Prado-Martinez, G., Garg Para *et al.* (2013) Dynamics of DNA methylation in recent human and great ape evolution. *PLOS Genetics*. https://doi.org/10.1371/journal.pgen.1003763.

Herskovits, M.J. (1955) *Cultural Anthropology*. New York: Knopf.

Hill, S.E. and Buss, B.M. (2008) The evolutionary psychology of envy. In R.H. Smith (ed.) *Envy: Theory and Research*. New York: Oxford University Press.

Hirsch, H. (1995) *Genocide and the Politics of Memory: Studying Death to Preserve Life*. Chapel Hill, NC: University of North Carolina Press.

Horner, V.A. and De Waal, F.B.M. (2009) Controlled studies of chimpanzee cultural transmission. *Progress in Brain Research, 178*, 3–15.

Horner, V.A., Whiten, A., Flynn, E. and De Waal, F.B.M. (2006) Faithful replication of foraging techniques along cultural transmission chains by chimpanzees and children. *Proceedings of the National Academy of Sciences USA, 103*, 13878–13883.

Humphrey, N. (1986) *The Inner Eye*. London: Faber & Faber.

Humphrey, N. (1992) *A History of the Mind*. London: Vintage.

Humphrey, N. (1993) *The Inner Eye* (new edition). London: Vintage.

Husserl, E. (1925; trans. 1977) *Phenomenological Psychology*. The Hague: Martinus Nijhoff.

Husserl, E. (1931; trans. 1960) *Cartesian Meditations: An Introduction to Phenomenology*. The Hague: Martinus Nijhoff.

Husserl, E. (1936; trans. 1970) *The Crisis of European Sciences and Transcendental Phenomenology*. Evanston, IL: Northwestern University Press.

Itani, J. and Nishimura, A. (1973) The study of infrahuman culture in Japan. In W. Montagna (ed.) *Precultural Primate Behaviour*, Chicago, IL: University of Chicago Press.

Jablonski, N.G. (2010) The Naked Truth. *Scientific American, 302*(2), 28–35.

Jablonski, N.G. (2016) The Naked Truth. *Scientific American, The Story of Us, 302*(2), 52–59.

Jackendoff, R. (1993) *Patterns in the Mind: Language and Human Nature*. Hemel Hempstead: Harvester Wheatsheaf.

Jacobs, M. (1992) *Freud*. London: Sage.

James, W. (1890) *The Principles of Psychology*. London: Macmillan.

Jarrett, C. (2011) The deadly sins. *The Psychologist, 24*(2), 98–104.

Jerison, H.J. (1973) *Evolution of Brain and Intelligence*. New York: Academic Press.

Johnson, M.H. (2005) *Developmental Cognitive Neuroscience: An Introduction* (2nd edition). Oxford: Blackwell.

Johnson, M.H. (2009) Developing human brain functions. *The Psychologist, 22*(11), 924–926.

Johnson, C.V. and Friedman, H.L. (2014) *The Praeger handbook of social justice and psychology*. Santa Barbara, CA: ABC-CLIO.

Jones, D. (2008) Running to catch the sun. *The Psychologist, 21*(7), 580–583.

Jones, S. (1994) *The Language of the Genes*. London: Flamingo.

Joseph, S. and Linley, P.A. (2006) Positive psychology versus the medical model? *American Psychologist*, May–June, 332–333.

Kahneman, D. (2013) *Thinking, Fast and Slow*. (Reprinted edition). New York: Farrar, Strauss & Giroux.

Kawai, M. (1965) Newly acquired pre-cultural behaviour of the natural troop of Japanese monkeys on Koshima Islet. *Primates, 6*, 1–30.

Kawamura, S. (1959) The process of sub-culture propagation among Japanese macaques. *Primates, 2*, 43–54.

Kemp, C. (2015) Back to the wild. *New Scientist, 226*(3024), 30–35.

Kerschner, I. (2016) Pardon plea by Adolf Eichmann, Nazi war criminal, is made public. *New York Times*, 27 Jan.

Kierkegaard, S. (1944) *The Concept of Dread* (trans. W. Lowrie). Princeton, NJ: Princeton University Press. (Originally published 1844.)

Kihlstrom, J.F. (1987) The cognitive unconscious. *Science, 237*(4821), 1445–1452.

Koch, C. (2009) A theory of consciousness. *Scientific American Mind, 20*(4), 16–19.

Koch, C. (2017) Does brain size matter? *Scientific American: Mysteries of the Mind, 26*(3), 18–23.

Koch, C. and Tononi, G. (2011) A test for consciousness. *Scientific American, 304*(6), 26–29.

Köhler, W. (1925) *The Mentality of Apes*. New York: Harcourt Brace.

Kolbert, E. (2018) Skin deep. *National Geographic, 233*(4), 28–45

Krause, J. *et al.* (2007) The derived FOXP2 variant of modern human was shared with Neanderthals. *Current Biology, 17*, 1–5.

Krause, J., Lalueza-Eox, C., Orlando, L. et al. (2007) The derived FOXP2 variant of modern humans was shared with Neanderthals. *Current Biology, 17*, 1908–1912.

Krueger, J.L. and Funder, D.C. (2004) Towards a balanced social psychology: Causes, consequences, and cures for the problem-seeking approach to social behaviour and cognition. *Behavioural & Brain Sciences, 27*, 313–376.

Lai, C.S., Fisher, S.E., Hurst, J.A., Vargha-Khadem, F., and Monaco, A.P. (2001) A novel forkhead-domain gene is mutated in a severe speech and language disorder. *Nature, 413*, 519–523.

Lamson, M.S. (1881) *Life and Education of Laura Dewey Bridgman, the Deaf, Dumb, and Blind Girl*. Boston: Houghton, Mifflin Co.

Lang, J. (2014) Against obedience: Hannah Arendt's overlooked challenge to social-psychological explanations of mass atrocity. *Theory & Psychology, 24*(5), 649–667

Langer, S.K. (1951) *Philosophy in a New Key*. New York: Mentor.

Latané, B. and Darley, J.M. (1970) *The Unresponsive Bystander: Why Does He Not Help?* New York: Appleton-Century-Croft.

Laungani, P.D. (2007) *Understanding Cross-Cultural Psychology*. London: Sage.

Lawton, G. (2013) Nudge in the right direction. *New Scientist, 218*(2922), 32–36.

Leakey, R. (1994) *The Origin of Humankind*. London: Weidenfeld & Nicolson.

Le Page, M. (2010) RNA rules, OK. *New Scientist, 206*(2765), 34–35.

Leslie, A.M. (1987) Pretence and representation: The origins of "theory of mind". *Psychological Review, 94*, 412–426.

Leslie, A.M. (1994) Pretending and believing: Issues in the theory of ToMM. *Cognition, 50*, 211–238.

Leslie, A.M. and Roth, D. (1993) What autism teaches us about metarepresentations. In S. Baron-Cohen, H. Tager-Flusberg and D.J. Cohen (eds.) *Understanding Other Minds: Perspectives from Autism*. Oxford: Oxford University Press.

Levy, N. (2006) Addiction and autonomy. *Canadian Journal of Philosophy, 36*, 427–447.

Levy, N. (2013) Addiction is not a brain disease (and it matters). *Frontiers in Psychiatry, 4*, doi:10.3389/fpsyt.2013.00024.

Lewis, M and Brooks-Gunn, J. (1979) *Social Cognition and the Acquisition of Self*. New York: Plenum.

Libet, B., Gleason, C.A., Wright, E.W., and Pearl, D.K. (1983) Time of conscious intention to act in relation to onset of cerebral activity (readiness potential): the unconscious initiation of a freely voluntary act. *Brain, 106*, 623–642.

Libet, B. (1985) Unconscious cerebral initiative and the role of conscious will in voluntary action. *Behavioural & Brain Sciences, 8*, 529–539.

Libet, B. (1994) A testable field theory of mind-brain interaction. *Journal of Consciousness Studies, 1*, 119–126.

Linley, P.A. (2008) Positive psychology (history). In S.J. Lopez (ed.) *The Encyclopaedia of Positive Psychology*. Oxford: Blackwell.

Lippmann, W. (1922) *Public Opinion*. New York: Harcourt.

Locke, J. (1690) *An Essay Concerning Human Understanding*. Oxford: P.H. Nidditch.

Locke, J.L. and Bogin, B. (2006) Language and life history: A new perspective on the development and evolution of human language. *Behavioural & Brain Sciences, 29*, 259–325.

Lodge, D. (2002) Sense and sensibility. *Guardian Review*, 2 November, 4–6.

Mackintosh, N.J. (1978) Cognitive or associative theories of conditioning: Implications of an analysis of blocking. In S.H. Hulse, M. Fowler and W.K. Honig (eds.) *Cognitive Processes in Animal Behaviour*. Hillsdale, NJ: Lawrence Erlbaum.

MacLean, P.D. (1973) *A Triune Concept of the Brain and Behaviour*. Toronto: University of Toronto Press.

MacLean, P.D. (1985) Evolutionary psychiatry and the triune brain. *Psychological Medicine, 15*, 219–221.

Macquarrie, J. (1972) *Existentialism*. Harmondsworth: Pelican.

Macquarrie, J. (1972) *Existentialism*. Harmondsworth: Penguin.

Malik, K. (2006) What science can and cannot tell us about human nature. In R. Headlam Wells and J. McFadden (eds.) *Human Nature: Fact and Fiction*. London: Continuum.

Mangan, B. (2007) Cognition, fringe consciousness, and the legacy of William James. In M. Velmans and S. Schneider (eds.) *The Blackwell Companion to Consciousness*. Oxford: Blackwell Publishing.

Mareschal, D., Johnson, M.H., Sirois, S. *et al.* (2007) *Neuroconstructivism: Vol.1. How the Brain Constructs Cognition*. Oxford: Oxford University Press.

Maslow, A.H. (1954) *Motivation and Personality*. New York: Harper.

Maslow, A.H. (1965) *Eupsychian Management*. New York: Irwin Dorsey.

Maslow, A.H. (1968) *Toward a Psychology of Being* (2nd edition). New York: Van Nostrand Reinhold.

Maslow, A.H. (1970) *Motivation and Personality* (2nd edition). New York: Harper & Row.

Max, D.T. (2017) Beyond human. *National Geographic, 231*(4), 40–63

Mayer, J. (2011) *Life in a Jar: The Irena Sendler Project*. Middlebury, VT: Long Trail Press.

McAdams, D.P. (2012) Meaning and personality. In P.T.P. Wong (ed.) *The Human Quest for Meaning: Theories, Research, and Applications* (2nd edition). New York: Routledge.

McConahay, J.B. (1986) Modern racism, ambivalence, and the Modern Racism Scale. In J.F. Dovidio and S.L. Gaertner (eds.) *Prejudice, Discrimination, and Racism*. New York: Academic Press.

McEwan, I. (2006) Literature, science and human nature. In R. Headlam Wells and J. McFadden (eds.) *Human Nature: Fact and Fiction*. London: Continuum.

McGregor, I. (2006) Offensive defensiveness. *Psychological Inquiry, 17*, 299–308.

McLean, C.Y., Reno, P.L., Pollen, A.A. *et al.* (2011) Human-specific loss of regulatory DNA and the evolution of human-specific traits. *Nature, 471*, 216–219. Doi:10.1038/nature09774 9 March, 2011.

McMillan, D. (2014) *How Could this Happen: Explaining the Holocaust*. New York: Basic Books.

McNeil, J.E. and Warrington, E.K. (1993) Prosopagnosia: A face-specific disorder. *Quarterly Journal of Experimental Psychology, 46A*, 1–10.

Merleau-Ponty, M. (1962) *The Phenomenology of Perception*. London: RKP.

Merleau-Ponty, M. (1968) *The Visible and the Invisible*. Evanston, ILL: Northwestern University Press.

Milgram, S. (1974) *Obedience to Authority*. New York: Harper Torchbooks.

Miller, A.G. (2016) Introduction and overview. In A.G. Miller (ed.) *The Social Psychology of Good and Evil*. New York: The Guilford Press.

Milton, J. (1667/1957) *John Milton: Complete Poems and Major Prose* (edited by M.Y. Hughes) New York: Odyssey Press.

Mitchell, P. (1997) *Introduction to Theory of Mind: Children, Autism and Apes*. London: Arnold.

Moghaddam, F.M. (2005) *Great Ideas in Psychology: A Cultural and Historical Introduction*. Oxford: Oneworld Publications.

Moghaddam, F.M. (2005) The staircase to terrorism: A psychological exploration. *American Psychologist, 60*(2), 161–169.

Moghaddam, F.M. (2009) De-radicalization and the staircase to terrorism. In D. Canter (ed.) *The Faces of Terrorism: Multidisciplinary Perspectives*. Chichester, UK: Wiley-Blackwell.

Moghaddam, F.M., Heckenlaible, V., Blackman, M. *et al.* (2016) Globalization and terrorism: The primacy of collective processes. In A.G. Miller (ed.) *The Social Psychology of Good and Evil*. New York: The Guilford Press.

Moghaddam, F.M., Taylor, D.M. and Wright, S.C. (1993) *Social Psychology in Cross-Cultural Perspective*. New York: W.H. Freeman.

Monin, B., Sawyer, P.J. and Marquez, M. (2008) Rejection of moral rebels: Resenting those who do the right thing. *Journal of Personality & Social Psychology, 95*, 76–93.

Monroe, A.E., Vohs, K.D. and Baumeister, F. (2016) Free will evolved for morality and culture. In A.G. Miller (ed.) *The Social Psychology of Good and Evil*. New York: The Guilford Press.

Morawski, J. (1982) Assessing psychology's moral heritage through our neglected utopias. *American Psychologist, 37*, 1092–1095.

Morea, P. (1990) *Personality: An Introduction to the Theories of Psychology*. Harmondsworth: Penguin.

Motluk, A. (2010) It's not what you've got … *New Scientist, 207*(2771), 38–41.

Nagel, T. (1974) What is it like to be a bat? *Philosophical Review, 83*, 435–450.

Neisser, U. (2008) Memory with a grain of salt. In H.H. Wood and A.S. Byatt (eds.) *Memory: An Anthology*. London: Chatto and Windus.

Nietzsche, F. (1974/1882) *The Gay Science/Joyful Wisdom* (trans. W. Kaufmann). London: Vintage.

Nietzsche, F. (1973/1886) *Beyond Good and Evil* (trans. R.J. Hollingdale). Harmondsworth: Penguin.

Nisbett, R.E. and Wilson, T.D. (1977) Telling more than we can know: verbal reports on mental processes. *Psychological Review, 84*, 231–259.

Nishida, T. (1987) Local traditions and cultural tradition. In B.B. Smuts, D.L. Cheney, R.M. Seyfarth, R.W. Wrangham, and T.T. Struhsaker (eds.) *Primate Societies*. Chicago: University of Chicago Press.

Oakley, K. (1957) *Man the Toolmaker*. London: British Museum (Natural History).

O'Donohue, W. and Ferguson, K.E. (2001) *The Psychology of B.F. Skinner*. Thousand Oaks, CA: Sage Publications.

Oliner, S.P. and Oliner, P.M. (1988) *The Altruistic Personality: The Rescuers of the Jews in Nazi Europe*. New York: Free Press.

Operario, D. and FIske, S.T. (2004) Stereotypes: Content, structures, processes and context. In M.B.Brewer and M. Hewstone (eds.) *Social Cognition*. Oxford: Blackwell Publishing.

Oppenheimer, S. (2007) What makes us human? – Our ancestors and the weather. In C. Pasternak (ed.) *What Makes Us Human?* Oxford: Oneworld.

Ornstein, R.E. (1976) *The Mind Field*. Oxford: Pergamon.

Pagel, M. (2012) *Wired for Culture: The Natural History of Human Cooperation*. London: Penguin Books.

Pasternak, C. (2007) Curiosity and quest. In C. Pasternak (ed.) *What Makes Us Human?* Oxford: Oneworld.

Patterson, F.G. (1978) The gestures of a gorilla: Language acquisition in another pongid. *Brain and Language, 5*, 72–97.

Patterson, F.G. (1980) Innovative use of language by a gorilla: A case study. In K. Nelson (ed.) *Children's Language*, Vol.2. New York: Gardner Press.

Patton, P. (2008/2009) One world, many minds. *Scientific American Mind, 19*(6), 72–79.

Pavlov, I. P. (1927) *Conditioned Reflexes*. Oxford: Oxford University Press.

Pettit, P. (2002) When burial begins. *British Archaeology, 66* (August).

Phelps, E.A., O'Connor, K.J., Cunningham, W.A. *et al.* (2000) Performance on indirect measures of race evaluation predicts amygdale activation. *Journal of Cognitive Neuroscience, 12*, 729–738.

Piliavin, I.M., Rodin, J. and Piliavin, J.A. (1969) Good samaritanism: An underground phenomenon? *Journal of Personality & Social Psychology, 1*(4), 289–299.

Piliavin, J.A., Dovidio, J.F., Gaertner, S.L. and Clark, R.D. (1981) *Emergency Interventions*. New York: Academic Press.

Pinker, S. (1994) *The Language Instinct*. New York: Morrow.

Pinker, S. and Jackendoff, R. (2005) The faculty of language: What's special about it? *Cognition, 95*, 201–236.

Plotnik, J.M., De Waal, F.B.M., and Reiss, D. (2006) Self-recognition in an Asian elephant. *Proceedings of the National Academy of Sciences of the USA. 103*, 17053–17057.

Plotnik, J.M. et al. (2014) Thinking with their trunks: Elephants use smell but not sound to locate food and exclude nonrewarding alternatives. *Animal Behaviour, 88,* 91–98.

Pollard, K.S. (2009) What makes us human? *Scientific American, 300*(5), 32–37.

Polster, M.F. (2014) Eve's Daughters: The forbidden heroism of women. In J.K. Zeig (ed.) *The Evolution of Psychotherapy, the Second Conference.* New York: Routledge.

Povinelli, D.J. (1993) Reconstructing the evolution of mind. *American Psychologist, 48,* 493–509.

Povinelli, D.J. (1998) … Maybe not. *Scientific American Presents, 9*(4), 67, 72–75.

Povinelli, D.J. (2000) *Folk Physics for Apes.* Oxford: Oxford University Press.

Prabhakar, S., Visel, A. and Akiyama, J.A. (2008) Human-specific gain of function in a Developmental Enhancer. *Science, 321*(5894), 1346–1350.

Premack, D. and Woodruff, G. (1978) Does the chimpanzee have a theory of mind? *Behavioural and Brain Sciences, 4,* 515–526.

Premack, D. (1971) Language in chimpanzee? *Science, 172,* 808–822.

Prior, H., Schwartz, A. and Gunturkun, O. (2008) Mirror-induced behaviour in the magpie (*Pica pica*): Evidence of self-recognition. *PLoS Biology, 6*(8).

Pyszczynski, T., Greenberg, J., and Kolole, S.L. (2004) Experimental existential psychology: Exploring the human confrontation with reality. In J. Greenberg, S.L. Koole and T. Pyszczynski (eds.) *Handbook of Experimental Existential Psychology.* New York: The Guilford Press.

Ramachandran, V.S. (1998) The unbearable likeness of being. *Independent on Sunday,* 22 November, 22–24.

Ramachandran, V.S. (2011) *The Tell-Tale Brain: Unlocking the Mysteries of Human Nature.* London: Windmill Books.

Rank, O. (1958) *Beyond Psychology.* New York: Dover Books. (Originally published 1941.)

Reicher, S. and Haslam, S.A. (2011) The shock of the old. *The Psychologist, 24*(9), 650–652.

Reicher, S. and Haslam, S.A. (2012) Obedience: Revisiting Milgram's shock experiments. In J.R. Smith and S.A. Haslam (eds.) *Social Psychology: Revisiting the Classic Studies.* Thousand Oaks, CA: Sage.

Reicher, S., Haslam, S.A. and Smith, J.R. (2012) Working toward the experimenter: Reconceptualizing obedience within the Milgram paradigm as identification-based followership. *Perspectives on Psychological Science, 7*(4), 315–324.

Reiss, D. and Marino, L. (2001) Mirror self-recognition in the bottlenose dolphin: A case of cognitive convergence. *Proceedings of the National Academy of Sciences of the USA. 98,* 5937–5942.

Reynolds, V. (1980) The rise and fall of human nature. In A.J. Chapman and D.M. Jones (eds.) *Models of Man.* Leicester: British Psychological Society.

Richards, G. (2010) *Putting Psychology in its Place: Critical Historical Perspectives* (3rd edition). London: Routledge.

Richerson, P.J. and Boyd, R. (2005) *Not by Genes Alone: How Culture Transformed Human Evolution.* Chicago: University of Chicago Press.

Ridley, M. (1999) *Genome: The Autobiography of a Species in 23 Chapters.* London: Fourth Estate.

Ridley, M. (2003) *Nature Via Nurture: Genes, Experience and What Makes Us Human.* London: Fourth Estate.

Rilling, J.K. and Insel, T.R. (1999) The primate neocortex in comparative perspective using magnetic resonance imaging. *Journal of Human Evolution, 37*(2), 191–223.

Roberts, A. (2009) *The Incredible Human Journey: The Story of How We Colonised the Planet.* London: Bloomsbury.

Rogers, C.R. (1951) *Client-Centred Therapy: Its Current Practice, Implications and Theory.* Boston, MA: Houghton-Mifflin.

Rogers, C.R. (1961) *On Becoming a Person: A Therapist's View of Psychotherapy*. Boston, MA: Houghton-Mifflin.

Rogers, C.R. (1983) *Freedom to Learn for the 80s*. Columbus, OH: Charles E. Merrill.

Rose, D. (2006) *Consciousness: Philosophical, Psychological and Neural Theories*. Oxford: Oxford University Press.

Rose, S. (1976) *The Conscious Brain* (revised edition). Harmondsworth: Penguin.

Rose, S. (2005) *The 21st-Century Brain: Explaining, Mending and Manipulating the Mind*. London: Vintage Books.

Ross, L., Lepper, M. and Ward, A. (2010) History of social psychology: Insights, challenges, and contributions to theory and application. In S.T. Fiske, D.T. Gilbert and G. Lindzey (eds.) *Handbook of Social Psychology* (5th edition, Vol. 2). New York: Wiley.

Rousseau, J.-J. (1979/1762) *Emile* (trans. A. Bloom). New York: Basic Books.

Rowan, J. (2001) *Ordinary Ecstasy: The Dialectics of Humanistic Psychology* (3rd edition). Hove: Brunner-Routledge.

Rumbaugh, D.M., Warner, H., and Von Glaserfeld, E. (1977) The Lana project: Origin and tactics. In D.M. Rumbaugh (ed.) *Language Learning by a Chimpanzee: The LANA Project*. New York: Academic Press.

Rycroft, C. (1966) Introduction. In C. Rycroft (ed.) *Psychoanalysis Observed*. London: Constable.

Sahakian, B.J. and Gottwald, J. (2017) *Sex, Lies, & Brain Scans: How fMRI Reveals What Really Goes on in our Minds*. Oxford: Oxford University Press.

Savage-Rumbaugh, S., Rumbaugh, D.M. and Boysen, S.L. (1980) Do apes use language? *American Scientist, 68*, 49–61.

Savin, H.B. (1973) Professors and psychological researchers: Conflicting values in conflicting roles. *Cognition, 21*, 147–149.

Schick, K.D. and Toth, M. (1993) *Making Silent Stones Speak*. London: Weidenfeld & Nicolson.

Schore, A. (2003) *Affect Dysregulation and Disorders of the Self*. New York: Norton.

Schroeder, D.A., Penner, L.A., Dovidio, J.F. and Piliavin, J.A. (1995) *The Psychology of Helping and Altruism: Problems and Puzzles*. New York: McGraw-Hill.

Searle, J.R. (2007) Biological naturalism In M. Velmans and S. Schneider (eds.) *The Blackwell Companion to Consciousness*. Oxford: Blackwell Publishing.

Sears, D.O. and Henry, P.J. (2003) The origins of symbolic racism. *Journal of Personality & Social Psychology, 85*, 259–275.

Sechenov, I.M. (1965/1863) *Reflexes of the Brain*. Cambridge, MA: MIT Press.

Seligman, M.E.P. (2003) Positive psychology: Fundamental assumptions. *The Psychologist, 16*(3), 126–127.

Seligman, M.E.P., Steen, T.A., Park, N. and Peterson, C. (2005) Positive psychology progress: Empirical validation of interventions. *American Psychologist, 60*, 410–421.

Shaver, K.G. (1987) *Principles of Social Psychology* (3rd edition). Hillsdale, NJ: Lawrence Erlbaum.

Sheskin, M. (2018) The inequality delusion. *New Scientist, 237*(3171), 28–31.

Shotter, J. (1975) *Images of Man in Psychological Research*. London: Methuen.

Simpson, J.C. (2000) It's all in the upbringing. *Johns Hopkins Magazine*, April. www.jhu.edu/~jhumag/0400web/35.html.

Simring, K.S. (2013) Accidental gluttons. *Scientific American, 24*(5), 26–33.

Skinner, B.F. (1938) *The Behaviour of Organisms*. New York: Appleton-Century-Crofts.

Skinner, B.F. (1948) *Walden Two*. New York: Macmillan.

Skinner, B.F. (1971) *Beyond Freedom and Dignity*. New York: Knopf.

Skinner, B.F. (1974) *About Behaviourism*. New York: Knopf.

Smith, R.H. (ed.) (2008) *Envy: Theory and Research*. New York: Oxford University Press.

Smith, R. (2013) *Between Mind and Nature: A History of Psychology*. London: Reaktion Books.

Snyder, M., Omoto, A.M. and Dwyer, P.C. (2016) Volunteerism: Multiple perspectives on benefits and costs. In A. G. Miller (ed.) *The Social Psychology of Good and Evil*. New York: The Guilford Press.

Sober, E. (1992) The evolution of altruism: Correlation, cost and benefit. *Biology & Philosophy*, 7, 177–188.

Solomon, S., Greenberg, J. and Pyszczynski, T. (1991a) A terror management theory of social behaviour: The psychological functions of self-esteem and cultural worldviews. In M. Zanna (ed.) *Advances In Experimental Social Psychology*, Vol. 24. Orlando, FL: Academic Press.

Solomon, S., Greenberg, J. and Pyszczynski, T. (1991b) A terror management theory of self-esteem. In C.R. Snyder and D. Forsyth (eds.) *Handbook of Social and Clinical Psychology: The Health Perspective*. New York: Pergamon Press.

Solomon, S., Greenberg, J. and Pyszczynski, T. (2004) The cultural animal: Twenty years of terror management theory and research. In J. Greenberg, S.L. Koole and T. Pyszczynski (eds.) *Handbook of Experimental Existential Psychology*. New York: The Guilford Press.

Southgate, V., Senju, A. and Csibra, G. (2007) Action anticipation through attribution of false beliefs by 2-year-olds. *Psychological Science, 18*, 587–592.

Starmans, C., Sheskin, M. and Bloom, P. (2017) Why people prefer unequal societies. *Nature Human Behaviour, 1*, 0082.

Staub, E. (1991) Psychological and cultural origins of extreme destructiveness and extreme altruism. In W. Kurtines, J. Gewirtz and J. Lamb (eds.) *Handbook of Moral Behaviour and Development*. New York: Erlbaum.

Stevens, A. and Price, J. (2000) *Evolutionary Psychiatry: A New Beginning* (2nd edition). London: Routledge.

Stout, D. (2016) Tales of a Stone Age neuroscientist. *Scientific American: The Story of Us, 25*(4), 28–35.

Suddendorf, T. (2010) Episodic memory versus episodic foresight: Similarities and differences. *WIRES Cognitive Science, 1*, 99–107.

Suddendorf, T. and Corballis, M.C. (1997) Mental time travel and the evolution of the human mind. *Genetic, Social, and General Psychology Monographs, 123*, 133–167.

Suddendorf, T. and Corballis, M.C. (2007) The evolution of foresight: What is mental time travel, and is it unique to humans? *Behavioural and Brain Sciences, 30*, 299–351.

Sulloway, F.J. (1979) *Freud, Biologist of the Mind: Beyond the Psychoanalytic Legend*. New York: Basic Books.

Tallis, R. (2013) Think brain scans reveal our innermost thoughts? Think again. *The Observer*, 2 June, 31.

Tangney, J.P., Blalock, D.V., Folk, J.B. and Stuewig, J. (2016) Evil persons or evil deeds?: What we've learned about incarcerated offenders. In A.G. Miller (ed.) *The Social Psychology of Good and Evil*. New York: The Guilford Press.

Tattersall, I. (2007) Human evolution and the human condition. In C. Pasternak (ed.) *What Makes Us Human?* Oxford: Oneworld.

Terbeck, S., Kahane, G., McTavish, S. and Savulescu, J. (2012) Propanolol reduces implicit negative racial bias. Psychopharmacology, *222*(3), 419–424.

Terrace, H.S. (1979) *Nim*. New York: Knopf.

Teichman, J. (1988) *Philosophy and the Mind*. Oxford: Blackwell.

Thorndike, E.L. (1898) Animal intelligence: An experimental study of the associative processes in animals. *Psychological Review Monograph Supplement 2* (Whole No. 8).

Thorne, B. (1992) *Carl Rogers*. London: Sage.

Tolman, E.C. (1948) Cognitive maps in rats and man. *Psychological Review, 55*, 189–208.

Tolman, E.C. and Honzik, C.H. (1930) Introduction and removal of reward and maze-learning in rats. *University of California Publications in Psychology, 4*, 257–275.

Tomasello, M. (1999) The human adaptation for culture. *Annual Review of Anthropology, 28*, 509–529.

Tomasello, M. and Call, J. (1997) *Primate Cognition*. New York: Oxford University Press.

Tononi, G. (2007) The information integration theory of consciousness. In M. Velmans and S. Schneider (eds.) *The Blackwell Companion to Consciousness*. Oxford: Blackwell Publishing.

Toulmin, S. (1977) From form to function: Philosophy and the history of science in the 1950s and now. *Daedalus, 106*, 143–162.

Triandis, H. (1994) *Culture and Social Behaviour*. New York: McGraw-Hill.

Trivers, R.L. (1974) Parent-offspring conflict. *American Zoologist, 14*, 249–264.

Tulving, E. (2002) Episodic memory: From mind to brain. *Annual Review of Psychology, 53*, 1–25.

Turner, J. (2000) *On the Origin of Human Evolutions*. Palo Alto, CA: Stanford University Press.

Turner, J.C. (2006) Tyranny, freedom, and social structure: Escaping our theoretical prisons. *British Journal of Social Psychology, 45*, 41–46.

Tversky, A. and Kahneman, D. (1973) Availability: A heuristic for judging frequency and probability. *Cognitive Psychology, 5*, 207–232.

Tversky, A. and Kahneman, D. (1974) Judgement under uncertainty: Heuristics and biases. *Science, 185*, 1124–1131.

Vargha-Khadem, F., Watkins, K.E., Alcock, K.J., Fletcher, P. and Passingham, R. (1995) Praxic and nonverbal cognitive deficits in a large family with a genetically transmitted speech and language disorder. *Proceedings of the National Academy of Science, USA, 92*, 930–933.

Velmans, M. (1991) Intersubjective science. *Journal of Consciousness Studies, 6*(2/3), 299–306.

Velmans, M. (2003) Preconscious free will. *Journal of Consciousness Studies, 10*(12), 42–61.

Visalberghi, E. and Fragaszy, D.M. (1990) Food washing behaviour in tufted capuchin monkeys (*Cebus paella*) and crabeating macaques (*Macaca fascularis*). *Animal Behaviour, 40*, 829–836.

Vollhardt, J.R. and Campbell-Obaid, M. (2016) The social psychology of genocide and mass atrocities. In A.G. Miller (ed.) *The Social Psychology of Good and Evil*. New York: The Guilford Press.

Waller, J. (2001) Perpetrators of genocide: An explanatory model of extraordinary human evil. *Journal of Hate Studies, 1*, 5–22.

Watkins, K.E., Dronkers, N.F. and Vargha-Khadem, F., (2002) Behavioural analysis of an inherited speech and language disorder: Comparison with acquired aphasia. *Brain, 125*, 452–464.

Watson, J.B. (1931) *Behaviourism* (2nd edition). London: Kegan Paul, Trench, Trubner & Co.l.

Watson, J.B. and Rayner, R. (1920) Conditioned emotional reactions. *Journal of Experimental Psychology, 3*(1), 1–14.

Walsh, R.T.G., Teo, T., and Baydala, A. (2014) *A Critical History and Philosophy of Psychology*. Cambridge: Cambridge University Press.

Walton, S. (2004) *Humanity: An Emotional History*. London: Atlantic Books.

Wearing, D. (2005) *Forever Today*. London: Corgi Books.

Webster, R.J. and Saucier, D.A. (2013) Angels and demons are among us: Assessing individual differences in belief in pure evil and belief in pure good. *Personality & Social Psychology Bulletin, 39*, 1455–1470.

Weiskrantz, L. (1986) *Blindsight: A Case Study and Implications*. Oxford: Oxford University Press.

Weiskrantz, L. (2007) The case of blindsight. In M. Velmans and S. Schneider (eds.) *The Blackwell Companion to Consciousness*. Oxford: Blackwell Publishing.

Whiten, A. (1999) The evolution of deep social mind in humans. In M. Corballis and S.E.G. Lea (eds.) *The Descent of Mind*. Oxford: Oxford University Press.

Whiten, A. (2007) The place of 'deep social mind' in the evolution of human nature. In C. Pasternak (ed.) *What Makes Us Human?* Oxford: Oneworld.

Whiten, A. and Byrne, R.W. (1988) Tactical deception in primates. *Behavioural & Brain Sciences*, 11, 233–244.

Whiten, A. and Erdal, D. (2012) The human socio-cognitive niche and its evolutionary origins. *Philosophical Transactions of the Royal Society B, 367*, 2119–2129.

Whiten, A., Horner, V. and De Waal, F.B.M. (2005) Conformity to cultural norms of food use in chimpanzees. *Nature, 437*, 737–740.

Wilber, K. (1983) *Eye to Eye: The Quest for the New Paradigm*. Garden City: Anchor.

Williamson, V. (2009) In search of the language of music. *The Psychologist, 22*(12), 1022–1025.

Wilson, G.T., O'Leary, K.D., Nathan, P.E. and Clark, L.A. (1996) *Abnormal Psychology: Integrating Perspectives*. Needham Heights, MA: Allyn and Bacon.

Wink, W. (1992) *Engaging the Powers: Discernment and Resistance in a World of Domination*. Minneapolis, MN: Augsburg Fortress.

Wise, S.M. (1999) *Rattling the Cage: Towards Legal Rights for Animals*. London: Profile Books.

Wolpert, L. (2007) Causal belief makes us human. In C. Pasternak (ed.) *What Makes Us Human?* Oxford: Oneworld.

World Health Organization (2008) *World Health Statistics 2008*. Geneva: W.H.O.

Yalom, I.D. (1980) *Existential Psychotherapy*. New York: Basic Books.

Yalom, I.D. (2008) *Staring at the Sun: Overcoming the Dread of Death*. London: Piatkus Books.

Zimbardo, P. (1969) The human choice: Individuation, reason, and order versus deindividuation, impulse, and chaos. In W.J. Arnold and D. Levine (eds.) *Nebraska Symposium on Motivation*. Lincoln, NA: University of Nebraska Press.

Zimbardo, P. (1971) The power and pathology of imprisonment. *Congressional Record* (Serial No. 15, Oct. 25). Hearing before Subcommittee No. 3 of Commission on the Judiciary, House of Representatives, 92nd Congress. *First Session on Corrections, Pt.III: Prisons, Prison Reform and Prisoners' Rights, CA*. Washington, DC: US Government Printing Office.

Zimbardo, P.G. and Ruch, F.L. (1977) *Psychology and Life* (2nd edition). New York: Scott Foreman.

Zimbardo, P. (2007) *The Lucifer Effect: Understanding How Good People Turn Evil*. New York: Random House.

Zimbardo, P.G. and Boyd, J. (2008) *The Time Paradox: The New Psychology of Time that will Change your Life*. New York: Simon & Schuster.

Zimbardo, P. (2018) A personal journey from evil to heroism. *Psychology Review, 24*(1), 2–4.

Zimbardo, P., Banks, W.C., Craig, H. and Jaffe, D. (1973) A Pirandellian prison: The mind is a formidable jailor. *New York Times Magazine*, 8 April, 38–60.

Zimbardo, P. and Ruch, F.L. (1977) *Psychology and Life* (2nd edition). New York: Scott Foreman.

Index

Note: Page numbers in italics indicate figures. Page numbers in bold indicate tables.